Profiting from Your Music and Sound Project Studio

Jeffrey P. Fisher

ALLWORTH PRESS
NEW YORK

D0681874

For Mom.
Your love and support gives me
the determination to chase my dreams.
Thank you.

© 2001 Jeffrey P. Fisher

All rights reserved. Copyright under Berne Copyright Convention, Universal Copyright Convention, and Pan-American Copyright Convention. No part of this book may be reproduced, stored in a retrieval system, or transmitted in any form, or by any means, electronic, mechanical, photocopying, recording, or otherwise, without prior permission of the publisher.

05   04   03   02   01   00   5   4   3   2   1

Published by Allworth Press
An imprint of Allworth Communications
10 East 23rd Street, New York, NY 10010

Cover design by Douglas Design Associates, New York, NY

Page composition/typography by RH Publishing Freelance, Lake Grove, NY

ISBN: 1-58115-100-4

Library of Congress Cataloging-in-Publication Data
Fisher, Jeffrey P. (Jeffrey Paul), 1963–
  Profiting from your music and sound project studio / Jeffrey P. Fisher.
     p.   cm.
Includes index.
  ISBN 1-58115-100-4
1. Sound recording industry—Vocational guidance.   2. Sound studios.
3. Music—Economic aspects.   I. Title.
ML3790.F593 2001
621.389'3'068—dc21   2001003496
                                                                  CIP

Printed in Canada

Table of Contents

Introduction

Every artist needs a workshop, a place where creativity and technology combine into meaningful art. For those of us in the music and sound industry, the recording studio is our workshop. These dark, secret rooms, stuffed with gear, were the primary way for music and sound artists to capture their performances. Then, the home recording revolution brought affordable audio technology to the masses. Unfortunately, this equipment was of inferior quality compared to its commercial counterparts. Home recording was looked down upon. Slowly and steadily, the technology and sound quality improved. The old "home recording" moniker gave way to a new production environment: the professional project studio. These personal, mostly home-based recording and production spaces let artists create high-quality work without the constraints and expenses imposed by the commercial studio.

Project studio recording has emerged as a formidable force and forever changed the commercial music and sound recording landscape. Today's technology enables project studios to complement and, in many cases, replace the commercial recording studio. While the impact of the project studio hasn't hastened the extinction of the large studio, it has forced commercial ventures to shift focus, concentrating on larger projects. This leaves a huge gap in the basic music and sound production world—the gap now filled by professionals working from their own project studios.

For many, having a project studio at one's disposal is no longer a luxury, but rather, a requirement. Musicians, composers, songwriters, producers, engineers, sound designers, voice artists, and other music and sound professionals use project studios to produce a diverse range of creative audiovisual content. Your project studio can not only function as a workshop for your original endeavors, but can also be an exciting and lucrative way to make money.

Profiting from Your Music and Sound Project Studio offers the definitive approach to establishing, promoting, managing, and succeeding with a professional music and sound project studio. Based on interviews with dozens of project studio owners, meticulous research into the burgeoning phenomenon, and my fifteen-plus years' experience working in the industry, this resource contains proven advice based on the real world of project studio recording. You now have access to the most complete, up-to-date, and practical information on the subject today.

What are the steps you must take to profit from your music and sound project studio?

* Choose and define your lifestyle
* Plan for the future and set goals
* Implement your plan
* Acquire the necessary resources required by your plan
* Diversify your music and sound project studio products and services
* Promote your capabilities ruthlessly
* Run your project studio as a business
* Make the most of all your resources
* Persist

This book provides the choices and the road map you need to succeed on any level. As with any good road map, you can choose the route to take. I provide the information, direction, and a little motivation along the way. But you are the navigator, solely responsible for your professional and personal life's journey. Whatever path you choose, be serious and dedicated. You can't start your project studio ad hoc and run it by the seat of your pants. Instead, run your project studio as a legitimate business, and you'll better reap all the rewards of your endeavors. That means developing the necessary technical skills demanded by your project studio, cultivating the right attitude that helps you realize your goals, nurturing your people skills, and mastering the business and career management knowledge you need to sustain your success. Study this book's tips, tricks, insight, methods, and tactics—then steal the best ideas, mold them to fit your particular strengths, and put them into action right away.

What You Get in This Book

Profiting from Your Music and Sound Project Studio explains the new project studio paradigm, helps you build your success framework, and provides the crucial details to help you thrive.

Before you can begin profiting from your project studio, you need to take care of some important, rudimentary planning, as described in chapter 3, Planning Your Project Studio Lifestyle.

Chapter 4, Acquiring the Necessary Resources, details how to set up a viable production environment that services your particular needs.

Transforming Your Gear and Career into a Moneymaking Machine (chapters 6 and 7) will lead you to discover how to diversify into related areas that can ensure your continued success.

Your Project Studio and the Internet (chapter 8) form a powerful partnership, including collaboration, promotion, and more.

Chapter 9, Preparing to Promote, covers this critical activity. If you don't promote your project studio effectively, you will fail miserably. This chapter, along with chapter 10, Unleashing Your Promotions, uncovers the secrets to finding, landing, and keeping clients.

Chapter 11, Starting and Managing Your Project Studio, supplies the best advice for setting up and running your project studio and addresses several ongoing issues that affect the success of your project studio.

Chapter 12, Pricing for Profit, shows you how to price your products and services.

Chapter 13, Make the Most of Your Project Studio Profits, helps you support your lifestyle through your creative work.

Also note, our relationship doesn't have to start or end with this book. I welcome hearing from you to answer your questions, debate the issues, and share in your success. You can e-mail me at *jpf@jeffreypfisher.com* or call me at (630) 378-4109. Also, there are updates, the latest industry news, and other additional information available to you on my Web site at *www.jeffreypfisher.com*.

Project Studio Survey

Project studios handle a variety of music and sound production tasks. The people who own and use these personal recording spaces also come from diverse backgrounds. Because of these two facts, coupled with the sheer lack of meaningful information on this book's topic, I hosted an informal survey of project studio owners to get their opinions on several vital issues. The survey itself was rather long and involved, but those who participated were diligent, candid, and generous with their responses. Their comments on the issues are sprinkled throughout the text, with the full results of certain survey questions presented at the close of pertinent chapters.

There were many more contributors to the survey than the fourteen people included here. To be fair, the answers provided by these other respondents were kept confidential and anonymous, some by request, others by my choice. I'd like to thank *all* the participants publicly for their support and assistance on making this book stronger.

♩ Tim Butler, Oakdale, Minnesota. After recording demos for his own band, followed by demos for other bands, Butler now composes background music for commercials, corporate presentations, and his own music CD library.

♩ Michael Carroll, aka Musik G, Generator Productions, Queens, New York. This is the basement project studio where Carroll works with vocalists and other artists.

♩ David Conley, Studio 103, Seattle, Washington, offers film scoring, songwriting, and orchestration services.

♩ Dave Davies, GSC Records, Saltspring Island, Canada. Davies runs his record label full-time from a dedicated studio on a lot next to his house. He also does music videos, TV commercials, voice-overs, and animations.

♩ Jeffery Dunnigan, Audio Lab, Boise, Idaho, handles local bands, sound effects and soundtracks for CD-ROMs and videos, jingles, and radio and TV ads.

♩ Ken Feldman, New York, New York. As a full-time professional sound engineer, Feldman's home project studio is primarily used for vocal and instrument overdubs on tracks to be completed at commercial facilities.

♩ Jimmy Graham, INDEBASEMENT Records and Audio Productions, Windsor, Ontario, Canada, handles album recording, original music, commercial production, mobile recording, CD/cassette duplication, and mastering.

♩ Harlan Hogan, Chicago, Illinois. Hogan uses his project studio to record his professional voice-overs for both commercial and nonbroadcast clients.

♩ J. Dennis Onopa , 24K Creative Musical Products, El Paso, Texas. A self-professed gear junkie, Onopa operates his project studio full time, doing mostly jingles and on-hold telephone productions.

♩ Jeremy Spencer, Sinfonia Productions, Calgary, Alberta, Canada. Spencer works part-time composing and recording his own material, writing music for theater and corporate videos, and distributing his own line of original relaxation music.

♩ Eric B. Thompson, Eric Thompson Music and Sound Services, Cary, North Carolina. Located in a loft-style bedroom of his townhouse, Thompson works part-time composing and recording radio and TV advertising jingles, movie and television scores, multimedia, and classical music concert pieces.

♪ James Utterback, Jimidi Records and Studios, Indianapolis, Indiana, specializes in music and graphic production for Internet, broadcast, and other communications avenues.

♪ Phil "the Tremolo King" Vanderyken, Planet B Productions, New Orleans, Louisiana. This is the part-time, home project studio where Vanderyken works on CDs of his own music and composes and designs sound for commercial clients.

♪ Frank Wyatt, Crafty Hands Studio, McLean, Virginia. Wyatt uses his project studio for his own band and also offers analog tape-to-CD archiving and Web sound design services.

1

Join the Project Studio Revolution

Now is *the greatest time* to be in the recording business. The range of equipment options available to the project studio today rivals that used by commercial studios. In some cases, it's the *same* gear. The sounds coming from project studios are often indistinguishable from their traditional commercial counterparts. Project studios no longer have to compromise or apologize. The playing field is level in terms of quality and sonic palettes. Raw talent is now the focus. It's "who can do a better job?" and not "what has a better sound?" And your talent will enable you to profit from your music and sound project studio.

You Can Do It

It's possible to set up a world-class recording rig at a tiny fraction of what it used to cost. With a computer-based system, you can even reduce the physical equipment needed, as most of the gear (recorder, signal processing, etc.) can reside "virtually" in the computer as software. This also saves on space, meaning you can locate your project studio in a corner of your living room. With a laptop and a lunch box full of gear (USB interface, mics, headphones, etc.), your project studio can go and be anywhere.

And you do not need tens of thousands of dollars invested in gear to make money. You can start small and stay small, or grow in whatever ways your personal goals demand. Also, you do not have to earn tens of thousands of dollars to profit nicely. You can keep your project studio as a tidy sideline business that lets you hone your chops and support your gear habit. Alternately, you may choose to expand into something bigger. You must define what profit means to you, and then pursue your personal vision of it.

"I believe that if this is something you want to do, you must be willing to commit yourself for the long haul," advised David Conley in the survey. "There will be times when your faith in your dream is tested . . . and I mean TESTED! Getting your project studio is a cool thing, because if you have an idea at 4:00 AM, you can get it on (virtual) tape, but it is only one step in a long road. It's a tool, like any other tool. A composer must have a studio if he or she is serious about accomplishing in this field. It's like the darkroom of the photographer or the workshop of the master mechanic. It goes with the territory."

Don't suffer the heartache expressed by one project studio owner: "My biggest regret in building a studio is that I didn't start twenty years ago." Instead, get started today. Follow the advice that another owner gives to all those contemplating starting their own project studio: "If you're even thinking about it—*do it now*! Don't wait until you have the money for the 'best' gear. You'll be waiting forever, because there's always something better coming out next NAMM, the International Music Products Association semi-annual trade show. Get started with whatever budget you have right now, and let your clients pay for more. Try to stay out of debt as much as possible, at least in the beginning. Keep your gear lust at bay, and buy only what you *really* need. Remember, tools do not replace talent."

What Is a Project Studio?

Most project studios feature an artist working primarily alone from his usually home-based production studio doing creative work using the tools of his trade. This artist can be a musician, composer, voice artist, sound effects designer, or other music-and-sound professional. The tools these artists use help them realize their ideas. The archetypal project studio functions as *your* personal workshop for expressing your creative ideas, rather than as a commercial facility for hire. That said, there are essentially four kinds of project studios in use today.

Artist Studio

This is a personal project studio owned and operated by a recording artist for the sole purpose of working on his or her own specific studio recordings. These artists rarely work on productions that aren't their own. An example would be a songwriter who produces her own CD, in whole or in part, from her own project studio.

Beck's *Midnite Vultures* was the prototypical artist project studio recording. The setup in Beck's Pasadena home comprised good mics, great preamps, a mixer for monitoring, and a Pro Tools rig. Engineer Mickey Petralia explained about working on the project, "It was like hanging out with your friends and making music. There was never any pressure, there was never a label or management. It was like sitting around your friend's home studio and just banging out some music. Sometimes, when you work that way, it has a vibe. You can capture stuff, more moments, that way, as opposed to, I think, in a studio."

Some project studios are temporarily set up in a home or rented property for the sole purpose of recording a single project. James Taylor's *Hourglass* was tracked at Martha's Vineyard. What started as just a simple recording of the band's rehearsal became the album's basic tracks. All the other overdubbing and sweetening went onto these tapes.

It is now possible to lock yourself away in some remote retreat, record, and then disassemble your project studio and finish the recordings elsewhere.

Project Studio for Private Use

Music and sound professionals use their project studios to produce a variety of recordings for different clients. The distinction between this form and the artist-in-residence is that in this case, the project studio owner works on other people's projects, not strictly his own. An example would be a composer who uses his studio to compose and record the soundtracks to several films a year. The composer, like other project studio owners who work similarly, is selling his *talent* to clients. The studio itself is inconsequential to the client. As one put it, "I am not open to business in the commercial studio sense. My project studio is a workshop for me to do my films and productions. I promote the artist/composer/producer. The studio is merely a tool. I don't want to open my doors as a commercial studio because of all the traffic that will result in my home and the wear and tear on the gear. This area is flooded with commercial studios; it is a rat race I do not wish to engage in."

Jan Hammer was one of the first to use a project studio for TV scores. He composed, recorded, and mixed all the music for the *Miami Vice* television series from his project studio, located in the dining room of his upstate New York farmhouse. He subsequently built a more permanent home studio in an adjacent barn on his property. Consisting of an open control room and live tracking room, Hammer uses the facility to continue his work. The control room accommodates his recording gear and electronic keyboard instruments, while the tracking room is more for live drums, piano, and guitar amps. Like many project studio owners, Hammer prefers to work alone. He carefully wired his studio to accommodate this one-man-band work ethic. He can play guitar while seated at the console (with the amp and speakers in the tracking room), and he can run the multitrack recorder using a remote while seated at the piano. According to Hammer's technical assistant, Andy Topeka, "Musicians like Jan want a place where they can go and make their music without technicians hanging over them."

Even some voice-over artists have project studios. They record their parts into hard-disk systems, mix the tracks, and deliver on CD or via modem. Using a phone patch, the producer can hear the recording and make suggestions to be assured of the final product. Now, the voice artist doesn't need to travel and can do more sessions in a day.

Project Studio for Public Use

Essentially, this is a small home studio acting as a commercial facility. Anyone can book time to record anything. These studios take in any work that comes their way. Here, the people buy the room itself—studio time—to make their own recordings. Though some people view these situations as low-budget competitors to commercial studios, they actually serve a useful purpose, picking up the clients large studios mostly ignore.

Project Studio for Fun

These personal spaces are dedicated to recording enthusiasts who may or may not move on to paying gigs. Since many of these project studios are in spare bedrooms, the industry media recently coined the moniker "guest room warrior" to represent this group.

What is important to note is that many project studios are hybrids of these forms. This fact enables most project studio owners to diversify their business in such ways that help them increase their profits. This product-and-service diversity is a fundamental concept driving this book's philosophy.

Project Studios in Action

New Age artist Patrick O'Hearn was happy to be recording at his home. In fact, he used his royalty advance and recording fund for one album to buy a Harrison mixing console. "I was able to persuade the label to [take] the money that would have been invested in the commercial studio and advance that to me to purchase the console," he told *Music Technology*. "Private Music was willing to include it in the recording fund, because as far as they were concerned, it wasn't going to cost any more than what we were used to shelling out for me to make a record. It was going to be infinitely beneficial to me and ultimately, if amortized over a few records, was going to bring down their costs considerably." On his next record, O'Hearn followed this route again and acquired a Sony 3324 digital multitrack. "I really don't make any profit on the records, but I have gained a remarkable home studio."

Rudy Sarzo (Quiet Riot) decided to build his studio for his own fun. He told *Home Recording*, "I'm able to work on any project I want here, big or small. I don't have heavy rent to pay. I don't have leases on any equipment, and there isn't a staff to support. I'm able to do what I want to do when I want to do it."

Conversely, composer Mark Isham built a studio capable of handling his film scoring duties in his backyard. He told *Keyboard* that "after having many studios set up in bedrooms and garages, I finally had the opportunity to build my dream studio." Featuring a large control room and separate tracking room, Isham's main instructions were to have the look of a New York loft. He's used the studio to complete his film scoring work for a number of projects.

David Conley has operated his project studio for five years. "I compose film scores, write songs, and orchestrate. I also produce live performances of classical music for broadcast, as well as many other radio programs. I frequently bring that work home." He was a studio musician at seventeen. His weekend band was offered a recording contract and tour. He never looked back, even though the band broke up. Later, he went to Cornish College of the Arts in Seattle and studied composition, graduating with honors. "My project studio started as a MIDI studio and grew as my needs changed. I used to play along with MIDI-recorded elements to two-track audiotape, but as my work as a songwriter grew more and more, I realized that the quality of my demos needed to improve." Conley now completely supports his family with the earnings from his production business.

Ken Feldman started his New York City home studio two years ago as "a side effect of buying gear to work as an audio engineer in Manhattan and buying gear that would allow me to work as a producer who is able to get excellent quality work done on great gear while keeping studio costs to a minimum." Ken has a B.A. in sound recording technology from SUNY Fredonia, and he's been working at studios and in live sound since graduating in 1990. Using money he makes as a professional sound engineer, Ken works from his project studio part-time, recording individual instruments or vocalists and digital eight-track demos with MIDI. He records tracks with the aim of taking his project studio work to a commercial facility for further work and mixing.

For over three years, Jimmy Graham has worked from his home project studio, handling full album recording and production, custom music tracks, voice-overs, commercials, karaoke recordings, mobile recording, and audio-program editing and mastering for local bands and businesses. With his recording engineering degree from the Recording Institute of Detroit and fifteen years as a professional musician/songwriter (guitar, vocals, bass, keys), his aim is to "give artists the ability to get high-quality recordings without bankrupting the band."

Harlan Hogan, a Chicago-based voice artist, provides some of his narration talents from his own project studio. He, like many other project studio owners, fell into the production side through osmosis. "I started doing audition tapes on cassette at my house, progressed to reel-to-reel, and emerged with a simple project studio, including an ISDN line for hookups around the world. I was forced by necessity to learn to record well and deliver finished tracks." Commercials are the real moneymakers, but nonbroadcast work (corporate industrials and educational productions) is his base. He also does phone-hold projects and recently expanded into writing spots and scripts and producing the narration. If the job is beyond his skill, Hogan prefers to go to a commercial studio and let the pros handle it. He feels the costs of doing it this way are far cheaper in the long run, as he would waste too much time trying to do something outside his area of expertise. He is also adamant that he's not in competition with the pros. "Yes, I have recording facilities for my personal use, but if the client needs the bells and whistles of a commercial studio, I urge them to go to the studio. But for simple projects, I can add value through my all-in-one package deal."

Why Are Project Studios So Popular?

There are five reasons why more and more music and sound professionals choose a project studio as their personal workspace.

Technology

Today's technology has put incredible power into our hands at prices that continue to plummet. For around $10,000, you can put together a studio that would have cost five to ten times as much less than a decade ago. Researching this book found me plowing through my filing cabinets for clippings of two decades of my favorite music industry articles. As I read through the material, I discovered a rather interesting, natural progression of technological change. We all thought MIDI was amazing. Compared to the power of today's digital audio workstations, that format seems like the Dark Ages. Ironically, there was one prominent thread that appeared from this backlog of industry observations: Technology would kill the music industry. The same dire prediction was repeated ad nauseam. Synthesizers and samplers would replace live players. MIDI would let everyone be a great composer. Commercial studios would disappear. And desktop studios would rule. None of these worries came true completely. Instead, our music and sound industry has evolved alongside the technology and continues to grow exponentially each year.

The yin-yang of technology is both exciting and troublesome, a blessing and a curse. We have so many great tools at our disposal that can make our music and sound work better and more creative. At the same time, the technology moves so fast that keeping up often squanders our precious resources of time and attention. It's plain hard work to understand the changes, and incorporating them into a project studio is often even more challenging. What do you do? Do you lock yourself away and avoid change? I don't think so. But you must use caution and restraint. If a client requests a new piece of gear, then you'd better jump on the bandwagon, but otherwise, I'd suggest you move cautiously in the technology maze. Constantly upgrading can play real havoc on your ability to actually get things done!

Electronic Musician recently reported the other side of this issue. As one up-and-coming artist confessed, "I don't want to invest all my money in equipment and then spend the time learning to use it all instead of developing myself as an artist." The same person went on to say that booking studio time was worse, because he always kept an eye on the clock. Although there are some dissenters, most of us embrace technological change as a welcome friend. It is, for us, the best way to put bread on our tables.

The Home-Based Family Business

The project studio is also part of a larger movement toward home-based businesses. Working from your home provides certain flexibility that helps many creative types thrive. Technology enabled this work-from-home revolution and has created a new "family business." Before industrialization, people worked together from their home to support the family. They grew their own food, made their own clothes, and generally divvied up the responsibilities to run the household. Everybody pitched in, because survival depended upon it. The move to industrialization, and the resulting shift of society toward consumerism, separated home and work life. Today, more people have returned to the home and have made it the center of both work and family. The entire household is once again contributing to the success of the family business. Jeffery Dunnigan's wife manages the studio and does the books while he concentrates on the music and engineering. Tim Butler relies on his spouse to "make phone calls to get contact names. She's much more sociable than me." Dave Davies adds, "My kids are involved in several aspects of the business."

Working for Yourself

Full-time employment in the music and sound industry is rare. This forces many to become self-employed, less by choice and more by necessity. The truth is, you have a much better chance of starting and succeeding with your own project studio business than trying to find a "job" in the industry. Today, 90 percent of the music industry is self-employed. Do you know what that really means? Nine out of every ten of the creative professionals in the industry run their own business! It would be a long shot to think you could ever land a music industry job, because there really is no such thing. We all just *rent* our talents. Therefore, you have only one alternative: Jettison the résumé. Instead, acquire solid business skills—how to manage people and projects, how to promote successfully, and how to manage your finances—combine them with your music and sound talent and you'll have the foundation on which to build your successful project studio business career.

Competitive Edge

The music and sound industry is highly competitive and rife with dedicated, innovative, and passionate professionals. Having access to the better tools can give many the edge they need to lead the crowd. We also work in a highly personal business that emphasizes delivering complete production services with minimal fuss. The industry also demands versatility, which forces you to become a jack-of-all-trades: finding clients, designing projects, writing contracts, paying the bills, playing all the instruments, finishing the mix, packaging a CD, sweeping the floor, and completing any number of related and ancillary tasks. When you run your own project studio, there will be a lot of work to do. Rest assured that there will be rewards for all your hard work as well.

Lower Cost, Increasing Income

Your project studio can be how you make a living, or it can just put some extra cash in your pocket. The project studio is the perfect marriage between artist and production. The low overhead of such a venture gives the artist freedom to create without the burden of the time clock ticking off dollars. Any reasonably well-equipped studio can turn out master- and broadcast-quality work. No longer is home recording an excuse for substandard work. Though many project studio owners work from a home studio, there is some amazing work coming from those basements and spare bedrooms.

Along with the lower costs comes the potential for higher income. Many projects are now contracted as package deals. For example, a package deal for a film composer means the composer is responsible

9

for all costs to produce the music: composing, arranging, recording costs, talent fees, and more. The package deal is why so many composers work from their own project studios, composing, playing, recording, and mixing all on their own. It's the only way to ensure they make any money on the deal.

Ye Olde Days

Before the home studio revolution, there was only one way to record: commercial facilities. Although there have always been small studios available at cheap rates for demos and such, it took major technological advances to bring real quality to the masses at prices that made sense. MIDI was one major step forward. Working from home, you could sequence your keyboard and drum machine parts, then take the sequence to a commercial recording studio and use all their gear to realize and finalize your musical ideas. Chances are, the commercial facility had an extensive MIDI setup, access to other gear, and professional experience to make your music even better.

Richard Souther took a similar route with his debut synth-based album, *Heirborne*. "Souther carefully sequenced more than twenty analog and digital synthesizers in advance of the actual recording," reported *Mix*. "The sessions were eventually completed by pulling a twenty-four–track mobile recording studio up to [Souther's] home studio and transferring the sequenced parts to tape. The album was later mixed at Larry Carlton's Room 335."

The Dawn of the Project Studio

The arrival of affordable digital multitracks really transformed home recording into the project studio we know today. The quality level jumped exponentially, and as the equipment improved further, the line between project studios and commercial studios blurred. Although entire projects start and end at commercial facilities, the project studio continues to impact the industry. Will the project studio dominate as the place from which music and sound originates? I doubt it. Most commercial studios have learned to coexist with the project studio phenomenon. There are certain advantages in commercial facilities, such as terrific room acoustics, the latest, greatest gear (such as microphones and outboard processing), access to big recording spaces, accurate mixing environments, and lastly, but surely most importantly, good people with professional experience.

Many commercial studios have even learned to cater to the special needs of project studios. Tracks start out in someone's living room and eventually make it into a commercial studio. Others record the basic tracks at the commercial studio, then return to the home project studio for track clean up, vocal and instrument overdubs, comping, and mix preparations. After all that work, they return to mix at the big studio. The Internet band phenomenon Fisher (no relation) recorded their album, *True North*, using this method. They went to a commercial studio to lay down drums, piano, and other acoustic instruments, used their home project studio to overdub vocals, guitars, and so forth, and finally went back to the commercial studio for the final mix.

Many people do the opposite by recording their basic tracks on digital equipment at their home project studio and then take either the tapes or the computer files to the commercial facility for final mixing. And, of course, some people do the entire project in their own project studio.

Glen Ballard claims he produced 75 percent of Alanis Morissette's *Jagged Little Pill* in his project studio, including mixing the entire album from the Alesis ADAT session tapes on his Euphonix console. He told *EQ*, "Everything was created in that environment, just the two of us. When we overdubbed drums and other musicians [at a commercial facility], that was kind of postproduction, almost."

Right now, by using portable hard disk drives or CD-ROMs, you can "hot swap" sessions and move from studio to studio with ease. Jeff Bova explained how this process works: As a popular synthesist, he sweetens tracks for many clients at his project studio. He told *Mix* that "hot swapping drives has made things totally transparent. Clients come here with material they've begun on Pro Tools and dropped to a hard drive or CD-ROM. I boot the session on my rig and continue to work. When we're done here, we drop to hard drive once again and send the drive off to wherever it's going next—upstairs or to some country."

The Growing Role of the Project Studio

The music and sound industry as a whole embraces a spirit of independence and interdependence. It's quite common for several professionals with their own project studios to work together on a project and then go their separate ways at its conclusion. These same people may unite periodically, in whole or in part, as new situations arise.

Also, project studios are not confined to music production. The real power of the project studio is its impact on other industries. For example, video postproduction often takes advantage of project studios. Once the program material is photographed, the film gets digitized for editing using a computer-based nonlinear editor (NLE). The director and editor work from the editor's project studio to edit the show. When the show is cut, copies are given to the composer and sound effects professionals. The composer spots the show with the director to determine where to place the music and what that music will sound like. The composer returns to his home project studio to complete the score. At his project studio, the sound designer spots the show to determine the placement of needed effects. These effects are recorded and synched to the picture. Another project studio handles the Foley effects, while still another finishes the Automatic Dialogue Replacement (ADR). The director, editor, composer, and sound designer meet at the dubbing stage to bring together all the elements to create the final program. Most of the work gets done in individual's project studios. Only the dubbing stage is done at the real commercial facility in this example.

As broadband, high-speed Internet access becomes ubiquitous, file sharing and long-distance collaboration will become the norm, rather than the exception. Throughout the whole process described above, the director can see and hear how the film is coming together without leaving his home or office. Everybody works together as if they were all in the same room—even if they are miles, even continents apart!

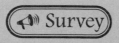 Survey

How did you get started with your project studio and why did you start it?

♩ My friend and I have been talking about getting some music put together and go the indie route, so acquiring a studio was the best bet to begin with.

♩ I grew tired of chasing the major label album deal with my original band, and it was getting too hard to make a decent living with the orchestra and lounge gigs in Las Vegas. So, I broke my original band up, quit the two-show bands, and moved to start afresh.

♩ I owned a software company that shipped around the world. I started making training videos for the programs and added a bit of audio gear throughout that time. I sold the company four years ago, but kept the audio/video part. When I built the dedicated building, I got deep into the audio side.

♩ Started out recording music as a personal hobby, then was approached, through a friend, to write music for theater. I now write a variety of scores for professional theater from time to time.

♩ It started out of necessity. I produce and release my own records, so I needed a place to save on studio time. I also produce my own radio show.

♩ A friend needed a space and some gear to record a local band. The twenty-five–track CD went on to becoming one of Canada's best-selling indie releases in the summer of 1998.

♩ I started by recording people in my basement on my four-track cassette machine. It looked like I was going to be recording people my whole life, whether I was in the business or not, so I decided to make it my business.

- ♪ Started a band, needed a place to practice and write my music.

- ♪ I bought an ADAT to record my band, and it just kept growing from there.

- ♩ I originally started a project, or artist's studio, because I found that I could compose and record myself cheaply because of the falling prices of music technology, and I could do it at any time of the day I wanted to.

- ♩ Got started by recording solo piano pieces with a four-track cassette recorder. The studio grew as I realized that one day, I could make a livelihood from my composing and arranging skills, indulging my passion.

- ♩ I started as a musician who wanted to provide music services to the business community. I think I neglected that community for the consumer market because of the home/office environment, but I intend on reengineering at a commercial location for the business community.

- ♩ I am a professional musician, play with a progressive rock group. We recently reformed, and my interest in doing my own studio for song development and as an income stream emerged.

- ♩ I got started around 1995 with a four-track and a microphone. I'd been playing, writing, and performing music for over ten years. My few experiences in professional studios had been disappointing and expensive. I knew I could do better.

- ♪ To create my own music, I started getting into digital recording.

- ♩ I got started with my project studio because I didn't have the money to go to a professional studio and complete an album. I started with a Boss DR-5 and have been building from there. I'm still building piece by piece.

(2)

Having What You Need to Succeed

T*he proper mental attitude* is an important asset you will need to develop. The first step is to align your personal and professional life into an integrated whole focused on building and sustaining your project studio as a business. I've met and worked with many talented people during my life. Those people who are successful exhibit several common characteristics. While these attributes are not solely responsible for their success, they are common ingredients you should consider cultivating in your career.

Passion

You must bring your desire to succeed to your project studio. Successful people are extremely passionate about their work. Ask one to talk about what she does, and her whole demeanor changes. There's a glow in the eyes; they become more animated and expressive. When you are excited, your enthusiasm and energy increase. When you are passionate, your outlook and "inlook" change. One person said, "It's like being in love!" That may indeed be true. Part of this passion stems from integrating your work with your personal aspirations. It's easy to be passionate about something you love doing.

Dedication

You must have a personal stake in your project studio. Its success is your success. Everything you do affects you personally; it is a reflection of you. That's why you must dedicate yourself to your career to sustain it. There is risk in going it alone, and if you are not serious about making your business viable, you will face failure. Dedication means being willing to buckle down and do whatever it takes to make it. You may need to sacrifice a little to realize your dreams. Don't look at these sacrifices as some form of denial. Instead, tell yourself you are focusing on what you really want and need.

Confidence

You wouldn't even consider starting your own project studio if you didn't feel you could make some money at it. You're prepared to take the risks because you trust your abilities. Possessing and projecting a strong self-image is one quality shared by many of the world's most successful people. They think and feel "can do," not "can't." While it's not unusual to be a little overwhelmed at times, exuding positive confidence at crucial junctures is a significant factor in continued prosperity.

There are several limiting behaviors that can interfere with your confidence. The most obvious is worry. While a little concern for outcomes acts as a check and balance in your life, too much worry can freeze you into inactivity. Procrastination is another form of self-sabotage that you must overcome as well. Close on its destructive heels is making excuses with ifs, ands, and buts. "I can't start yet, because I need a better microphone, better recorder, better fill-in-the-blank." You should also try to eliminate envy and self-pity from your life. These are horribly destructive forces that can adversely interfere with your personal and professional life.

Do you ever feel that if only you had more time, you could be more creative? Do you think that if only you had more money, you could buy more gear and make your project studio even better? Often, when facing the dreaded blank page, artists look for excuses. If that's you, consider this: All artists must create under resource limitations. You have to do the best you can, given the time, money, and other assets you have available. An infinite amount of time will rarely yield a better piece of art. Instead, you'd probably never finish anything. Economics and the vagaries of life always put constraints on the creative process. But that is what it is all about: doing your best under the circumstances. You must catch the muse, harness its power, and use instinct, craft, and talent to transform the indefinable into something tangible. So, forget about the "if only . . ." and just get started creating with what you have around you and inside you right now.

Also, it's hard to objectively evaluate your own skills. Sometimes, you just have to put your work out into the world and see what happens. Ultimately, the clients who hire you will be the final judge of your competency! Sometimes, what you really need is a little push from someone who's been there. Look for a mentor, or perhaps just call on someone whom you admire. Take her to lunch, and pick her brain or just listen politely as she reminisces about the past. Alternately, hire someone for help. Bring in another pro engineer to run a few sessions, and peek over his shoulder. If you need help in a specific area, hire the appropriate person (accountant, promotion expert, etc.). These tactics are paths to gain the confidence you need to push ahead.

Mastery of Their Talent and Art

One personality trait that contributes to the confidence factor mentioned above is that most successful people simply know what they are doing. Rarely does someone sit down and decide to start a project studio. Usually, it's a logical series of steps that finds you one day immersed in this business. Along the way, you collect the skills necessary to do the work. What ordinarily occurs along that same route is a realization of who you really are. When you make the journey of self-discovery while accumulating real-world skills, you emerge as a potent force, ready to face the daily challenges presented to you.

Creative Temperament

Diversifying your project studio is a real key to making your business successful. There is another benefit to diversity besides the monetary gains: Many creative people get bored too easily and welcome exciting, new challenges to their life. If that is you, diversifying your project studio can help you better satisfy your creative spirit. There will be more and varied work to do that keeps you from falling into the pit of drudgery and routine. Personally, I'm constantly juggling several disparate enterprises to maintain both my financial and emotional health. My project studio business specializes in music, sound, and graphic design for new media. I'm constantly augmenting my *Melomania* music library. I also regularly consult with other people and companies to help

17

them start, build, and sustain their creative businesses through specific promotional techniques. I regularly write new, update old, and promote all my books and other music and sound business success resources. There's a serious music enterprise in perpetual production. And there are many other projects, large or small, worthwhile or frivolous, capturing my attention at any given moment.

Take-Charge Attitude

You can't sit around on your hands and wait for something—anything—to happen. You must take initiative and be proactive from the start. Nothing is going to happen unless you make it so. Accepting full responsibility for your success means you have to work hard to maintain it. You need to be aggressive, not sheepish about promoting your work. Let's say you have a few projects running, some money in the bank, and things are going well for you. Now is the time to celebrate. Hooray! However, now is not the time to become too complacent. Use caution before you reward yourself. You can't risk neglecting matters completely. It's far too easy to lose sight of your goals when you're busy or when everything seems so fine. Check to see if you're still on track. Make sure you keep promoting and trying to land new gigs. Don't let the euphoria of apparent success breed laziness. Business invariably has a way of taking a downturn and catching you off guard. Are you prepared?

Self-Reliance and Motivation

When you work on your own, you are responsible for everything. If *you* don't do the work, who will? You can't blame anyone, nor can you delegate your tasks to an underling. It's your baby, and you better be ready to work hard. If you need someone hovering over your shoulder urging you on, you'd better seriously re-evaluate your chosen profession. You must motivate yourself to get to the desk each day and do what has to be done. Procrastination and sloth have no place in your life if you plan on profiting from your music and sound project studio.

The project studio business can be a lonely job. You may be forced to sit in front of your computer for days, editing endless takes of a voice-over into a coherent production. If you don't work well or effectively on your own, you might find it difficult to run your project studio. On the other side, you may have a bevy of clients parading about your room, leaving you little solitary time. That may be exactly what you need, while another might find that horrifying. Some people love the freedom of the project studio, while others hate the demands. Striking your balance is the key.

Knowing Your Strengths and Weaknesses

Part of planning means examining your skills, talents, and ambitions. You really need to objectively evaluate what you bring to your venture. Through that exploration, you'll uncover your particular power and, hopefully, recognize your shortcomings, too. To be successful, you must always work your strengths and either try to overcome your weaknesses or get help to fill the void. In essence, you use your strengths to your greatest ability and reap the most from them. Likewise, downplay your weaker facets to avoid problems. Don't force yourself into situations that don't fit with your particular skill set. For instance, you may be an outgoing person who responds well in front of people. You won't want to lock yourself in your studio with little client contact.

Thick Skin

You must learn not to take rejection personally. I know this advice is somewhat contradictory to what I've said above. While you are totally responsible for the success and failure of your project studio business and career, don't take every little setback as utter failure on your part. Learn to separate circumstances you can't control from those you can. Sometimes, people will hang up on you or—believe it or not—actually not like the work you've done for them. Strive to do your best at all times, but don't dwell over mistakes or short-sighted clients.

Entrepreneurial Spirit

People who are in business for themselves get it. People who have never worked on their own simply don't get it. I'm not being impertinent here. Working on your own, for yourself, requires a certain mind-set that few possess. Entrepreneurs want to be a success on their own and on their own terms. They don't want to punch a clock and collect a pay check. They get a certain satisfaction from supporting their lifestyle through mostly their own toil. It doesn't require an encyclopedic knowledge of business, but it does take a keen sense of what being in business means and what it takes to build and sustain one. Those who fail with their small business ventures too often neglect the importance of this point. Doing the creative work in your project studio is only one part of the whole business scene. You can't neglect the other aspects, such as promotion, bookkeeping, and so forth. Being self-employed is never easy. With self-employment comes a bevy of concerns that can create undue stress. Because you're faced with constantly drumming up work, I compare it to being on a job-search treadmill. You're forever sending out promotional material (résumés), meeting with prospective clients (job interviews), and following up. You fail to land the gig, but you keep working at it, because your livelihood depends upon it.

People who possess this entrepreneurial spirit thrive on these demands. People who don't have what it takes sometimes crumble under the pressures. While I believe you can acquire the skills necessary to be in business for yourself, if you don't have the mental focus or real desire to make it on your own, you will have troubles along the way. So, how do you know whether you have what it takes? You need to seriously evaluate your life goals and make plans. There is more on these subjects later.

Commitment to Success

Though it seems obvious, many people unknowingly forget this crucial step. Before you begin to plan where you want to go and how you'll get there, you must first make this fundamental mental transition. Pledging yourself to making your project studio career the success you envision goes a long way toward helping you actualize that goal. You can't take a wishy-washy, half-hearted stance on this issue. It's not a wait-and-see proposition. You must fully comprehend the ramifications of making the leap to professional project studio owner and dedicate yourself to making it real.

Skills You Must Master to Succeed with Your Goals

It's obvious you need the technical skills necessary to record, mix, and master music and sound projects. You probably already possess these skills, or you wouldn't have chosen this career path in the first place. However, you can't successfully manage your project studio without some additional skills. Those old, clichéd three R's apply: readin', 'riting, and 'rithmetic. Also, follow the advice from psychologist John Rosemond, who says that we all should learn the other three R's: "respectful, responsible, and resourceful." I would also add honesty, confidence, tolerance, compassion, enthusiasm, and patience to this list. Adapt the way you think to these principles, and practice cultivating these qualities. You will never regret mastering these skills, as they will serve you throughout your life.

Learning the Ropes

Sound engineers used to work their way through the ranks at commercial facilities. They would start as gofer, move to second engineer, and after a myriad of sessions, eventually get their big break as a full-fledged engineer. Along the way, the senior engineers would teach recording techniques and how to be an effective part of the creative team. Today, many people learn from their project studios and sacrifice the apprenticeship that so typified a past sound engineer's course of study. With so much information available in magazines, books, and the Web, the fledgling music and sound engineer can acquire a vast amount of practical industry knowledge. To this information, it is critical to add real-world experience, gleaned by working closely with others. This interaction is vital. Many project studio owners are one-person shops and have infrequent contact with the outside world. This stifles the creativity and objectivity of the project studio. Getting out and working alongside other music and sound professionals is generally the only cure.

Besides, you can learn a great deal from a seasoned professional by just watching him or her work for a few hours or days. Mark Hudson (of Hudson Brothers fame) spoke of working with legendary engineer Geoff Emerick on the mixing for Ringo Starr's *Vertical Man*. "That was a lesson for me," he told *Electronic Musician*. "If every engineer in the industry watched Geoff Emerick for a day, they'd either quit or completely change their way of thinking. I learned a lot from watching him work." Ken Feldman echoed Hudson's comment. "Hire a pro engineer for a project or two, so you can watch and see other—possibly better—ways of using your gear to its maximum potential."

21

People Skills

You will work with a lot of people throughout your career. That means you better quickly develop the right attitude that enables you to work effectively with both the good and bad people the world brings to your doorstep. This ain't easy. Sure, some clients are a dream and love everything you do. Others can be so nitpicky that it almost drives you insane. Remember who signs the check, though. That's the person you must please. Sometimes, you might not agree with what they want. Go ahead and offer an alternative, but be prepared to do it their way in the end.

Writing

Bad relationships with clients and vendors are a primary reason for business failure. Poor communication is frequently cited as the major reason these relationships go sour. Therefore, you must also learn to communicate effectively when running your own project studio.

The writing you send out into the world is a reflection of you. Make sure it delivers the image and message you are trying to convey. If you can't write a cohesive sentence, you'd better take some time to practice. Concentrate on delivering your message quickly, simply, and clearly. Nobody will ever complain or be turned off by plain prose. They will, however, highly suspect your professionalism when faced with rambling, unfocused text loaded with grammatical and spelling errors. Rewriting is the real secret to good writing that communicates well. Go ahead and scribble down those first thoughts. However, make sure you carefully review your words, make necessary changes, and only then create the final draft.

Speaking

Your project studio will demand you to be in constant contact with people on the phone and in person. As with writing, your oral delivery can sometimes make or break you. Practice speaking slowly, clearly, and confidently. Try to be friendly and enthusiastic when you speak. Record your voice and listen to it. Do you hear any major problems you could easily overcome? In promotional situations, it might be helpful to script and learn some pat answers to common questions. Knowing what you need to say can help you communicate better in pressure situations.

Listening

In the creative sphere in which we work, there are some rather gregarious individuals who tend to dominate conversations. Get two talkers in a room together and nothing gets done because they keep cutting each other off. As the professional who is mostly called upon to help others solve their problems, you must master your *listening* skills. Your clients will invariably tell you what they really want. If you're talking all the time, you'll never hear what you need to know. Active listening takes concentration, patience, and discipline. You must pay attention to what the other person says and try to read between the lines. You'll need discipline, so that when you feel you need to say something, you know you should keep your mouth shut instead.

Researching

You must learn how to find the information you need to operate your project studio and also, how to use what you do find intelligently. For example, if you don't know who your clients are or will be, or what they do or where they come from, how can you successfully launch your project studio? Who is your market? Who is your competition? Are there any industry trends that might affect your business? These are question you may need to answer, and knowing how to find the right information is an important skill for you to have.

Studying

Don't ever stop learning. Become a lifelong student. Try to constantly expand your knowledge base, because that lets you greatly expand your opportunities for success, too. Take classes that let you master new skills or sharpen your current ones. Read to learn and to grow. Regularly read your local paper, a major metropolitan paper, a weekly news magazine, the industry trades, and other books and magazines, both inside and outside your interests. Another key way to truly grow as a professional is to experience more in your life. Consider travel, volunteer work, interning, or working part-time in another field to expand your horizons. Get a mentor who supplies the filler for the gaps in your knowledge.

The best way to break into a new field or area is to learn about it firsthand. Look for a project that lets you test the waters. Let's say you've been doing music, but now you want to land voice-over recordings. Is there a small advertiser, perhaps even a charity or local school event, for whom you could prepare a promotional spot for little or no money? It's a win-win situation, as you gain valuable experience and they get the audio work they need free (or at little cost). If you're a smart, ruthless self-promoter, you'll leverage that initial success to get more similar projects. Ask this initial client to provide a testimonial and reference that you can use to promote your new service to others.

For the musically inclined, take up another instrument. For example, if you play keys, take up guitar. You'll gain useful, new perspectives that can trigger creativity. I wanted to learn the flute, so I bought a cheap bamboo flute and gained a fresh perspective on my music at the same time. You might consider taking some lessons on both your chosen instrument and/or a new acquisition. The discipline and guided instruction can help you find new ways to express yourself.

Go back to school, and take some classes in either related or unrelated fields. The different viewpoint provided by a good teacher can be refreshing. Having a group of peers can also help you kick around ideas and provide a needed spark. I've found that taking a class in a wholly unrelated area has an even greater impact on your current work. The fresh outlook provided by a new subject can rekindle your fire and deliver ideas you wouldn't have thought of without the change. Never be afraid to look outside the boundaries and stretch yourself a little. I followed my own advice and decided to try Tai Chi for the reasons outlined above. Specifically, I always had an interest in Eastern philosophy, and I feel Tai Chi is the physical embodiment of that philosophy's fundamental concepts. I also needed to immerse myself in something completely different from my usual music, sound, and writing work. Concentrating on the movements helps clear my head and refresh my work direction. Plus, I desperately needed to get some more exercise!

Rudimentary Business Background

Since you know that running your own project studio business is the only way to be successful, you need to acquire the basic business skills necessary to be effective. Learn business math, so you can better handle your personal and professional finances. This book provides the initial information you need. However, you may require refinements to the sensible advice offered here. That should motivate you to acquire the additional business information you need that supports your particular situation.

Basic Electronics Knowledge

When I took Sound Engineering 101 in college (the only sound course I've ever had in my life), the teacher spent the entire quarter on one subject: the amplifier circuit. His contention was that the amplifier circuit is the basis for almost all analog music components. If you knew how an amplifier worked, including the components that comprise it, you knew most of what you needed to know about electronics. After building that foundation, you could move on to other sound topics— in Sound Engineering 102! I never took another course on sound engineering. I did, however take classes on musical acoustics (how instruments create their sounds) and room acoustics (the action of sound in an environment). These three courses concluded my formal education in sound production. The rest of my knowledge came through trial and error, coupled with lifelong self-study.

You will be better off if you gain a basic understanding of electronics, too. Do you know how an amplifier works? Do you know how to solder a cable? Do you know the basic parts of electronics—op-amps, capacitors, resistors, diodes, transformers, transistors, IC chips—and what they do? How do these components affect your sound? Even a rudimentary understanding of electronics can come in handy. I also feel that knowing the basic physics of sound can be invaluable.

Strong Computer Skills

Do you know computers? Chances are, you will use a computer for your project studio business, even build your entire business around one. Consequently, you really need to know how to troubleshoot it or hire someone who can! My entire business revolves around my computers, so they are central to my continued livelihood. I suspect that many of my project studio colleagues rely on their computers more than any single component. And, as technology continues to promote the computer hardware and software platform for audio production, the PC's central role will become paramount.

As any PC owner can testify, it's tough to keep the box working. Add in the demands of audio production to the already-teetering stability of the current PC crop, and well, it all adds up to one frustrating experience. You can't just use a PC; you have to baby-sit it, nurture it, feed it, and generally take care of its every whim. Once in a while, the box will reward you with a trouble-free session (I once went a whole week without a problem . . . I was on vacation!). Unfortunately, without some geeky hacker knowledge, you will be at a severe disadvantage when facing inevitable "PC quirks." If you have to wait endlessly on hold for technical support, you will waste valuable time that could be better spent more productively. Instead, learn all you can about your computer system (and other gear for that matter), so that you can keep everything in sound working order. Specifically, you need to learn how to:

- Run diagnostics
- Install, uninstall, and reinstall software
- Recover from big failures
- Get around little failures
- Make a boot disk, update it regularly, check to make sure it works, and keep it in a safe place!
- Upgrade with caution

The latest and greatest is not always bug-free. I absolutely hate putting down new software, because I know I'm going to have some problem. Once I get the PC working well, with the components I need, I try to leave it all alone. It takes something really enticing to get me to risk an upgrade. And OS upgrades? Forget about them. I'm always intentionally two years behind.

There is some fine software by the folks at Symantec (*www.symantec.com*) that has saved and continues to save my butt when it comes to computing. I recommend their Norton Utilities, Anti-Virus, and Internet Security products.

Get Help

If you find that your skills in any of these areas are not as good as they should be, swallow your pride and work hard toward improving them. Go back to school, pick up some books on the subject, and practice using these skills regularly with the aim of improving them.

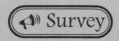

Survey

What do you consider to be your greatest strengths?

- My will to succeed. I have a serious problem with failure.

- My use of creativity in my approach to problem solving.

- Idea man, plus pit bull tenacity on follow-through.

- Musical creativity and the ability to write music in virtually any style.

- That I am a multi-instrumentalist/vocalist and proficient in many musical styles.

- Music production, people skills.

- Resourcefulness. I may not have all of the fanciest gear in the world, but I don't let that stand in the way of me getting the sound I want.

- I am very sociable and talented. I can spot trends pretty well, too.

- My ability to compose and record quality music quickly.

What do you consider to be your weakness?

- I have a problem getting inspiration; sometimes it's there, and sometimes it's not.

- My lack of marketing knowledge.

- Day-to-day management.

- Knowing what to say and present to prospective clients. I'm also weak in that I never really know what to quote people when it comes down to the money issues.

- That I'm a solitary person who finds it difficult to go around all the time and make new contacts. I like to play with/collaborate with other musicians, but I don't enjoy "networking."

♪ Mixing.

♪ Dealing with the business end of things, i.e., getting paid.

♪ I always have too many things going on at one time.

♪ My "people skills."

♪ Though I have formidable keyboard chops, I have no improvisational ability; this suffers from never really jamming freely with a band, let alone gigging.

♪ Inability to judge my own weaknesses (and lyrics).

♪ Bad temper! Easily bored. Stubborn. Sometimes too attached to my own artistic temperament and vision. Sometimes disorganized and spreading myself too thin.

♪ My wanting to be able to do it all myself.

Do you keep your professional and personal life separate, or are they integrated? Do you find this situation a problem? Please explain why.

♪ My personal life and professional are integrated. Everyone I am affiliated with is into music and wanting to get a studio together. So, my pleasure is my profession.

♪ Nearly fully integrated, probably because of the intense amount of hours I work and the studio being *in* my home. I do not find this a problem; it is who I am.

♪ I melt them together as much as I can, and love it.

♪ My professional life and personal life are deeply integrated, largely because my business is based on relationships with my clients. Sometimes, it's a problem, because I'm by nature a private person.

♪ Sometimes, it's hard to do things with the kids trying to "play" the keyboard! I pretty much have to juggle and find time to promote myself. My wife is, fortunately, *very* supportive and gives me her never-ending encouragement.

- ♪ Even when I leave the studio, I'm still a musician, and since my wife works in the studio and my daughter is frequently hanging around, things are pretty well integrated, and I love it.

- ♪ They've always been integrated for me, because music has always been such a big part of my life.

- ♪ Keep them separate—when I work, I work; when I play, I play.

- ♪ Keep separate. Never mix business with family. It never works out.

3

Planning Your Project Studio Lifestyle

*I*f *you have decided,* after reading the last chapter, that you possess the qualities and the drive to succeed, you are now ready to design (or redesign) your business/lifestyle. The six planning steps are:

- Evaluate your current situation
- Make goals
- Determine the resources you require
- Create a plan
- Implement it
- Review and measure your progress

Where Are You Now?

The first step toward planning your successful project studio is to carefully evaluate your experience, talent, and current situation.

- What are your personal skills (personality, temperament, etc.)?
- What are your professional skills (business knowledge, math, management, etc.)?
- What are your industry skills? (musician, sound engineer, etc.)?
- What are your greatest strengths?
- What do you consider to be your weakness?
- How can you fix what you lack?

Where Do You Wish to Go?

With a careful understanding of your present position, turn your attention toward making specific goals. Imaginative, creative, and passionate artists are those who not only know what they want to do, but also know how they will get there. Don't just make goals for your project studio. Think in terms of personal, professional, family and relationship, and community goals. Since you will use your project studio to support your lifestyle, make sure your plan reflects the other aspects of your life. You also need to make short-term, long-term, and life goals in each of these categories. A short-term goal is usually something you can complete quickly, such as landing a gig that pays enough to upgrade your computer system. Long-term goals always have a distant time horizon. Your life goal indicates the ultimate direction of your life.

Making sure your goals are reasonably realistic is another critical component. Don't say "I will make a million dollars in the next six months" when you've never made more than $40,000 to date. Also, express your goals as a positive. Don't say, "I will quit my job before the end of the year." Instead write down, "I will replace my current job income with income earned through my project studio before the end of the year."

What Do You Need to Reach Those Goals?

Now that you know what you expect from your hard work, determine the many resources you need to get where you want to go. Answer these questions:

- Who will do the work?
- What skills are needed?
- Where will the work be done?
- What equipment is needed to do the work?
- How much money is required?

The next chapter concentrates fully on this subject, and you should review it before you complete this part of your plan.

How Will You Reach Your Goals?

You need to draft a plan of action that lets you move toward your goals with the resources you have available. Don't say, "I want to make money with my project studio." That's too vague. Instead say, "I will earn $20,000 from my project studio by the end of the year." The best plans are specific and measurable. In this example, if your bank account shows a meager gain on December 31, you'll know you didn't meet your goal. Include the necessary elements that support your plan, too. Your plan can be as detailed as you want or just a simple outline of various goals. You should write this plan down and keep it nearby. It's useful to check off your progress as you move along. That also helps you see the big picture during temporary setbacks.

Get Started

Realizing your goals can sometimes be a daunting proposition. You are at point A and you want to get to point Z. If that seems out of reach, focus on getting from point A to point B, then C, and so on. Reaching minor milestones and collecting achievements along the way will keep you on track. As I said in my *Ruthless Self-promotion in the Music Industry* book, "Success comes through careful diligence." It is through working your plan, day in and day out, that you will achieve the goals you've set for yourself. You will become the success you want, need, and deserve.

Review and Measure Your Progress

Your plan is useless if you don't periodically analyze it. Examine your goals to see if you are proceeding as planned. Minor detours are acceptable, but major alterations probably require you to start this planning process all over again. Staying up-to-date with your planning enables you to concentrate on those situations that perpetuate your success. Are you bringing in enough money to pay your bills and hopefully save a little, too? Are you doing as well as you would if you were employed full-time? Compare yourself to others doing similar work. Use the rates cited elsewhere in this book as a starting point. Also, many professional organizations publish more extensive rate surveys that can really help you pin down the right numbers. For example, I do commercial music, and *Film Music* magazine (*www.film-*

musicmag.com) publishes a rate survey each year that provides invaluable insight into the "going rate." I compare my rates to the survey to make sure I'm in line with industry norms.

What is your return on investment? If you're not making 10 to 20 percent (or better), you might be better off investing your money elsewhere. You should have a profit of at least $100 to $200 for every $1,000 you've invested in your business. Stocks average 10 percent a year; you should be beating that with your project studio business. I use this litmus test when deciding whether or not I should purchase new gear. If I spend $300 on a new gadget, it should enable me to earn at least $60 a year (20 percent return) from using it. If not, the same $300 invested in stocks would probably yield a much better return.

Look closely at all your activities or profit centers. Compare the expense of maintaining the activity to the revenue it brings in. Are you spending too much time on activities that provide little real gain? Look at the overall picture. Where is your effort reaping the most reward? It's probably time to let the pipe dreams go and concentrate on the real money. What is your sales and earnings growth? Most bookkeeping software lets you compare just about any period to another. Over the years, some clear trends will appear. Using this real-world financial data helps you make better, more informed decisions when faced with creating a new product or service (or killing off unprofitable activities altogether).

Ask your clients to evaluate how you are doing. Do they like what you offer and how you treat them? Are there ideas they suggest that you could implement? Are they satisfied with where your business is right now and where it appears to be heading? Are they leaving you or worried you might leave them? Try putting together what I call a "kitchen cabinet." Gather a few different people of varied backgrounds and form a sort of executive advisory board. This should be an informal group whose purpose is to help you run your business better. Meet quarterly (at your kitchen table is optional) as a group and discuss the various aspects of your business. While it would be nice if this cabinet included your lawyer, accountant, and others, that might be too costly. I suggest you bring in family, friends, business peers, even some good clients, and use this time to find solutions to problems and to bounce ideas around. You may be pleasantly surprised by the insight provided by these sessions. Use what you discover to improve your business management.

Follow your heart, but pay attention to your gut. Sometimes, your heart can be a little naive. It doesn't always recognize the reality of a situation. If that's the case for you, ask your stomach for a more realistic evaluation. If you have this queasy feeling in your belly, there's a good chance that something's not quite right. Also, don't forget about your personal goals. Working for yourself can be very satisfying, outside of the bread it puts on your family's table. Are you leading the successful life you wish to lead and in the way that only you want to lead it?

Your Darkest Hour

During your review you may discover that you are not where you'd like to be. How can you get back on track? Try these strategies:

'Fess Up

There's nothing better than a heartfelt catharsis to free your mind and body. Find a trusted friend or significant other who will let you dump on them until you get everything out. Make sure this kind soul understands the rules: You are not looking for solutions, you just need to vent a little and let it all go. Needless to say, you will owe this person big time after just such a bitch session. Offer to return the favor or buy them a wonderful, extravagant dinner.

If you're not comfortable with this idea, or if you can't find the right person, pick up pen and paper and write it all down. I suggest not using the computer. Pen in hand on paper is very intimate and lets you write in free form without searching for a mouse or correcting your spelling. One more refinement: Put the pen to the page, and don't pick it up until you are completely finished (or run out of paper, whichever comes first). Once you've scribbled, scratched, and scrawled your thoughts down, fold up the paper and stick it in a drawer. Wait a few days, and read the letter again. You will be surprised by what you wrote. If your situation has changed, destroy the paper and move on. If your situation is still stalled, repeat the whole process again, but this time look for constructive solutions.

Watch out for self-sabotage, too. Author Laurence Boldt offers this method for recognizing and overcoming the obstacles we sometimes put in our own way. Ask and answer these questions: "What did you do to sabotage your own action? How did you do it? Why did you do this? When did you do this? Who helped you accomplish this act? What and how will you fix it and prevent it from happening again?"

Fool Around

What happens in this business is that you start out building your project studio to work exclusively on your own stuff. Then, you realize you need to make some money to pay for your investment (not to mention the other trappings of life). So, you start taking on other projects, and soon you are so busy that you have little time left to work on your own stuff (or you're too tired and creatively exhausted). I know when I'm busy, I sometimes feel guilty if I take time to write a tune, jam on guitar, or surf the Net. But you *must* take breaks to rest your ears, mind, and body. And you must pursue your own passions to feed your soul. Give yourself permission to have fun and play! Don't go too far, though. Clear you head, then get back to working toward your goals when you feel refreshed.

Listen and Learn

Put on your favorite music or sound projects, and rediscover what made you choose this profession in the first place. For me, the Beatles remind me of my love of songwriting. David Torn reminds me to look outside the norm for creative solutions. Torn also exposes my limitations as a guitarist, which compels me to improve my technique. Bernard Herrmann reminds me of my affection for scoring soundtracks. Jan Hammer reminds me of why I built my project studio in the first place. And the original *Star Wars* trilogy on video reminds me that you can put together an incredible soundtrack with a minimum of tools (and one Ben Burdt).

You can also listen on a more critical level to help shed some light on your situation. Drop in a CD, and try to figure it all out. Try to figure out the chords. Try to figure out how they recorded it. How did the engineer get *that* sound? Try to recreate the project in your own way. First, try to do it verbatim, then try to make it different. Recreate the soundtrack to part of a movie: dialogue, sound effects, Foley, and music. You will learn a lot with these exercises.

Listen to music and sound projects you otherwise don't. Pick up some tracks in a new genre and give them a spin. Ask the neighbor kid to borrow her 'NSync CD if you don't want to get caught buying it at the local music store. Check out a television show, even a documentary, for a view of how other people put soundtracks together. Turn on the radio and carefully examine what you hear. In other words, do a little research and apply what you learn toward improving your own particular situation.

Get Clear

It's time for you to clear the clutter from your life. Get rid of physical items you no longer use or need. Let go of your mental rubbish, including old grudges (forgive and forget), prejudices, unsubstantiated notions, and other ideas that impede your progress. Finally, challenge your current beliefs and attitudes. Why do you think/act the way you do? This kind of mental spring cleaning can open your mind to new possibilities and perhaps more opportunities.

Formal Business Plan

You should consider drafting a formal business plan for your project studio business. A detailed plan such as this can serve as the road map that guides your career. The same formal document will be required should you go for a bank loan or try to attract potential investors. To create your plan you need to carefully ask and answer these questions:

- What is your business?
- What will your business be called?
- How will it be organized?
- What are the products and/or services you will offer?
- What will you charge for these products and services?
- What are your plans for the future?
  - What are your personal goals?
  - What are your strategic goals for your business and the action plans to achieve them?
- What is your financial plan?
  - What are your current business assets?
  - Start-up costs?
  - Sales projections for the next five years?
  - Expense projections for the next five years?
  - Personal assets and liabilities?
- What is your promotion plan?
  - Who and where are your clients?
  - What do they want and need?

- How will you reach these people?
- Why should they buy from you?
- Who are your competitors?
- What makes you different from these competitors?
- What specific promotions will you use?
- What additional items should you include?
  - Pictures of your project studio
  - Promotional material
  - CD demo
  - Testimonials or other letters of recommendation
  - Personal information, including copies of tax returns

Create a Budget

Don't ignore the financial aspect when doing your planning. Mention the word "budget," and most people's eyes glaze over. A budget is a tool, not a yoke or a joke. A budget has two sides: income goals and expense projections. Don't do one part of the budget without considering the other. Establishing a basic budget helps you keep careful watch over your business income and expenses. How do you know how much money you need to make if you don't know how much you spend? When asked whether they had an expense budget for the project studio, one survey reply said, "It costs about $2,500 per month to keep the doors open and the equipment from being repossessed." Do you know what *your* dollar figure is? Not controlling costs and not managing your income are main contributing factors to business failure.

If you're starting out, you'll need to make some guesses. If you've been established for some time, you should already have an accurate idea of your typical financial transactions. With the budget in hand, you can see if you are overspending (or underearning) and can take steps to correct problems before they spiral out of control. Follow the steps outlined in chapter 13 to determine your expenses and income needs, and then draft your formal budget.

Keys to Building and Sustaining Your Project Studio Lifestyle

As you work through these planning stages, you will realize the demands required by your creative career. The planning helps you focus on what really must happen to achieve the goals you set for yourself. What will also emerge are nine specific characteristics that contribute to the longevity of your project studio business.

Do What You Enjoy

This is perhaps the simplest advice, but it is, nevertheless, echoed endlessly by the wholly successful people of our world. When you work your true vocation, you will glide through the day effortlessly. You'll face each new challenge aggressively and bask in the good fortune when your endeavors prevail. Frank Wyatt told me, "This may be a difficult process, but it is work that I really love. I am so into doing it well that the days fly by without a moment of boredom, and my only concerns are in the sounds being created around me. It is definitely worth the effort, hopefully financially eventually, but already in the satisfaction that I am doing what I love and can give it 100 percent without regret." Tim Butler added, "Now that I'm building my own business as a soundtrack/jingle composer, I actually get to use every skill and every talent I have, all at once, to make this work. It's all come together perfectly for me. What a great career!"

Get Serious about Your Career

Your project studio can't be something you do until something better comes along. You must devote all your energy and resources toward making it work. The best way to get serious is to begin to run your career as a small business. You don't freelance; you don't work on the side; you don't moonlight. *You operate your own business.* Combining your heart's desire with earning money is one path to an integrated, whole life. I know many people say they would love to just work for the money and leave the job behind when they walk out the door each night. Truth be told, most really successful people have combined their work and personal lives in such ways that help them reach both their goals: money to support their lifestyle and work they adore that is truly fulfilling.

Make Appropriate Sacrifices

You can't have it all—so choose wisely. It is my firm belief that you can have anything you want in life. Unfortunately, you can't have *every-*

thing you want. To be successful usually requires you to sacrifice some things. First, decide what it is you really want, and then, focus your energy on only those aspects that enable you to reach those goals. The rest you must give up or, at the very least, greatly reduce your involvement in them.

Put Together a Team

You can't run a profitable project studio business career without other people. You need clients, obviously, and you may need other help realizing your vision. Find people whom you can trust, but always be reasonably cautious with your alliances and partnerships. You should develop relationships with other professionals right away. Some people you may use only occasionally, while others may become more integral members of your team, even permanent employees. "My day-to-day management skills are not so good," confessed Dave Davies, "so, I hired a manager to take care of all daily activity. I also use a part-time assistant engineer. I do everything else."

Follow these steps when choosing your team members:

- Carefully define your needs. Choosing the right adviser or associate is easier when you know what you want in the first place. You may think you need a copywriter for your promotional brochure, when what you *really* need is a marketing specialist to develop an overall promotional plan for you.
- Find possible candidates. Once you know what you need, select several possible people or firms, and prepare to interview each selection. Ask your family, friends, and other business associates for leads to the professionals you need. Most people are rather candid when it comes to recommending professional services. Your friend is not going to send you to a loser lawyer, so you can take most references seriously.
- Contact these candidates, and request information about their services. Use this information to narrow the field. You may need to set up meetings with the most promising people. For example, you might have a session player come in and audition, or you might review your situa-

tion with a new accountant before selecting the right firm. Make sure you get the answers you need, so that you can make the best possible selection.

You need to exercise some restraint with the people you add to your team. Don't make promises you can't keep, and also make sure you take their judgments with a grain of salt. Remember the age-old adage: "If it sound too good to be true, it probably is."

Before you hire any service provider, product supplier, independent contractor, or employee, follow this process to make sure everything goes smoothly:

- Define the problem or specific need. It's not good enough to say, "I need more sales." A better approach would be to break that down to several little problems. "I need to increase the number of leads from my promotions." Do you see that by focusing narrowly, you better define the problem? This helps both you and your contractor do a better job.
- Take time to present your precise objectives. This step helps ensure that you and your prospective contractor are on the same page. For example: "I want a brochure to describe my project studio and highlight my work. It should be short, simple, and work both as a printed piece and on the Web."
- Agree on the project specifics. Make sure the approach, fee, and completion date fit your objectives fully and that the proposed approach either solves your problem or fulfills your needs completely. Don't let the contractor try to sell you products and services you don't need.
- Divide up the work. Who is responsible for what aspects of the project? If you've hired a duplicator to make CDs, but you haven't finished the master, you can't expect them to make copies until you deliver your part first.
- Get regular updates. The longer the project takes, the more communication you need. On big projects, I prefer to be walked through step-by-step and fully informed of each milestone. Smaller projects might not require as much intervention. Let your gut be the judge.

- Carefully review the work. If the job is not to your satisfaction, demand restitution. If the job met or exceeded your expectations, reward the contractor accordingly with more projects. Tell those who screw up exactly what went wrong and how they can improve their work in the future. If their shoddy work continues, tell them you're choosing another source and why.

One final key member of your team is a valued partner. This partner doesn't need to be a legal partner. While you don't need a sycophant, it can be helpful to have a cheerleader, someone with whom you can celebrate during your greatest victories, who also doubles as a sympathetic shoulder in times of strife. It's even better if this kindred spirit is also "made of rubber," to bounce ideas off of, too. While you might not depend on this person for every final decision, he or she can be a strong contributor to you and your project studio's continued success. Not surprisingly, many project studio owners depend on the support of their spouses. "My wife supports me 100 percent," said Tim Butler. "She totally supports my desire to do this as a full-time profession." Phil Vanderyken concurred: "My wife is a partner. She does annoying little jobs such as sending packages. She's also my biggest critic—which I find invaluable!"

Learn to Be Creative on Demand

I've always been enamored by the creative process. Is there a secret formula to creativity? Entire books have addressed this issue, and one common thread seems to have emerged. New experiences enable people to be more creative. The more you experience with your life, the more you will be inspired. Now, being a professional means being creative on demand. This kind of creativity is usually more technique and craft. The more technically skilled you are, the easier it is for you to find solutions. However, to move beyond the typical response when facing problems requires looking beyond the obvious. If you never really expand your life through having new experiences, you'll face a difficult time tapping your innate creativity.

Think about it. Doesn't something new almost always inspire you and spark your creativity? Have you ever found a new patch on your synth and been inspired to write a new song? Have you ever plugged in a new gizmo only to find yourself using it in new, creative ways you'd never imagined? Have you ever experienced a highly emotional moment in your life that has resulted in your creating something? New experiences breed creativity, while solid technical skills help you harness your muse. Understanding these fundamental creativity ingredients should inspire you to always focus on learning and experiencing more every day. So, commit yourself right now to both sharpening your technical skills and bringing new experiences into your life.

Also, make sure you give your creativity a regular workout through practice. Cultivating and enhancing your creativity should be part of your daily routine. You can't make music on demand unless you've honed your craft first. You can't do novel sound tricks unless you already possess expert knowledge about how your gear works and how to use it to get the sounds you need. Of course, serendipity plays a role in all creative endeavors, but without a firm technical foundation, you may not recognize those serendipitous moments when they arrive.

Another creativity booster is harnessing your youthful exuberance. Children learn through play. They try things out to see what happens. They rarely take the "that'll never work" attitude that frequently plagues adults. As we get older, we often get a little too set in our ways. We are not as open to new ideas as younger people tend to be. This can severely limit the creative flow. In the music and sound world, creativity and craft are tantamount. Though it is fundamental to learn a little from the experience of others, it is equally vital to sometimes let go of old ideas and reinvent the wheel. Along that path, you may also reinvent yourself.

On a more practical level, the vagaries of the project studio business create work opportunities that can arise quite quickly. That means you need to be prepared to deliver with a minimum of time and resources. Deadlines can freeze some people into inactivity, while others thrive on the pressure. If you are the former, I suggest you work hard to prepare shortcuts that enable you to work faster and better when under tight constraints. Setting up your studio for efficiency and taking time to get organized can do wonders in these situations. Arrange your life to complete the tasks necessary to meet the deadline and work diligently. Do what must be done to get the job done right. Burn the midnight oil. Farm out some work to another firm. Let your domestic demands decline (laundry, dishes, etc.). Break up the big project into smaller chunks that you can complete bit by bit. If you thrive on pressure, you probably didn't need any advice.

It's Okay to Make Some Mistakes

When you made a mistake, Mom always told you to chalk it up to experience. I prefer to think that mistakes are the tuition you pay to learn a valuable lesson. How much does it cost to attend the School of Hard Knocks? That depends on what your mistakes are, of course. I always say it is better to make a $500 mistake rather than a $5,000 error. However, what is really most important to remember is that after you've paid for the class, make sure you never repeat it. We all make mistakes. So what? It's only the fool who doesn't learn from them.

Balance Your Work and Personal Life

You will love working from your own project studio—the clear majority already does. You will work hard sustaining your success. At the same time, you will love the flexibility of being on your own. You will love the myriad challenges, both creative and business-related, that will come your way. You will save time and be more productive (no commute!). You will have more time for your relationships, especially your family. You will devote more time to what is really important to you, including giving more to others and your community. As Paul and Sarah Edwards said in their *Working from Home* book, "It can be either a dream come true or a nightmare, depending on what you do. It's 100 percent up to you!"

Unfortunately, when you are in business for yourself, the job starts to consume your personal life. There is a constant siren's call from your desk urging you to return and finish more work. Many people find keeping work and life separate a great challenge. Others love the integration. In either case, I've found that taking a few steps can satisfy both notions.

- Keep regular business hours. This helps your mind separate work from play.
- Demand quiet, private time from your family. Make sure they know when you are working and that you expect their cooperation.
- Separate business functions from personal ones. For instance, have a telephone line just for the project studio, and let it ring only there. That way, you won't be tempted to grab the business line during dinner.

- If you can physically separate your project studio from your home's personal space, do so. Some project studio owners have their gear in the living room. Walking past all those reminders would be difficult for some. It's easier to close the door at the end of the day and go "home."
- Reduce the personal distractions. Because you work from your home, people love to drop by, take you to lunch, ask you to watch the kids, and so forth. You need to find an acceptable balance for your life.

Accept Change and Growth as the Inevitable By-Products of Your Success

While attending a client's holiday party, I heard the host remark as he looked around the room, "Where did all these people come from?" His humble little business had grown exponentially. He told me, "All these people are living their life because of me. They depend on me." It was at that moment that his success was made completely real for him.

Sometimes things don't turn out as you expected. As John Lennon so poignantly said, "Life is what happens to you while you're busy making other plans." If you carefully review your goals and measure your milestones, you shouldn't arrive too far from your destination. However, I must confess that I'm not doing quite what I expected at my project studio when I began Fisher Creative Group over a decade ago. Sure, I'm doing some things that I always dreamed about, but I'm also into ventures that I never envisioned when I turned in my notice at my former full-time job. Overall, I'm happy with my progress. I want to make sure you follow these steps, so you are ultimately happy with the way life turns out for you, too.

Keep Your Life in Perspective

The United Nations estimates that 30 percent of the world's population lives on less than $1 a day. Furthermore, up to 85 percent of these unfortunate people are illiterate, with a majority having a life expectancy of half the Western average. It's the kind of sobering news that can really put life in perspective for you. I was sitting around thinking about how big a hard drive I should put in my next computer when I read this. One-third of the world is far more worried about

45

their next meal. To them, thirty-two versus forty-five gigabytes just doesn't seem particularly important. My point for sharing this information is simple: You must always appreciate what you have. As your parents probably said time and again, there are many people less fortunate than you . . . so eat your broccoli. I'm sure there is something we all can do to help those in need. And I leave that up to you to do in your own private way, as I feel charity is a highly personal thing.

The Taoists say that "life is the gift." No matter what is happening in your life right now, you should express gratitude and enjoy it. Meeting the challenges of daily life is what living is all about. If you start to drift away from your central purpose, take a minute to look around at all that you have. I'm not talking about material goods or bank balances. I'm talking about children, your spouse or significant other, family, friends, relationships, talents, your music and other art, and your soul. Celebrate what you already have. Savor what you have already achieved. Enjoy being who and what you are. And always be grateful for the real fortune in your life. In light of these depressing U.N. findings, these are the things that really matter. Don't you agree?

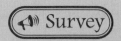 Survey

Do you have a formal business plan for your studio? If yes, can you summarize it briefly?

Though the vast majority of respondents had carefully defined goals, few had any real formal business plan. Those who had plans said it would take too long to explain. Here are the typical responses:

♪ I've just been taking it step by step and learning as I go.

♪ Make a good record, and they will come, and come again, and tell their friends. That's the plan that's been working for nine years.

♩ [My plan] establishes one, three, and five year goals, with controls for measuring progress. It is based more on project completion than on money, although income and expenses are considered. [BRAVO!]

Do you have a formal marketing plan for your studio? If yes, can you summarize it briefly?

As with the formal business plan, few people had written down their plans on promoting and marketing their project studio and career. Though many listed the promotions they use, their "plans" were not particularly useful.

Do you have specific income goals for your project studio?

♩ If my project studio can give me back what I put into it as far as my final product goes, then I will be satisfied.

♩ I rethought my philosophy over the summer. I am now making projections and working towards meeting them.

♪ No. The success of the sale(s) is the goal; the money is just a means of keeping score.

♪ To earn $5,000 by next spring.

♪ I'm trying to get into new fields, so I'm not sure what the income potential is to make realistic goals.

♪ Average $300 to $500 per week.

♪ This year, we're hoping to break the $100,000 mark.

♪ $50,000 by 2003; $100,000 by 2005.

♪ $500 a month.

♩ Yes, to annually exceed the monetary value of my full-time livelihood (salary and benefits combined), so that I can pursue my music business as a livelihood.

What are your plans for the short term? Long term?

♩ Short-term plans are to release my group album and my solo album, and to try and successfully market them to my audience. Long-term is to get a distribution deal through a major label.

♩ Unfortunately, I do not have clearly defined goals at the moment. I would like to be recording and producing music that people enjoy listening to.

♪ Push my current artists as far as I can, and keep my ears open for others like them.

♩ To continue banging on doors (when time permits) and build a reputation as a trustworthy and useful sound-track composer.

♪ Pursue film/multimedia work.

♩ I would like to expand my studio (short term). I would like to rebuild my studio from scratch (long term).

♩ Short term: become more steady as far as incoming business (not two hours today and fourteen tomorrow!!). Long term: establish myself with more professional acts as a producer, work with pro-indie and major label acts.

♩ We are branching out into things like booking and production, because we need to offer more to get people in the studio. People are able to have their neighbor record them and have it sound pretty good. We need to offer our customers an opportunity to be part of a '"scene"' if they come here.

♩ Keep expanding my client prospects. Long term, to earn my living ($50,000 to $100,000) doing this full time.

♩ Short term: wrap my head around the studio, experimenting with my gear, writing, and recording. Long term: working full time at my home studio, recording tracks for other artists, digital media, film and television, etc.

♪ Long term: I want to be Danny Elfman.

(4)
Acquiring the Necessary Resources

After *you determine your plan,* turn your attention to finding all the resources you need to put your plan into action. Generally, you need music and sound sources (such as instruments), people who play or use these music and sound sources, and equipment to record, manipulate, and distribute those music and sound elements. You may need to acquire certain skills or work with people who possess particular skills. You may need new gear to launch or augment your project studio setup. If you haven't already, you may need to find a place to locate your business. And lastly, you may have to uncover money sources to fund your plan. Getting these resources may be either an all-at-once or a gradual proposition. Most people build their business up over time, using a portion of the proceeds from successful gigs to fund their needs. Don't make the mistake of feeling you need everything in place before you can get started. Always make the most of whatever resources you have at your disposal right now.

How to Choose the Right Gear for Your Project Studio

One common thread that ran throughout the project studio survey conducted for this book was that gear mistakes were made by nearly everyone. Many bought gear they didn't need or that didn't work the way they expected. The reason this happens is because they didn't fully evaluate their situation, set some goals, and then buy only what would meet their needs. "Know *why* you need a piece of equipment before you buy," advised Michael Carroll. "Don't just buy stuff because it may look cool in your studio, because if you do, you will have a room full of equipment that's not paying for itself. Shop around to get the best price on equipment, and do your homework before you buy. Most of all, learn all your equipment inside and out, and you will love yourself for it later!"

If you get a little too much into gear, your project studio can become a money pit, sucking up every spare cent you have. Don't let that happen. Buy the basics, and only grab new gear when you know you'll need it. Since you can have virtually anything shipped overnight (or even download it straight from the Web), there's no reason not to wait for the demand. Before you rush out and spend your savings outfitting your project studio with the latest, greatest sound toys, take a minute to complete your answers to these questions:

- What gear do you have already?
- What do you consider to be the gaps, and why?
- What do you *really* need right now?
- When and how will you get it?

Next, carefully and fully evaluate your answers. Don't listen to salespeople, read ads, or devour magazine reviews at this point. The time to consult these sources is *after* you've already chosen the direction you will go and the *very basic* gear list that will get you there! How do you determine your basic needs? The two key questions are:

- What do/will you record?
- How do/will you record it?

Do you record live drums? Then you will need a bunch of microphones, cables, and stands, a good mixer with decent microphone pre-amplifiers, a couple of compressors, several effects devices, and more. You say you don't record drum kits? Then you don't need that gear and would probably never use it! Do you record keyboards? You need a good MIDI sequencing program, a simple mixer, and probably some outboard signal processing. If you only have one keyboard (or use software synths and samplers), you don't need the mixer, because you'll just hook up the output of your keyboard into the input of your recording device or stream the soft synth's output to your hard disk recording system. Oh, you say you're planning on adding a rack of synths and samplers in the future? I'd suggest you wait until you do so before investing in a large mixer you don't need and will rarely use.

There's little need for fancy mixers, multichannel sound cards, or racks of signal processing gear if you will just overdub one track at a time and mix on your computer. At my studio, almost everything I record is an overdub. All that I require is a monitor mix of existing tracks to play along with and mono/stereo input for whatever part I'm adding next. For example, on a recent song, I built a drum loop, over-dubbed a mono keyboard bass part, overdubbed a stereo acoustic guitar, added a stereo sampled piano part, and recorded a double-tracked lead vocal. The song was tracked and mixed on my computer, mastered there, too, and burned directly to a CD. Stereo in and out on my sound card (and no mixer) was all I needed for this project and just about any other project that I do in my studio.

Jeremy Spencer offered this sensible advice: "Don't get into debt buying gear that you don't really need. If possible, get by with equipment you already own, and buy things as projects come along. I pump out stuff for professional theaters with my minuscule setup, but everything does what I need it to." Jimmy Graham concurred: "If you can't afford the gear, wait. Nine times out of ten, you don't need it that bad anyway!" .

As you contemplate adding new gear, follow this five-step process to help you decide if it's the right move: strategy, research, goals, budget, buy/pass.

Strategy

Develop a strategy that lets you objectively evaluate your needs and wants, industry trends, client demands, and profitability.

- Are you considering or already offering a new product or service that requires special equipment?
- What industry trends are pressuring you to expand your studio (the growth of 5.1 surround, for instance)?
- What are your clients asking for?
- What specific gear do you want/need?
- Can you make (more) money with this gear?

For example, your client needs surround-sound mixing, and that means you must upgrade your studio. What is the bare minimum you need? By carefully examining your needs, you can begin to find the right gear and then go shopping. For this client, you might need:

- Mixing console or software-based surround mixer with eight buses (six for the 5.1 surround and two for the stereo bus).
- Eight-track storage, outboard MDM (modular digital multitrack) or computer DAW (digital audio workstation). These are for *additional* storage of the surround mix, not the original session tapes.
- Surround-sound monitoring, comprising five matched monitors and a subwoofer. Self-powered monitors are great here, as you can easily route the mixer bus channels to the speakers. This setup must be carefully fit into your room to make sure your monitoring is accurate.
- Surround encoder to monitor your mix in progress.

Research

After you determine what you need and why, get into research mode by carefully consulting the music trade press, reading reviews, asking your peers, and so forth. Take the trade magazine reviews with a grain of salt, as most of the products they review are made by companies who also spend advertising dollars at the magazine. Instead, look for disinterested third parties, such as those found on Harmony-Central (*www.harmony-central.com*) and at the Web Audio Forums (*www.audioforums.com*).

Set Goals

Establish specific guidelines for the gear you need, such as when you plan to get it, what you will use it for, and how you will charge for using it (or recoup your costs). "Over ten years ago, I sketched out a dream list of gear I wanted to have for a studio. Now, my studio is almost exactly as I had dreamed, outside of technology innovations I didn't foresee," recalled David Conley. For those just starting out, he also suggested you "try as best as possible to anticipate your needs by a close examination of what you wish to do. Ask questions of people who have done what you want to do, and research, research, research your gear before you buy."

Budget

Decide how you will acquire the gear—cash, credit, lease, rent—and set a budget. For most gear purchases, you should use savings and pay cash for the purchase. It's no good to finance your project studio using high-interest credit card debt. You might consider leasing the gear in certain circumstances, but unless it is a major capital purchase, not too many dealers will set up lease terms for you. Don't overlook renting equipment. This differs from leasing, because you only need the equipment for a short period—one session, for instance. I've had to rent mixdown decks to accommodate client demands; there was no reason for me to own them.

One way to get the money for studio upgrades is to start a rainy day fund. Establish a savings account at your bank, and channel 5 to 10 percent of your gross billings to the account. When you've accumulated enough cash, buy the gear. Another strategy is to aggressively pursue a new gig that lets you earn the money you need. For example, my company had produced a video for a client. Once completed, I also suggested the company place the video on its Web site, and that my company would handle the necessary encoding. The client agreed. This additional service paid for the video capture card and software I wanted for my project studio. In another case, I was lusting after a sample CD. So, I picked up the phone and suggested to another past client that he should update his phone hold messages. He agreed. My client received new promotional phone messages, and I bought the cool sample CD I wanted.

Buy/Pass

After working through these steps, you should have a good idea of whether the expense is worth it. If you decide this is the right move, buy the gear; otherwise, pass this time around and move on.

Robert Rich has recorded and mixed over a dozen albums from his garage project studio. Rich uses a combination of MDMs and hard disk technology to record his unusual ambient music. He supplements his income with producing and mastering gigs. "I tend to only buy new stuff when I absolutely need it," he told *Keyboard*. "I'm trying to live off my recordings. It gets too expensive to keep upgrading every time something new comes out."

Basic Project Studio Gear

The problem with talking about gear in a book such as this is that by the time it comes out, the information will be outdated. Therefore, I decided to take a more generic approach to the gear issue that would help you understand and choose the *fundamental* equipment you need, leaving the specific research and choice up to you. Every project studio needs the following basic components:

- Music and sound sources to record
- Devices to capture that audio
- Equipment that stores the captured audio
- Methods to hear the captured audio
- Ways to manipulate the captured audio
- Media to redistribute the final music and sound

Most of us rarely have the luxury of building a complete, viable project studio from scratch. Usually, it's built over time, adding and subtracting gear along the way. You must be careful with your choices, or you'll find yourself surrounded by outdated and useless recording technology. Taking the time to choose either timeless gear or gear with a clear upgrade path is definitely a sound investment. Timeless gear includes high-quality microphones, preamps, and compressors. Gear with upgrade possibilities include software-based sound processors and their ilk. Also, when you design your project studio, make sure you plan for expansion. Technology changes, your business mix will change, and your project studio must be flexible enough to adapt to these changes. It's no good building custom cable lengths and maxing out the rack, only to find you have to move and build it all again in another space.

Music and Sound Sources to Record

First and foremost on your project studio list is having the appropriate sound-producing stuff. What you need depends on the project studio services you offer. Typically, this includes music gear such as pianos, synthesizers, samplers, guitars, basses, other string and wind instruments, drums and percussion instruments, and so forth. Some of these instruments may be hardware-based or computer-based virtual instruments. Other sound-producing gear includes sample CDs, music and loop libraries, sound effects CDs, etc. You also need the services of people to either play the instruments or provide their other talents—sung or spoken vocals, for instance. To get an idea of what some of your peers are using at their project studios, read the survey that concludes this chapter.

Devices to Capture That Audio

You need equipment that allows you to capture the audio produced in your project studio. For acoustic gear (guitars, piano, drums, and voice) you need high-quality microphones and high-quality microphone/instrument preamps. There are two types of microphones most used today: dynamic and condenser. Dynamic microphones generate their own signal. The diaphragm in the mic housing moves analogously to the sound waves propagating it. This diaphragm is connected to a tiny magnet surrounded by a coil of wire (this is a basic electric generator). The sound waves are then converted to a low-level analogous electrical signal. You need a mic preamp to boost this low signal to recordable levels. Condenser mics need power to work. The cheapest rely on a battery (electret-condensers), while the best use power supplied by a mixer or mic preamp. This is called "phantom power" and is standardized at forty-eight volts.

Dynamic mics, such as the infamous Shure SM57 or SM58, are ideal all-purpose mics. They work for vocals, guitar amps, acoustic guitars, and some drums. The Sennheiser MD 42/II is another good choice for general recording. If you buy no other mic, get one of these. When you are serious about your project studio, you are going to need a high-quality condenser mic. Condensers are best used to capture the real detail in a performance. They are warm, accurate, and quiet. Many impart a specific sound and are chosen for that reason. Vintage mics, such as the AKG C12, Neumann U47, U87, and KM184 are ubiquitous high-quality, expensive choices. Large-diaphragm condensers are a must for vocals and acoustic instruments. You will never regret investing money in one really good microphone. Fortunately, there are many medium-priced microphones that can serve you well. Notably are the Shure KSM32, the Rode NT1, and the Marshall MXL-2001/2003. Do your research at these Web sites:

- Shure (*www.shure.com*)
- Sennheiser (*www.sennheiser.com*)

- Event Electronics (*www.eventelectronics.com*)
- Marshall (*www.mxlmics.com*)

Don't forget that the microphone is only part of the sound. The better the mic, the more your need for a great-sounding microphone preamp. Most mixers have the suitable mic preamps that boost the low mic signal up to a usable level. Some mixers even supply the needed phantom power required by condenser microphones. However, some inexpensive mixers have mic preamps that are not of the highest quality. There has been a trend in recent years to use dedicated mic preamps connected directly to the recorder, bypassing the mixer channels. This strategy keeps your signal path uncomplicated and short: mic to mic preamp to recorder. Several manufacturers offer a variety of external, stand-alone mic preamps that are ideal for project studio recordings. Some mic preamps use tubes to amplify the signal, while others use solid state electronics. Instead of a multichannel mixer, you can use a mono or stereo channel strip, the equivalent of one or two mixer channels. These include microphone and instrument preamps, sometimes coupled to stand-alone EQ, compressors, and noise gates. They range in price from very affordable to top-of-the-line, such as those offered by Avalon and Focusrite. Make sure you test several preamps along with the mics you choose to discover the best combination for your needs.

- Avalon (*www.avalondesign.com*)
- Focusrite (*www.focusrite.com*)

The other type of preamp you need is one for interfacing with certain musical instruments. To record an electric guitar or bass without an amplifier/speaker combination, you need an instrument preamp that takes the low signal put out by these instruments up to the level needed for recording. Some mic preamps also accommodate instruments. Related to this are the new amp simulators that let you plug in an electric guitar or bass and call up digitally modeled simulations of classic gear. The most famous of these are the Line 6 Pod and the Johnson J-Station.

- Line 6 (*www.line6.com*)
- Johnson (*www.johnson-amp.com*)

You may need a mixer at your project studio. A mixer essentially lets you combine multiple sound sources in various ways and deliver these combinations in new ways. Most mixers have mic and instrument preamps, equalization, level and pan controls, and more. If you need external mixer control, you can choose from feature-laden digital mixers or high-quality analog boards. Make sure you understand that your need for a mixer is largely dependent on the sound sources you will record and mix and how many you need to record or mix at once. If you have a lot of hardware—sound-generating and signal-processing—you will need a dedicated mixer to manage your audio to and from the multitrack recorder. Some stand-alone DAWs have built-in mixers, but are usually limited in scope. If you only have a single keyboard, you can get by without a mixer. Conversely, if you are going to record bands playing live in your project studio, you will need a mixer to handle all the elements (multiple mics and instruments playing simultaneously). If you are a solo soundtrack composer recording one thing at a time, you probably won't need a mixer or can get by with just a small, simple line mixer. I use my old analog mixer only for rehearsals and monitoring. Sometimes, I'll set up a scratch track on my keyboards and rehearse guitar and vocal parts at the same time, using my mixer to balance the parts. Other times, I use the mixer for creating different headphone monitor mixes for other performers.

For the computer-based project studio, the mixing utilities found in multitrack audio software are all you may really need. You can control volume, pan, EQ, and effects levels for each track and instantly recall all your settings. This kind of mix automation brings the added flexibility and power that is nearly impossible in the traditional analog world. Mixing on computer is not as much fun as sitting at a dedicated mixer and diddling knobs and faders until it sounds good. It's more work at the computer, but automation as described above coupled to instantly-recallable parameters make it a better choice today. When you're working with persnickety clients who insist on change after change, you'll appreciate how you can save multiple projects and mixes until the client says, "Yes!" Also, there are control surfaces available that talk to your software, letting you make changes with "hardware" that affect your software, just as you did with your old analog gear. There's more on this topic later.

Other Odds and Ends

One tiny component that needs discussing at this point is all the cables you need to effectively hook up the gear in your project studio. Cables aren't sexy, so they usually get the least regard. However, you need high-quality cables for your critical components or you risk adversely affecting your sound. Also, carefully lay out your gear to keep power, audio, digital, and MIDI cables separated. If you must cross power cables with others, do so at a right angle to minimize interference. Another important consideration is to keep all your audio signal paths as short as possible, using the least amount of cable you can. Mark Howard of Cumberland Records offered *Home Recording* this advice: "Have a really clean signal path. I always go straight from the microphone to the mic pre, [and then] straight to the tape machine, using really good wire. No compression. No EQ. If you can get it to sound right with almost nothing in the signal path, it makes it really easy to mix." Also, create a signal flow chart of your project studio that shows where everything goes. This can be a block diagram or a wiring scheme. If you use a patch bay, be sure to clearly identify the connections.

Another area that needs addressing is power. Every project studio needs clean electricity. Get one of those combination line stabilizer, noise filter, surge protector, voltage regulator, and backup power supply devices. Why risk losing valuable work to a short brownout, or watch as your gear investment burns up during a power surge? This is insurance that no project studio should neglect. My computer workstation plugs into one, while the rest of my gear goes to another. When I shut down the studio completely, I disconnect these power supplies from the mains, as an extra measure of security.

Equipment That Stores the Captured Audio

No matter what projects you land, you will need a multitrack recorder at your project studio. There are hardware- and software-based systems available.

- The stand-alone digital audio workstation (DAW). These "portable studio"-type devices combine a mixer, onboard signal processing, and multitrack recorder in one package. The most well known is the Roland VS series (*www.roland.com*).
- The stand-alone hardware system, comprising either tape and hard disk choices. The modular digital multitrack (MDM), first popularized by the Alesis ADAT and then the

Tascam DA-88, are the most well-known and used systems. Glen Ballard recorded Alanis Morissette's *Jagged Little Pill* entirely on ADATs. I believe the tape-based MDM format will disappear and be supplanted by the hard drive. Many people invested in this gear, as it was the first viable and affordable way to get into digital recording. Today, that is simply not the case, as computer speed and resources have dropped in price, while increasing their power exponentially. The new crop of MDMs are all hard disk–based and can interface with either digital or analog mixers.

- Alesis (*www.alesis.com*)
- Tascam (*www.tascam.com*)

- Computer and software-based DAW with hard disk recording, MIDI sequencing, and virtual mixing. There are DAW products supplied by several manufacturers. The most famous and most widely used is Digidesign's Pro Tools. Other systems include Ensoniq's PARIS and several software-based components that can use hardware from other manufacturers. As computers become even faster and infinitely more powerful, the virtual studio will really be the way to go. For the price of a decent system, you will have access to world-class tools. Plus, your projects will be easily exported to other formats, making them compatible with the rest of the world. External hard drives give you additional portability. You can take your drive anywhere to complete work. If you use a computer DAW running, say, Pro Tools, you have compatibility with much of the outside world.

- Digidesign (*www.digidesign.com*)
- Ensoniq (*www.ensoniq.com*)

✕ Digital vs. Analog

The computer is quickly becoming the centerpiece for most project studios. Even the staunchest supporters of analog and modular digital gear are turning to the virtual studio for their work. Today, you want to be in the digital domain with as much of your project studio components as possible. Even the low-end digital formats are better than most analog gear. I started on four-track cassette, then moved to eight-track cassette before going PC-based. It was a huge jump. I'd become rather adept at getting great sounds off my less-than-stellar analog gear, but the move to digital surprised me. I could finally record what I heard, and it played back exactly, without a modicum of fuss. I also love the nondestructive nature of digital. I can make edits, move takes around, change parameters, and not affect my original recordings in any way. It's much akin to word processing with sound. If I'm not sure I like something, I save the file, make the change, and then hear the difference. I can go backward or forward with ease.

Digital audio primer

- **Sampling frequency**: the number of snapshots taken of an analog waveform. CD quality is 44.1 kHz, or 44,100 snapshots or samples per second.
- **Bit resolution**: the number of bits used to describe each sample's amplitude or waveform height. Sixteen bits essentially means the sample is rounded to the nearest point of 65,536 possible steps.
- **Quantization error**: analog waveforms are smooth, while a digital waveform is comprised of discrete levels or steps. Some analog information falls between these stair steps. This distortion of the analog signal is called quantization error.

- Using more bits is one way to overcome this obstacle. Moving to twenty-four bits reduces the distances between the digital stair steps and correspondingly reduces the quantization errors.
- Dithering adds broadband noise to a digital signal to help mask digital distortion, especially on low-level signals. It is most useful when moving from one bit depth to another (e.g., audio master at twenty-four bits to sixteen-bit CD release).

Going Virtual

If you choose to go the computer route, you need some additional components besides the basic PC and software. You need an audio interface to take the analog signals of the real world and digitize them to the format the computer needs. A high-quality pro sound card is required for serious work. Much like the mixer discussion from above, if you need to record multiple sound sources simultaneously, you will need a multichannel sound card. Others can get by with stereo in/out. The sound card must also be full duplex, meaning it must be able to record and play back at the same time. If you plan to use MIDI on the computer, you will also need a suitable MIDI interface and MIDI sequencer software.

The quality of the sound going into a computer-based DAW is a function of its analog-to-digital converters (ADCs). Many budget sound cards do not use the best ADCs. The high-quality, professional cards simply sound better, even if you don't need their extra features. Some people even prefer to use dedicated ADCs, especially those made by Apogee, to digitize their precious audio. With the dawn of DVD audio, which supports multichannel 24-bit/96 kHz files, you will ultimately need to migrate to that format. Most sound cards still sit in the 16/44.1 world, but more and more are making the transformation.

Today, you don't even need a sound card to get audio in and out of your PC. The Universal Serial Bus (USB) has emerged as a viable method of moving data both in and out of a PC. Originally utilizing MIDI interfaces, audio devices quickly acquired USB interfaces and have now grown to encompass and support sophisticated DAWs. With its 12-Mbps (megabits per second) bandwidth and self-power (USB sends power to the attached device, meaning no external power supply is needed), the USB port is quickly being embraced by the audio production community. Ultimately, Firewire will emerge as a method for getting audio (and video) into and out of the computer. It has tremendous bandwidth and promises to be useful new technology.

What is particularly great about both USB- and Firewire-enabled devices is their quick plug-and-play connection. No longer are you forced to crack open the PC, install a card, install drivers, and troubleshoot the installation. You plug it in, install a driver, and go! These devices are also hot-swappable, which means you can plug and unplug devices without having to reboot your system. You can get both USB and Firewire MIDI and audio interfaces. For example, you could plug a small USB interface into a laptop for a very basic project studio. The newer models offer analog inputs (mic, line), digital I/O, mixing, multi-effects, routing, headphone connections, and more. Products from Roland, Tascam, and Event Electronics include analog and digital I/O, MIDI I/O, and faders, buttons, and knobs that you can configure to run your PC-based software. This area is in great flux, so I urge you to follow the trades to see if this hardware interface is better for you.

- Roland (*www.edirol.com*)
- Tascam (*www.tascam.com*)
- Event Electronics (*www.event1.com*)

Methods to Hear the Captured Audio

It's no good making sounds and recording them if you can't hear what you've done. Accurate monitoring is crucial to your project studio, as the speakers you use must reflect what others will hear when they listen to your work. Your monitoring system should consist of decent passive speakers powered by a high-quality amplifier, or self-powered monitor speakers that include their own built-in amplifier. I use two sets of monitors. Those at my computer help me check the music and sound destined for computer-based productions, while the mains are for checking projects slated for CD or other full-range venues. The placement of the speakers, the levels you listen at, and the room the speakers are in all affect the sound you hear. These issues are so important that I give them much greater coverage in the next chapter. Another type of monitor you will need is headphones. If you record singers, voice artists, or any acoustic instruments, you will need them for the talent to use during tracking and overdubbing.

Ways to Manipulate the Captured Audio

While the function of a microphone is to capture a sound accurately and the function of a recorder is to reproduce that sound faithfully, the real power in the project studio comes when you work sonic magic on the audio you record. Every project studio needs signal processing equipment. Using signal processing to restore problem audio or creatively manipulate the raw sound is the norm for music and sound production. The choices include:

- **Equalization (EQ)** lets you change the tonal characteristics of a sound.
- **Dynamics processing (compression/limiting)** lets you transform the apparent loudness and softness of a sound, including reducing or expanding its dynamic range.
- **Spatial processing (delay, reverb)** lets you create an artificial room ambience in which to place a sound.
- **Temporal and pitch processing** let you change either the time and/or pitch of sounds.
- **Special effects** generally let you superimpose different qualities onto a sound, such as adding a chorus effect to a guitar.

Signal processing comes in two flavors: dedicated outboard hardware and computer-based software plug-ins. The hardware can be used when recording or when mixing, while the plug-ins are almost always used during mixing. Many people swear by certain pieces of dedicated outboard gear. However, advanced digital modeling now makes it possible to program software-based plug-ins to recreate the sounds of infamous external gear. While there is a bevy of affordable and robust plug-ins, unfortunately, there are several formats, and some plug-ins only work with certain software platforms. Many people also complain about how difficult it is to manipulate tiny onscreen buttons and knobs. Yet, having access to an enormous range of sonic utilities makes these minor inconveniences palatable. If your project studio will be computer-based, you should seriously consider replacing any outboard processors with their virtual counterparts.

Media to Redistribute the Final Music and Sound

The multitrack session recordings are only one part of the final product. You need a way to combine the disparate elements into a single media file for distribution. You need a mixdown medium to hold your final mix. You may mix in mono, stereo, or 5.1. While you can mix to traditional analog machines, DAT, or an eight-track MDM, today, the vast majority of work is done on computer and distributed digitally (as files or on CD).

For basic editing, cleaning up, signal processing, and mastering, a computer-based two-track editor is mandatory. What's especially wonderful about digital stereo editing is that you can really put your audio under the microscope. You can literally edit the data by the sample. Even if you decide to go with a hardware multitrack, consider also getting a computer for digital editing of your stereo mixes. There are several choices from a variety of manufacturers, and it's best to check them out (download their demos) before deciding which one is right for you.

The next crucial part of your final project is being able to create master CDs in-house by adding a CD burner. This format allows you to make audio and data CDs, giving you the most compatibility with the outside world. Hot-swappable hard drives are also popular ways to move data from place to place. Finally, you'll want a high-speed Internet connection to deliver audio files to clients via e-mail or FTP (see chapter 8 for more details).

Keeping Up

The constant change of technology is a great challenge for project studio owners. Everything moves so swiftly that you're forced to devote some time to following the trends. You can't neglect this area, but don't let it consume your free time. Read the industry magazines, and visit a few of the popular Web sites regularly.

- *Electronic Musician (www.emusician.com)*
- *EQ (www.eqmag.com)*
- *Home Recording (www.homerecordingmag.com)*
- Home Recording forum at About.com (*http://homerecording.about.com*)
- *Keyboard (www.keyboard.com)*
- *Mix (www.mixonline.com)*

Jeffrey's Virtual Studio

I was reasonably satisfied with my studio for some time. It was fine for demo projects and most of the low- and medium-budget productions that came my way. All the time, I lusted after gear I read about and heard being used. One day, I realized that my studio hadn't kept up with the times. There had been a huge jump in technology and an even larger drop in prices. Having a powerful, flexible, and all-digital project studio was completely within my grasp. I resolved to pare down my project studio and concentrate on mastering a few tools and forgetting about all the other gear. This new rig needed to be high-quality, versatile, and able to handle the wildly disparate projects that come my way, conducive to getting ideas down quickly, and use a minimum of pieces.

I then carefully reviewed the kinds of projects I do and what they required. I realized that I never record more than one instrument at a time. Usually, this is a voice (sung or spoken), guitar, bass, or percussion track overdub. I'd never recorded a live drum kit or group here either. Next, I looked at my goals. My plans were simple: to continue to do similar projects as I had in the past. This two-step analysis helped me make a few critical decisions about my studio.

I chose to create a virtual studio, based entirely around a computer. Since staying in the digital domain was so important, choosing a computer-based multitrack was the best solution. It was gear with a clear upgrade path, expandable, and gave me access to affordable tools I could only dream about a few years ago. The virtual studio has some clear advantages. It's a modular approach, because different software can do different things, but it's still an overall, all-in-one solution. Computers also make working easier. What used to take hours now happens instantaneously. Sending work back and forth and collaborating over long distances is also a snap with a computer and Internet connection. The computer also presents new ways to do old things, such as new software-based samplers and synths (including recreations of vintage gear). There is also new technology for sound-making and manipulation, such as granular synthesis. Plus, any new approaches to music and sound creation and manipulation will first be available in the software world. It makes sense to be there today!

Gear Choices

Figuring out what you need for a computer-based virtual studio is often far easier than outfitting a traditional studio. To adapt the strategy presented earlier, you need a way to get music and sound into the computer, including high-quality microphones, high-quality microphone/instrument preamps, and a sound card (full-duplex to record and play at same time) or a USB interface (sound card, mixer, effects all-in-one); the computer itself and the software running on it, including digital audio recording and editing and perhaps MIDI recording and editing; and a way to get the sound out of the computer, including high-quality monitor speakers and a CD burner for masters. Here's my new setup:

- Hardware
  - PIII with CD-writer and Sound Blaster Live! sound card
  - Johnson J-station guitar/bass amp modeling and effects
  - Joe-Meek VC3 microphone/instrument preamp
  - Marshall MXL-2001 microphone with shock mount for voice/acoustic instruments
  - Wireless headphones
  - Cables
- Software
  - Sonic Foundry's Acid Pro 2.0, Vegas Video 2.0, and Sound Forge XP
  - Propellerhead's Reason software (with integrated synths, samplers, and drum machine)
  - RBC Voice Tweaker
  - T-racks mastering software
  - Various sample CDs for use with Acid
  - Easy CD Creator software
  - Blank CDs
- Old stuff (already had and still use)
  - Mic stand
  - Monitor speakers and amp
  - Shure SM57 microphone
  - Ibanez electric and Aria acoustic guitars
  - Ensoniq SD-1/32 synthesizer (I usually record this direct to the computer in stereo, sometimes through J-station/VC3 first)

Setup in Action

Here's how I typically use my virtual project studio. Vocals (sung and spoken) and other acoustic instruments find their way to the computer via either the MXL-2001 or the SM-57 mics and the VC3 preamp. Choosing a couple of high-quality microphones was vital. I tried several and settled on the Marshall MXL-2001. It is a fine condenser microphone that I just love on voice and acoustic guitar. My trusty old SM-57 is a good all-purpose mic to cover other situations. I chose the Joe Meek VC3 preamp for its sound. This is really a single-channel strip with a preamp, opto-compressor, and EQ all in one. The mic preamp is clean and crisp, while the compressor, instead of being linear and transparent as most compressors try to be, has a sound to it that reminds me of the infamous LA-2A compressor/limiter. Electric guitars and bass pass through the Johnson J-station on their way to the computer. Using these two main tools in this configuration keeps the signal path short. I connect the VC3 directly to the sound-card input using a high-quality one-foot cable. The digital out of the J-station also connects to the sound card through its digital S/PDIF connection, keeping the sound in the digital domain, further increasing quality.

I do have a small mixer that I use for monitoring or submixing hardware-based keyboard parts and for routing new material. Because my studio/control room is a combined space, I often cut tracks with headphones. Usually, that means one pair for the artist and one pair for the engineer (me). The mixer helps me deliver a specific balance to the performer while I monitor the recording itself.

I use my SD-1/32 for keyboard tracks by composing with its onboard sequencer before recording the *audio only* to the computer. When you dump your MIDI tracks to multitrack as audio, you keep everything in one place and can manipulate and treat them as other tracks (mixing, signal processing, etc.). I love the onboard sequencer on my synth and have never felt I needed a software program to handle my MIDI chores. I'd rather *play* my keyboard parts into Vegas (or create simple sequences and drop them into Acid or Vegas) than sequence them on the computer. The old method of combining MIDI-sequenced tracks with digital audio is a holdover from when storing digital audio was expensive. But today, the cost of hard drives and RAM is minuscule compared to days past. Also, having a bunch of synth modules requires a fancy mixer and a separate mixdown deck (as opposed to keeping it on the computer, mixing directly to a file, and burning a CD).

Of course, the ultimate method is to use software synths and samplers right on the computer itself, export those performances to your digital multitrack, and away you go. Software-based sound modules give you unheard-of flexibility. Most virtual synths are accurately modeled after specific equipment, while the virtual samplers let you expand your sonic palette exponentially. Currently, I use Propellerhead's Reason to create my keyboard and effects parts on the computer. My hardware keyboard will soon be relegated to the trifling task of MIDI note supplier; I'll use it to play the notes, but rarely let it contribute any sounds.

Aside from my guitars, the only other composition tools are the various sample CDs that provide other sounds and textures not created in the studio. Sonic Foundry's Acid Pro software has become my main tool for composing music. Acid is loop-based software that lets you drag and drop sound loops to its grid, and then automatically adjusts the tempo and key of each loop to match the song. What you really do is sequence samples to make a sonic collage using existing and new music and sound tracks. With my growing library of sample CDs, along with my own original loops and tracks, I've been quite happy with my output. With Acid, it is just so fast and easy to get a thirty- or sixty-second radio spot together. Another reason I like using sample loops is that they give me access to instruments and performances I'd never get otherwise. Sure, I'd love a real sitar on my latest track, but I had a hard time finding a player. So, I resorted to stringing together performances from a sample CD. I got my sitar, which helped me realize the vision I had for my song.

Although you can create finished projects within Acid Pro, the real power to this configuration is exporting the Acid tracks to another digital multitrack and sweetening the mix there. Using Acid Pro, I lay down a basic track using original and purchased loops. Once the basic track is complete, I export the individual tracks to a folder on the hard drive. I then launch Vegas Video and bring the Acid tracks up. I next layer other parts with the basic tracks (vocals, lead guitar, effects—whatever the track needs). Using many effects and mixing tools, I use Vegas to create the final stereo master.

For digital multitracking, Vegas Video is hard to beat. The program is simple to use, but very powerful. Also, you get a bevy of DirectX effects to instantly expand your sonic palette. Automation through volume, pan, and effects envelopes gives you considerable control over your mix, too. One particular favorite effect is the RBC Voice Tweaker. It works in real time to correct minor (and major) intonation problems and can automatically tune vocal performances. The T-racks mastering software is a stand-alone application that emulates tube EQ, compression, and limiting and is my final step for mastering music on the computer.

- Get more information about Acid Pro and Vegas Video from Sonic Foundry at *www.sonicfoundry.com*.
- Grab the RBC Voice Tweaker at *www.rbcaudio.com*.
- For more on T-racks, go to *www.t-racks.com*.
- Find all kinds of free, shareware, and demo software utilities, multitracks, MIDI, DirectX, and VST plug-ins and more at *www.sonicspot.com* or *www.thedirectxfiles.com*.
- Get Reason information at Propellerhead Software at *www.propellerheads.se*.

A Typical Project

Perhaps you might find it useful to study a project done at my project studio. The basic scenario for phone hold messages is to record a voice track of various mini-radiolike ads and accompany that with a music track. I usually record the voice tracks into Sound Forge XP. I use it instead of my multitrack software because of the way it places multiple takes in the same file. This is how one of my recent sessions went: The recording setup was my MXL-2001 microphone connected to the VC3 preamp and from there directly to the computer sound card input. The talent went to my little vocal booth, and I sat at the computer, monitoring on headphones.

After setting levels, doing a test recording, and checking the test's sound on regular studio monitor speakers, the session began in earnest. I created a folder on the hard drive to hold the project files and recorded each on-hold message into its own file. If a line was blown, we'd pick it up and finish recording in the same file. If the voice talent really goofed up, we dumped the file and started again. If the take was good, I kept it by naming it with a number that corresponded with the on-hold message ad, i.e., first ad = 001, second ad = 002, etc. This technique kept each raw on-hold ad in its own file in one folder.

After the voice talent left, I cleaned up each take by deleting the blown lines, replacing the good takes, and so forth. I turned to house-cleaning chores by trimming the starts and ends, making each ad complete and ready to run. Next, I removed every breath and lip smack by either deleting it and moving the words together or by selecting the breath waveform and reducing its volume to nothing (-inf). Last, I compressed each track gently and then normalized the output to 98 percent. These cleaned-up master takes were saved to new .wav files, leaving the original raw tracks available in an emergency. At this point, all I had to do was choose some appropriate music tracks from my *Melomania* music library CDs and put the project together.

I started Vegas with a new project and dragged and dropped the voice-over master takes to track one, moving them around so that there were appropriate gaps between on-hold messages. Next, I dragged and dropped the music segments to track two. Vegas automatically cross-fades when you drop a track on another. I set the level of the voice track to 0, the level of the music to -12. By adding a volume envelope to the music track, I could reduce its volume (or duck it) under the voice during certain portions. It's easy to draw a volume envelope to lower the music level, because you can literally see the waveforms. Drop the level 6 to 8 dB during the voice, and slope the in-and-out of the volume envelope gently. This way, the music moves down gently to leave space for the voice and then rises up equally gently when the voice track ends. I saved the Vegas project file and mixed the final version to a monaural .wav file. I launched my CD writer and burned a CD from the .wav file for distribution to the on-hold system. Once the project was done, I also created a backup data CD with the raw voice takes, master voice-over tracks, Vegas project file, all the music tracks, final mixed .wav files, and the project notes. I could then delete the files from my computer hard drive.

My total time invested was fifteen minutes recording voice, twenty minutes editing and cleaning up tracks, and another ten minutes arranging and mixing. *No, that is NOT a misprint. It took me only ten minutes to complete the final piece.* Please don't tell my clients!

Money Resources

To get money to start your project studio or to fund a major expenditure such as new gear, CD duplication, and such, you should consider these resources.

Be conservative. You do not need to have everything in place before launching your venture. It's fine to start with some basic equipment and augment as the needs arise and the money flows in. Set up that rainy-day fund as mentioned earlier. If you have a day job, channel some of that money toward building or expanding your project studio.

Ask friends and relatives for financial help. I know this can be a tricky subject, but you can address it creatively. You could set up a formal agreement between yourself and another party, where he or she gives you a loan and you promise to pay it back following agreed-upon terms. You can trade or barter services in lieu of cash.

It may be time to start charging more for your services. Alternately, devote more time to paying projects and get help for other tasks. Sometimes, it's cheaper to hire someone to do something rather than do it yourself. Hire a temp, a subcontractor, an intern, even your kids. For example, I never considered using messenger services and often wasted an hour picking up and delivering materials. I currently charge around $100 an hour, while the typical messenger costs under $30. Now, instead of jumping in the car, I call the service. Another way to bring in more money is to pare your expenses down to the bone. When you spend less, you make more. Do you really need that subscription? Membership? Name-brand coffee every morning? You can also pass on your business expenses to clients, such as charging back long-distance phone charges, delivery services, and supplies (tapes, CDs, etc.).

You can use your credit cards carefully for short-term financing. One technique you might consider is the "same-as-cash" deals offered by many companies. This is essentially an interest-free payment plan. You order the product for something akin to three payments of $29.95. The company takes your credit card number and charges you equal installments spread over time, usually once a month for three to six months. They bill you the same day each month, too, until the full amount is paid in full. The standard grace period on your credit card lets you float some of your out-of-pocket costs, too. When a major purchase is coming up, wait for your card to roll over, and then buy. This gives you the thirty day billing cycle plus the twenty-five day grace period before you have to pay. That means you get fifty-five days to raise the money to pay off the balance. Combining these techniques can let you get gear or supplies today and pay for them over time (without incurring finance charges or interest). That gives you more time to earn (or collect!) the cash you need. Let me remind you that these strategies are *only* for managing your cash flow. Try to pay for items with cash-on-hand and finance very little. I never spend unless I either have the money or know the money is forthcoming (like an invoice due in the future, quarterly royalties, and so on). Unfortunately, sometimes your cash flow can get squeezed, and you need to get creative.

If you are really in a pinch, you can try to get a conventional bank or Small Business Association (SBA) loan for your fledgling business, or even tap your home equity. I'd think carefully about either decision before adding debt to what can be an already-tenuous situation.

You can raise money from your current clients, too. If you land a major project, ask for an advance to get started, or bill in installments to keep cash coming in at regular intervals. If you need to make a major purchase on behalf of clients, you can ask them to pay you earlier to cover the bill.

Invoice promptly, and shorten your credit terms. Don't let people who owe you money off the hook. Get tough and get paid! Ask your suppliers for liberal credit terms. It's usually common practice to pay most invoices in thirty days. That buys you some time. You can try to negotiate longer terms or progress payments, too. Take advantage of all credit terms offered to you, so that you pay many of your bills at the last minute. In essence, get people to pay you faster, and pay your own bills slower.

Consider leasing or renting over buying equipment that you may need only occasionally. There is no need to buy every piece of gear available on the off chance you might need it someday. You'll find that with a basic setup, you can do much of what you need. If your equipment falls short, consider renting for short-term needs, such as a microphone or mixdown deck. Consider leasing high-cost gear instead of buying when you don't have the money you need to buy, but can cover the leasing payments easily. You will have a hard time finding equipment to lease, though, with the exception of very expensive items.

Barter products and services with other people. For example, give the guitarist free studio time in exchange for her playing on one of your tracks. Note that the IRS has specific rules governing bartering in business situations. Essentially, you record the exchange as typical business income and expenses. If the trade is like/kind, the effect on your taxes is zero. Using the above example, have the guitarist bill you for her time, and you bill her the same amount for your studio time.

75

The two invoices effectively cancel each other out, and you have the paper trail you need for tax recording.

While the SBA and other U.S. government agencies provide information and some services to help get your business started, getting a government grant from a state or the feds to start or run your business is next to impossible. However, other countries, such as Canada, have specific programs in place to help you out. It pays for you to research this area thoroughly.

If you are a corporation, you can issue stocks and bonds, as described in your corporate by-laws. This can be a formal way to raise cash for business expansion. Even if you are not a corporation, you could issue ad hoc stocks and bonds to friends and family. This wouldn't be much different than a loan, except that you could issue many smaller increments instead of just one big loan to one person. Talk with a lawyer or other financial adviser before considering this option.

Collaborating with Other People

Another resource you need for your project studio is other people with whom you collaborate and work. You already learned why having additional people resources can help you build your project studio business effectively and help you take care of mundane matters. Follow the advice about putting together your team in chapter 3. However, let's say you need to find some voice talent for a project. How do you go about finding these people? Most major cities have a directory of creative talent—advertising agencies, freelance artists, voice talent, etc.—or a resource of some kind. Contact your local Chamber of Commerce to find out how to get your copy. Your local library can also help. Try the theater department at your local community college or university for actors and actresses who want to do this kind of work. You might be able to trade them for a demo tape instead of cash. A speaker's forum might lend some good pipes. Check your yellow pages for the nearest Toastmaster's Club. You can also contact the two major performers' unions, the American Federation of Television and Radio Artists (AFTRA) and the Screen Actors Guild (SAG), for possible candidates. Here's how to select the best talent:

- Collect demo reels from five to eight prospects
- Listen and evaluate these reels

- Narrow your choice to three possible candidates
- Interview each candidate about styles, fees, deadlines, and project ideas
- Do a simple test spot to narrow your choice further
- Make your final selection

Two large databases of the recording industry are at *www.artistpro.com* and *www.1212.com*. You can find musicians, studios, equipment, engineers, and even gigs.

Your Most Critical Resource

The last resource you need for your project studio is clients. Since that means promotion, I send you to chapters 9 and 10 for the specific details on this crucial subject.

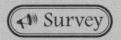 Survey

How did you acquire the money to start your project studio?

Most project studio owners used personal savings and proceeds from other day jobs to fund their gear habit. A comment from one typified the responses: "I built it one piece at a time!" Interestingly, several people sold existing, unrelated businesses and used those proceeds to fund their project studio.

♩ I was given the money as an investment. To date, have spent roughly $10,000, with plans still for more.

♪ Invested money I was making as an engineer into recording gear.

♩ When I was in college, I would get the financial aid overpay and invest it in rudimentary studio equipment. It was, inevitably, the best move I could have made, because I now completely support myself and my family with the earnings from my production business.

♪ Personal bank loan.

♪ Credit card debt.

♪ Mostly credit cards. I've since consolidated it in a home equity loan.

♩ Aside from being a musician and buying one piece at a time, I used the time-honored American way: beg, borrow, and steal.

♪ Day job.

What kind of gear do you have in your project studio?
(Be specific).

What gear is everybody using at their project studios? Unfortunately, there were no clear trends. Except for one studio using analog multitrack, the rest were digital in some way: MDM, stand-alone DAWs, and computer-based DAWs. Some people had lists several pages long, while others were getting by with a tiny complement of modern technology. Here are a few sample lists:

♩ VS 880; (3) VSR 880; Mackie 32X8; Tascam MMI; DBX dual tube preamp; several headphone amps; EMU ESI-32 sampler; Mac PPC computer; Sony RDAT; Alesis D4; Simmons drum pads; too many effects to mention; many mics, including C3000's, 414's, Solidtube, and more; several guitars; Digitech IPS 33B harmonizer; Digitech GSP 21 Legend guitar preamp; and more.

♩ Ensoniq ASR 10 sampler (keyboard version), Tascam 246 portastudio, Roland JV2080, Luxman 4 channel amp, Teac cassette deck, Koss monitors, Fender Stage Lead guitar amp, Les Paul electric guitar, Ibanez acoustic, Pentium 233 running Cakewalk V 8.0.

♩ Macintosh 9600 with MOTU Performer and Emagic Logic; iMac and Compaq something-or-other (I just inherited the PC—I haven't found a use for it yet); Roland VS-1680 and VS-880 with Zips and CD-R burner; MOTU MIDI Timepiece XT interface and JL Cooper rev2 MIDI patchbay; Panasonic SV3800 DAT; Teac and Sony CD players; Tascam mk2 cassette deck, Alesis twelve-channel submixer; DBX patchbay; various mics—main vocal mic: Rode NT2; Fatar SL-880 master keyboard controller; Roland JP8000; Roland JV1080 with expansion cards; Korg Wavestation SR; Korg N1R; Emu e6400 sampler with CD-R drive; Alesis Nanopiano module; Alesis SR16; Roland V-Drum custom drum set; Epiphone electric guitar; Yamaha trombone; various other ethnic instruments and percussion: didgeridoo, balalaika, djembe, doumbek, shakers, etc.

♩ Roland VS-840 Digital Mixing Workstation, 64 Virtual tracks/8 playback, with SCSI 100mb Zip drive, Power Mac

6100/66 (Mac OS8.6, 2 Gig hard drive, 40 Mb RAM, Poweruser external CD drive, 14" monitor), Mac Laserwriter Pro printer, Muratec F-70 fax machine, Steinberg Cubasis AV-Sequencer software, Opcode MIDI Translator 2, Roland DJ-70 Sampler/Keyboard with 3.5" floppy drive, JBL 4206 Studio Monitor 6.5 woofer with titanium tweeters, Philips-CDR880 CD recorder, Hitachi-HTA35F-Amplifier, Sony TC-W435 cassette deck, NAD-5240 CD player, Radio Shack stereo audio-source selector, Audio Technics-ATH-M2X headphones, Technic 1200 turntable, Gemini-PMX-7 Trickmaster mixer, Shure SM58 microphone, ART-Tube Pac pre-amplifier/compressor, Monster cable throughout.

♪ VS880ex, CD burner. [Now, that's a clean setup!—JPF]

♩ Twenty-four tracks of ADAT, Mackie 8 bus, KRK monitors, Tascam DAT recorder, Tascam CD burner, Alesis QS7.1 synth, Yamaha sequencer, SR-16 drum machine, Alesis compresser, Micro Verb 3, Quadra verb, ART FX, Aphex preamps, Aphex "Easy Rider" compresser, Rane Mojo 31 band EQ., Shure SM57's and SM58's.

♩ PC with Hewlett-Packard laser printer; Tascam DA-20 stereo DAT recorder; Roland VS-880 and Roland VS-1680 hard disk recorders with CD burner; Tannoy Reveal Active stereo bookshelf monitors; Korg C 5000 digital, touch-weighted, full-length piano; three Newpoint surge protectors; Martin Sigma acoustic guitar; Yamaha TQ5 sound module; Alesis NanoPiano sound module; Ensoniq EPS-16+ sampler with Apple CD drive; CAD 95 condenser mic.

♩ Boss BR-8 digital recorder, Alesis SR-16 drum machine, a POD, an Alesis 3630 compressor, a dual fifteen-band EQ, an ART FX-1 effects processor, a ZOOM 505 guitar pedal, a Strat, an Ibanez Artstar guitar, a Fender acoustic, an ElCheapo mic, and a JVC dual cassette mixdown deck. I borrow other equipment as needed.

What gear acquisitions are you planning for the near future? Distant future?

♪ I am looking into getting a console mixer (a Yamaha O2R), as well as the new Sony DMXR-100.

♪ More 414's, more VSR 880's, new Mac G4 with velocity engine.

♪ DAT, outboard effect rack, decent mixer.

♩ Near future: upgrade preamps and AD converters (some high-end tube preamp and maybe Apogee converters), more microphones—I'd really like a Neumann. Also, the Alesis Masterlink looks interesting, more sample CD-ROMs and sounds for the sound library; more ethnic/world instruments (I'm kind of a collector). Distant future (when I move the studio to a bigger place): Mackie d8b or whatever the current equivalent is; ProTools or stand-alone hard disk recorders; I'd love a Kurzweil 2600 workstation; more mics, sounds, and world instruments.

♪ Alesis QSR6.1 keyboards and/or Ensoniq ASR X Pro.

♪ More effects and processing software.

♩ Finalizer, Masterlink, more mics, and better stands. Later? A bigger, nicer board (an SSL or Neve preferably), a *real* (not ADAT) digital multitrack.

♪ Need better mics.

♪ A good $500 to $1,000 condenser mic.

♪ I would love to trade up to a new dual processor G4 Mac. Perhaps get a nice vocal mic.

♪ I plan to upgrade my palette of orchestral samples.

♪ More microphones near future. Two more DA78's and larger digital mixing console later.

♩ Mic preamps, tube and solid state compressor, low-end condenser mic(s), drum machine, sampler, various toys (such as a little vintage tube amp).

♪ Compressor, new vocal mics, more ergonomic chair.

♪ Professional controller (maybe Triton) and various compression, processors, etc.

♪ I don't need any new gear just now. When I need more tracks, I rent time at another facility.

5

Setting Up Your Project Studio for Maximum Profit

Y*ou don't have to think hard* to realize that some important people work from their home. The President's Oval Office is just a few steps from the living quarters. Home-based advantages are many, because technology lets you accomplish so much more, both efficiently and productively, from a comfortable environment. If you want to cut tracks in your birthday suit, you can! A home project studio can be cheaper to run than one located at a commercial site. You can have a flexible work schedule (I like to take Fridays off in the summer), no commuting (unless you have to visit clients), tons of legitimate tax deductions (including the oft-cited home office deduction), and more.

You may choose to locate your project studio in a commercial space. This will greatly increase your expenses, but it can be a more conducive environment for others. Carmen Rizzo told *Home Recording* that he never wanted to own a studio and especially didn't want one in his home. After several years of collecting gear and people wandering through his house, he decided to rent space. He divided a large, old building into a control room, tracking room, and lounge. If he can't record what he needs in-house, he gets it done at a commercial facility, then brings the recordings back to his project studio. "It's one of the vibe-iest places . . . a home-grown vibe, which I like." Rizzo prefers to work on his own projects and doesn't hire out the space either.

You can also choose to locate your project studio as part of another space, teaming up with a commercial studio or other production house, for example. Jeff Bova, whose project studio is located in the basement at Avatar Studios in New York, told *Mix*, "I get many benefits out of being based here in Avatar. From the beginning, I was given access to the entire facility. My clients get all the amenities they would expect from a major studio [when they] are working in my project space."

Locating Your Project Studio

Whether you keep you project studio at home, as most of us do, or locate it elsewhere, you need to choose a specific plan for the space. Most project studios are one-room affairs, meaning the control room and studio (or recording space) share the same real estate. Rare is the project studio that has a dedicated tracking room. Usually, there's nothing more than a small isolation booth or a room down the hall that's pressed into service as needed. This is why you will want to concentrate most of your time and money on the main control room, as that is where the majority of your work will take place. Fill this space with your gear, comfortable work surfaces, furniture, decorations, and, of course, acoustic treatments that ensure what you record and mix plays back faithfully.

Choosing a suitable room in your home is usually quite easy. Spare bedrooms, basements, attics, and garages are the typical choices. A few people set up in corners of their living rooms, but I feel a dedicated space is probably better both for work and for your off-hours sanity. Choose the biggest room you have available. Bigger rooms are somewhat easier to control acoustically than smaller, boxy rooms. If you can get beyond the fifteen-foot dimension in your room, you have a great starting base for your combined control room/studio.

If you are building from scratch, or rehabing a room, consider keeping it somewhat live sounding. If you make it too dead, it will be a hard place to record and mix in. If you keep it somewhat live in your initial approach, it's usually easier to deaden the space later by adding appropriate sound control treatments.

Pierre Marchand, who records Sarah McLachlan's albums at his Wild Sky Studios in a remote area outside Montreal, takes the large control room approach: "I prefer to be in the same room as the artist at all times," he told *Mix*. "I never use iso booths or recording areas; everything is recorded around the console. I go for performance. I put up a mic, and if it sounds good, wonderful, if not, I move the mic or try another mic. I'd rather have present only the people who are making music and capture that with the gear."

Typical Studio Layout

The combination control room and studio is usually acceptable for most jobs. Some project studio owners may use other rooms for recording instruments (e.g., guitar amps in a bathroom or stairway) or employ small isolation booths for vocals and solo instruments. The typical layout is built around either the mixer, with outboard gear nearby, or around the computer DAW in a virtual studio. Your monitoring position is the most critical element of your project studio layout. You will want to determine the optimum placement for your speakers first. Once you have them in place, then you can turn your attention to placing the other gear and amenities around your room. There is specific monitor placement and basic acoustic treatment information later in this chapter.

Plan your studio layout on paper first before you physically get to work. Run some test sessions on paper to see if the layout makes sense. Is the gear you use the easiest to get to? Can you expand easily? Once you're satisfied, set up the gear according to the blueprint. Don't hook everything up yet. Just get it working enough to test the real-world viability of your paper layout. Give the room a test spin for a day or two. Make any adjustments, and then finalize the installation.

I've found that creating several distinct workstations is a terrific solution. Since I do most of my work at the computer, it is my main workstation. I also have a mixing station (used mainly for submixing and monitor mixing), keyboard station, and an effects rig, mostly for guitar sounds. This mixing area, combined with the effects rig and keyboard area, is also another area for composing and routing songs and soundtracks. The area is ideal for working out beats and synth lines, sound programming, arranging, and just jamming and practicing. Though it is my main mix position, I often mix on the computer speakers first, then test and adjust mixes on the full monitors later. This way of working means rolling back and forth across the room from computer to mixing sweet spot, though. There is a small isolation booth for recording voice, acoustic guitar, solo instruments, and hand percussion. Adjacent to that is a lounge area for meetings, reading, writing, composing, phone calls, and naps. My project studio is also my business office, so it includes filing cabinets, bookshelves, storage, and other office trappings. Also, outside the work area is a play area for my young son, who does his thing while I do mine.

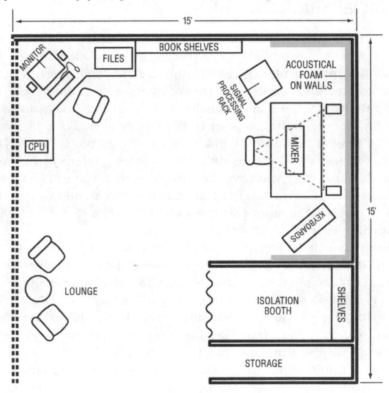

The BBC Radiophonic Workshop follows one of my favorite project studio layouts. Using several little rooms crammed with gear, the Workshop provides the sounds and music of the BBC. These suites use a simple, modular approach, with MIDI gear and sequencing. The gear is arranged on a C-shaped table. The mixer, main keyboard controller, and monitors are opposite the open end. Racks of other gear fill out the table. The BBC doesn't install the equipment; it's all transportable and dropped in to meet a composer's or sound designer's need. With audio links to more traditional studios and control rooms, these suites tackle the work and send it down the line for further sweetening.

Brian Tankersley and Mark Miller built their project studio around a ninety-six–track Ensoniq PARIS DAW. What was, according to Tankersley, going to be a utility for comping vocals turned out to sound good enough for serious production work. They reported in *Mix* that "this ninety-six–track PARIS system has 120 analog inputs, seventy-two analog outputs, and sixty digital I/Os directly into the DAW, with no external console." Another unique aspect of this Nashville studio is the control room setup. "We decided to build a large control room (20' x 30') with three separate workstations, each acoustically treated. Players at these stations face the console, and they have the option of putting on headphones or using monitors that can be positioned close," Tankersley said. One benefit to working with their unique arrangement is that with everybody working together in the control room, the creative process is nurtured. "Being able to yell at each other across the room and achieve a common spirit is the goal of our operation."

Many project studio owners keep their gear in portable racks. This lets them create a sort of building block studio that they can use both at home or elsewhere. If you have gear and projects always in a state of flux, this arrangement can work well for you, too. Kevin Antunes, the musical director and keyboardist for 'NSync and others, tours with his own project studio, which he uses for songwriting, production, and tour preparation. He told *Keyboard* it all fits into a 390-pound case, comprising an Akai MPC2000, Yamaha 01V digital mixer, powered speakers, Macintosh G3 computer, Tascam DA-98, Glyph hot-swappable hard drive, and various other components.

Furniture

Once you have a good idea of the gear in your project studio, you can put together the furniture you need to support it. You can take a modular approach, buying racks, stands, desks, chairs, bookshelves, and so forth, or you can opt for all-in-one solutions provided by some manufacturers. If you're so inclined, you can build your project studio furniture yourself, usually for far less than purchasing already-made. Plus, your layout can be customized to your precise needs, giving the room a nice, neat, integrated, professional look. My studio is more of a hodgepodge of gear and furniture collected over the years. Although the layout is workable and comfortable, it doesn't have that "slick" look.

Get a good desk for your main workstation. You will spend a lot of time at that surface; make sure it works for you. Also, don't skimp when it comes to your main chair. When asked about gear acquisitions, one survey respondent actually put "a more ergonomic chair" first on the wish list. Invest in a quality chair that's right for you; it's essential to your comfort and long-term health. Take a few for a test sit at several stores. Don't wince at the price tag of the one that ends up feeling the best. Since you will log a lot of time on that fabric-covered frame, take extra care to make the best choice. Also, if you have carpeted floors, get a good antistatic mat for under your chair at the computer.

- Omnirax Studio Furniture (*www.omnirax.com*)
- Quik-Lok (*www.quiklok.com*)
- Raxxess (*www.raxxess.com*)
- One of my favorite places to get great, inexpensive furniture and accessories is Ikea. If you are fortunate to live near one of their superstores, check out their line of office furniture, lighting, and other neat stuff for your project studio (*www.ikea.com*).

✖ One-Room Recording Tips

If you've taken reasonable steps to make the room sound good, it's usually a matter of setting up the gear and hitting "Record." Guitar, bass, and electronic keyboards can be recorded directly into a mixer or preamp, making single-room recording and monitoring a snap. For recording vocals and acoustic instruments with open mics, either build a small isolation booth and/or follow these tips:

- Monitor on headphones. You may need multiple pairs and perhaps separate monitor mixes—one for the talent and another for the engineer. Wireless headphones can really come in handy here (see below).

- You can monitor on speakers if you keep the level low. Make sure you face the mic away from the speaker to avoid unwanted leakage or feedback. In this setup, it may be wise to use a noise gate set to close down when no sound is present.

- In either situation—headphones or low-level monitoring—you should record some test tracks and carefully listen back through your regular monitors at normal levels to make sure everything sounds right.

- Jon Durant (Alchemy Records) recorded his *Anatomy of a Wish* from his basement project studio. "It's a 20' x 12' basement with a carpeted floor," he told *Home Recording*. "The gear is distributed in different locations throughout the room." He's even recorded live drums in the space, rolling back the tape to make changes and then recording additional takes. Unusually, Durant prefers the limitations of an eight-track MDM. "I'm a minimalist, and I really like to force myself into working within the framework of what I've got."

Recording Alone

As a project studio owner, you may need to record yourself. How do you set levels, control your hardware and software, and deliver a solid performance at the same time? If you can, hire another person or press a family member to come in and assist you in engineering these sessions. Not having to worry about the gear can free your mind for more creative expression. Concentrating on performance while letting the mundane tasks fall to another pair of hands will improve your work. If you can't find help, consider adding some specialized gear to make recording yourself easier. Wireless headphones let you walk around with ease between your workstation and instrument, while a wireless remote control lets you control the main features of your recorder from a distance. My 900 MHz wireless headphones let me wander around so I can diddle knobs at the rack, mouse around the computer, run to the iso booth, grab my guitar, lay down a few takes, then back to the computer, again and again—without tripping over cables or getting tangled up. When I'm recording my own vocals, hand percussion, and acoustic guitar, this setup makes playing and engineering a snap. And that frees me to concentrate on performance, without the gear destroying the vibe. The Keyspan Digital Media Remote (*www.keyspan.com*) connects to the USB port and gives me a handheld TV/VCR-type remote for my computer. I use it to control several Vegas Video functions from my isolation booth ten feet away.

When you record yourself, you may need to do several practice runs before you find the balance you need. Do several takes to get levels down and the sound right. Play a track, listen back on your monitors, tweak settings, and so on, until you are satisfied. Once you establish these baselines, write them down to make future sessions easier. Once I've set levels for my voice and guitar playing, I can start each session with those basic settings (mic placements, levels, effects setting, etc.), record a trial take, tweak the settings, and then record proper.

Session Notebook

You should also consider keeping a session notebook of every project you work on. This information can be invaluable for other sessions. Record settings, microphone setups, ideas that worked, tests that failed, funny stories, and anything else that you feel might be useful in the future. Keep this book up-to-date and organized, so that it becomes a useful reference for you. Recording software lets you save many of the "console" and "effects" settings you create. You no longer need to write down every parameter, because you can recall the settings with a click. Vegas even lets you save effects chains (two or more effects linked in specific combinations). Another must-have is a camera to document your sessions. This is especially useful for remembering a particular mic setup. Get a cheap Polaroid or digital camera, and snap away. File these pictures along with pertinent notes in your notebook.

As one person put it in *Home Recording*, "Perhaps the best part of working out of the house is never having to put away your toys." This can really be an advantage. You can spend hours getting things to sound right, and then leave the setup alone. You don't have to tear everything down for the next session. One studio I worked at spent days getting their drum kit to sound fantastic. After that, nobody was allowed to touch anything. The real benefit to this strategy was that anyone recording there could simply sit down, bang away, and get a consistently good drum sound. It really saved time, especially for demos, in which this studio specialized. You can do the same thing with a miked piano, acoustic guitar, even console and signal processing settings. Why reset your gear if you're the only one using it? A commercial studio doesn't always have that luxury.

Aesthetics

What attracts people to a recording studio? Award-winning engineer Ed Cherney told *Mix* magazine: "cleanliness, that everything works, and a friendly, considerate, and articulate staff. You want to talk to someone who is knowledgeable, can confirm the room and rate to you, and is going to be able to handle whatever your setup is. You want people who know what they are talking about and can commit to fulfilling your needs. If the studio isn't taken care of cosmetically, then you wonder about the reliability of the equipment [and people]." "The atmosphere of a studio is very important," added producer Eddie Kramer. "It's got to be like home." While these professionals are referring to commercial environments, their attitude applies completely to your project studio. The same reasons that made you start your own project studio are many of the same reasons clients will come to call. It should feel good and be conducive to creativity. "The best thing that ever happened with my project studio," explained Ken Feldman, "was getting incredible vocals done in my apartment by allowing the artist to feel very relaxed and at home."

Just because your project studio is in a spare bedroom doesn't mean it has to look like one. Personalize your space, and make it conducive to creative work. Let the room reflect the image you are trying to convey about what you sell. Keep it warm, inviting, bright, cheerful, and homey. Surround yourself with your success—awards, posters from your latest projects, CD covers, and so forth. Jack Joseph Puig's studio (L.A.'s Ocean Way, Studio A) has its hallway walls covered with the console tape strips from his sessions. He's decorated the studio in an eclectic style, with colored lights, candles, sculptures, tapestries, band posters, and a medieval banquet table, to create a nice vibe for the talent working there. As one studio owner put it, "Create an environment with more of a bed-and-breakfast feeling, rather than a hotel."

Choose an appropriate paint for the walls. Create a flexible lighting plot, with a combination of task lighting, overall lighting, and mood lighting. Add bookshelves, filing cabinets, and so forth to hide the clutter. Disguise all the wires, too. Don't forget about the floor; low-pile industrial carpeting is probably best. If you will have clients visiting, you need other amenities for them, such as a separate work surface, comfy seating, extra phone, and so forth. I know a computer programmer who worked from a makeshift desk comprised of an old door with sawhorses for support in a basement with a bare bulb for lighting. How can anyone work in such Dickensian squalor? My space is nothing fancy, just comfortable for me, with enough of my personality to make it interesting for my rare visitors.

Producer Mark Hudson, in his interview with *Electronic Musician,* stated that he is reluctant to allow technology to interfere with the way he makes music. Hudson's studio is in "a converted office above a Thai restaurant in West Los Angeles. I decided to make this little place with a vibe of doom. I put up cool lighting and some great memorabilia, and suddenly my demos started sounding amazing. I didn't know why this was happening, because my equipment is somewhat antiquated. I don't have Pro Tools or any other fancy stuff, just microphones stretched out to where the noise is, so that it gets on tape." Using Tascam DA88s, a Mackie mixer, some vintage gear (mics, preamps, and so forth), Hudson recorded tracks for Aerosmith and for Ringo Starr's *Vertical Man* CD. Hudson often tracks live and worries very little about isolation. He goes for emotion, vibe, and performance. "Get the performance at the moment—and then the mixdown is when you get meticulous."

Security

If you have an investment in equipment at your project studio, you should consider taking reasonable security steps to protect it, inside and out. Inside security would be locked cabinets for storing easily-stolen items, such as microphones. If you have clients coming to your studio, you don't want stuff to go missing. Consider a fireproof safe to store that expensive gear, valuable backups, and so forth. Outside security would be the typical security system to stop burglars from breaking in and making off with your gear. I also suggest not letting people know what you have in your house. Don't brag about your contents; don't leave empty boxes at the end of your driveway that announce to the world that you just bought a new state-of-the-art computer. If you have a lot of people coming to your studio, this tactic doesn't work, but for others, it's an extra measure of security.

Studio Tool Kit

Don't neglect your need for a simple repair kit for your project studio. Equipment has the unfortunate tendency to break down at the most inappropriate moment—usually in the middle of a crucial client session. If you are electronically adept, you might opt for cable testers, soldering iron, solder, pliers, and other such tools. Otherwise, have ample backups of all your gear, such as extra microphones and cables. Make sure you have a good supply of basic necessities: blank CDs, labels, instrument strings, and so forth. Definitely have software backups of your computer programs, along with notes about tweaks and so forth. You might just need to reinstall something to solve a recurrent problem. Have owner's manuals for all your gear at hand. Have your session notebook in hard copy and on the computer. Lastly, you might consider having an on-call technician who can troubleshoot your rig. You should find and build a relationship with this person *before* you get in a bind.

Preventive maintenance is always the best strategy. Check everything regularly, and give your gear a good workout before every critical session. Take notes of failures during sessions, and fix them right away.

- Keep your owner's manuals for all your gear. Follow the manufacturer guidelines for proper cleaning, storage, and so forth.
- Get dust covers to protect your gear.
- Keep gear out of the elements (heat, cold, direct sunlight, etc.).
- Keep liquid and food away from your gear. Drinks are only allowed in my lounge area, where there is no equipment within several feet.
- Use antistatic spray on fabrics around your gear. Use an antistatic chair mat, too.
- Use good quality surge protectors and/or uninterruptable power supplies (UPS). Since those cheapo surge protectors offer very little protection, you can skip them.
- Something will go wrong; prepare in advance by having crucial backups.

Project Studio Acoustics

You have two problems that you must solve with the acoustics of your project studio. One, keep noise out and keep your sound in. In other words, don't let the outside environment intrude on your recordings; at the same time, don't disturb the neighbors. Two, reduce the side effects caused by the room itself on what you record. You need to be fully aware of the sound characteristics of your room, because if it unnaturally affects what you hear, your mixes will suffer. The first problem requires soundproofing, while the second requires acoustic treatment of the room itself.

Soundproof Your Project Studio

Chances are, your project studio is in your home. If you record with microphones, you are going to want to make sure that outside noise doesn't get into your project studio and ruin your recordings. You can't have a truck that's rumbling by destroy a vocal take. If you don't record with microphones, outside noise doesn't really affect you. However, everybody still needs to take reasonable precautions to prevent the music and sound escaping from your studio and disturbing others.

Sound travels through both air and structure. Make your room airtight, and you eliminate some leakage. However, only mass *really* blocks sound. The more massive your structure, the more sound you can block. Foam, blankets, and pillows have little mass and offer minimal help. High-frequency sounds are easy to control and attenuate, while bass frequencies require extreme measures to control and dissipate. A large, low-frequency wave, such as the sound of an amplified bass guitar, will go right through a piece of foam and through most typical wall constructions, airtight or not. Though the wall will attenuate or lower the sound level somewhat, it usually takes more mass to be truly effective. Concrete walls and other such construction techniques provide the needed mass.

The amount of volume loss through a particular structure is expressed as its sound transmission class (STC). A typical single-family home wall, floor, and ceiling comprised of 5/8" drywall over 2x4 studs has 30 to 35 STC. That means it will reduce the level of sound passing through it by about 30 to 35 decibels (dB). Adding high-density insulation in the wall cavities can add an additional 5 to 10 STC. Adding a layer of Celotex brand sound block over the drywall, along with the insulation inside, can take the room to 45 STC. There is even a high-density acoustic vinyl that is only 1/8" thick that can add as much as 27 STC to a wall, without significantly increasing its depth. A concrete block wall filled with sand or mortar has a 50 to 55 STC. Of course, a window or hollow door can effectively eliminate the gains realized by these wall, floor, and ceiling structural enhancements. Solid doors and double-glass configurations are necessary to match the other soundproofing. Alongside that, you need special ways to deliver heated and air-conditioned air to the recording space through special sound-attenuating duct work.

What about structure-borne noise? Your studio is connected to the outside world in some way. Sound travels through objects, such as steel, and enters and leaves your studio through sympathetic vibration. The bass guitar rattles the floor; the floor is concrete with steel rebar. The rebar takes the thumping sound to your neighbor down the hall. In addition to increasing the mass of your studio structure, you need to build a room within a room. You essentially isolate your room from the rest of the structure. This isolation stops structure-borne noise, while the wall construction attenuates the airborne noise.

Another noise you may need to reduce is that generated by your equipment. Computers are noisy beasts. You can try locating them in other rooms or closets and use long cables or wireless solutions for the mouse and keyboard. You could also build isolation booths for the noisiest gear using high-density foam. Raxxess (*www.raxxess.com*) makes a sound isolation cabinet that you could use.

Soundproofing takes time, energy, and money. If you do it wrong, you could deplete your savings and be no better off than if you'd done nothing. It will take a lot of money to keep airplane noise out of your studio, when the better solution might be to find another location. Though I live in a busy neighborhood, I've never had a take ruined by outside noise. I have, however, had takes ruined by inside noise, such as the heater kicking in during a take. The real problem with soundproofing is it can be very expensive to do right, and you can't take it with you. After investing several thousand dollars soundproofing a room, you might decide to move.

If you live in attached housing or multiple-unit buildings, you are going to need to do everything you can to peacefully coexist with your neighbors. If you'll be jamming into the night or working odd hours with the levels cranked, you'll need to soundproof accordingly. You might consider monitoring at lower levels and even using headphones when you can. Avoid recording drum kits, loud guitars, and other dB hogs. Either record these instruments elsewhere, or use drum machines and amp modeling instead of miking guitar or bass cabinets.

Soundproofing is a huge subject beyond what's included here. If you feel you need to take drastic measures to soundproof your recording space, let me send you to these two resources: *Building a Recording Studio* by Jeff Cooper and *Sound Studio Construction on a Budget* by F. Alton Everest. You should take reasonable means to attenuate the sound coming into and leaving your project studio, but concentrate on making your room accurately reflect what's coming out of the speakers.

Make the Room Sound Good

Rooms affect the frequency balance in ways that make it difficult to know whether it is the recording or the room changing the sound. You can't just make the whole room dead (or worse, dead at high frequencies, with too much soft absorption). If your room colors your sound, your mixes will not be transportable; they will sound wrong in other listening environments.

There are three main acoustic principles that concern project studios: echo, flutter echo, and room resonances. Echo is the distinct repetition of a sound wave. To be perceived as an echo, the reflected sound must arrive about thirty-five milliseconds (ms) after the initial sound. Sound travels 1.1 feet per millisecond. So, the travel time for a wave would have to cover seventeen feet to the reflecting surface and the seventeen-foot return trip to the original sound source. For most project studios, this distance is not a problem. Only large rooms need to deal with distinct echoes.

Smaller rooms have the problem of flutter echo. Flutter echo is a stream of distinct echoes that build up between two reflective, usually parallel, surfaces. Clap your hands once sharply in a hotel or apartment hallway to hear the ringing sound of flutter echo between the two parallel walls.

The real problem with small rooms is that they build up frequencies and introduce unnatural effects into the sound. These room resonances, called standing waves, simultaneously emphasize some frequencies and cancel others. Due to these phase anomalies, some sounds seem louder, while others sound softer. This filter looks like a comb on an oscilloscope, showing distinct notched frequency bands, some attenuated, others enhanced. If you don't know of this comb filtering effect, you may compensate during recording or mixing. The result is, your recordings may sound different when played elsewhere.

The dimensions of the room dictate its primary resonant frequencies using this mathematical formula: **Frequency of standing wave =**

1130/(2 x the room dimensions). A twelve-foot room has an axial standing wave at 47 Hz, about the frequency of a low F on a bass guitar. Standing waves also affect harmonics (or multiples) of the fundamental frequency, meaning that 94 Hz, 141 Hz, and so on are emphasized in this example. It is the fundamental frequency and these first few harmonics that do the most damage. Therefore, the higher the frequency of the standing wave, the more adversely it can affect your audio. Since small rooms have relatively high-frequency room resonances, they suffer the most.

Try to avoid small rooms with symmetrical designs. A 10' x 10' x 8' room would be a terrible place for your studio, while an 11' x 15' x 8' may be better. The different room dimensions mean different resonances are helping to flatten the overall frequency response of the room. Odd-shaped rooms can sometimes be a good choice, too. Your best solution is to choose a large space for your project studio control room and carefully treat it with acoustic products.

Absorption, Reflection, and Diffusion

Unfortunately, a few sheets of acoustic foam will not solve all your acoustic problems. Porous materials, such as foam, fabric, carpet, and so on work wonders on high-frequency sound waves. Most low-frequency waves are not affected by such treatment. You can absorb low-frequency sound with a resonant cavity, called a bass trap, but the depth required for it to work effectively precludes its use in most small rooms. There are some technological advances that can help the small studio control these bass waves. Along with the usual mid- to high-frequency acoustic foam absorbers, you can get special foam-based bass traps that work in corners to reduce low-frequency buildup. Also, there is a tubular bass trap, called Tube Traps, that works well. Not sending really deep bass into your room is another tactic you can employ. This subject is discussed in the monitoring section later.

Avoid parallel surfaces and you will not have any flutter echo in your room. That's easy to say but hard to do. Most project studios in spare bedrooms are fixed with parallel walls. The best solution is to break up the walls with gear, furniture, decorative items, bookshelves, keyboard stands, gear racks, and so forth. You can place alternating sound absorbers and diffusers strategically around the room to reduce reflections, too.

You also need to use diffusion to break up sound waves and spread them around the room. Because sound loses energy as it strikes a surface, the more surfaces in your room, the less likely the chance for standing waves to build up. Scattering the sound in many directions eliminates standing waves (or at least reduces their effects), reduces echo and flutter echo, evens out the natural reverberation decay of the room, and generally helps mask the side effects of small rooms. Anything that makes a flat surface bumpy is the key here. A bookshelf filled with books and other doodads, for instance, can act as a good diffuser.

The ideal acoustical treatment achieves broadband absorption and diffusion with the goal of leveling the frequency response of the room. Use foam panels of varying thickness to absorb sound. Use diffuser panels to disperse sound around the room, and use high-density corner traps to control and reduce those troublesome low-frequency sounds. Peter D'Antonio of RPG Diffusor Systems said, "A balanced design should be sought, using all the ingredients of the acoustical palette, namely absorption, reflection, and diffusion." So, don't overdue just one area of control. Mix it up by addressing each issue equally.

As you plan out the acoustic response of your project studio, consider following the popular "live end/diffuse end" (LEDE) concept. Basically, you absorb all frequencies near the monitor speakers, so you hear their sound first, then diffuse the sound after it passes your ears into the room. Strategic placement of broadband foam absorbers, and bass traps in the front of the control room, coupled to diffusers in the middle and rear of the room, work in tandem to make the room more accurate. Proper near-field monitoring completes the setup. You may still need to place absorbers in the rear of the room to reduce flutter echo and standing waves, while additional bass trapping may be needed in all corners and sometimes along where the wall and ceiling meet.

Several providers of acoustic products have created complete, affordable solutions to improving the sound of small rooms. These acoustic-solutions-in-a-box comprise various sound absorbing and diffusing elements that work in tandem to absorb troublesome broadband frequencies, reduce the reflectivity of adjacent, parallel surfaces, and diffuse the sound to better fill the space.

- Acoustic Sciences Corporation (*www.tubetrap.com*)
- Acoustics First (*www.acousticsfirst.com*)

- Auralex Acoustics (*www.auralex.com*)
- RPG Diffusor Systems (*www.rpgdiffusors.com*)

While you can invest in many fancy and expensive acoustic treatments, don't neglect some inexpensive solutions. Those heavy, quilted moving blankets work quite well in a variety of situations. Hanging several from the ceiling to form a small box or tent creates an instant isolation booth. Better still, make one box out of blankets, leave an airspace of eight to twelve inches, and then make another box around it with more blankets. Hang them loosely with many corrugations (like a stage curtain) for the best result. The mids to highs will be severely attenuated, while the deep basses will pass through, move around your room, and try to get back in, but they will be reasonably attenuated, too. This setup is great for recording acoustic guitar, voice, electric guitar amps, and many other instruments: horns, flute, percussion, and so on. You can also build a similar system temporarily around your monitors and mixer for critical mixing operations. You will hear the speakers and virtually eliminate the room from affecting your sound. You can take down the blankets, fold them up, and store them when you don't need them. If you don't like the way the moving blankets look, cover them with some nicer cotton fabric.

Studio, Too

Most project studios have a combination recording room/ control room, so treating the control room takes care of most recordings, too. However, some people record in another space for its distinct sound and don't worry too much about acoustic anomalies. If you have a dedicated tracking space besides your control room, you can choose to treat its acoustics or leave its sound alone (it may still need noise control, though). For Beck's *Midnite Vultures*, engineer Mickey Petralia told *Mix,* "We'd be doing horns in the living room. The room had a giant ceiling about twenty feet, and it was just wide open. It had a pretty room sound to it. [We recorded] drums in a storage room downstairs, which offered a very tight sound."

Many project studio owners prefer to have a recording space that is somewhat more live with a specific sound, while the control room is somewhat more dead with controlled acoustics. In your tracking room, you can vary the sound of your space in simple ways. Create a hard surface area and install a heavy drape that you can pull over the wall when you require a more dead sound. You may also want a mostly dead and quiet isolation booth for some situations. A dead room can be disconcerting for some performers, so give them a little reverb in their headphones to compensate.

Monitors

Another acoustic treatment you should consider concerns your speakers. Since small room dimensions accentuate some bass frequencies while reducing others, causing an inaccurate reproduction of the sound, combining small, professional, near-field monitors with reasonable acoustical treatment can ensure your project studio accurately reflects what you record. Near-field monitors don't generate the deep bass that can really ruin the sound in a small control room. Small speakers roll off the bass, starting at 125 Hz, with about a 15 dB reduction by 40 Hz (the low E on a bass guitar). Most three to four-inch acoustic foam has no trouble handling 125 Hz on up. Using foam along with these monitors gives you solid control over the sound of your monitors in your room. Add a few corner bass traps, and you can whip the room into shape quite easily.

Near-field monitoring eliminates many room problems by moving the speakers closer to your ears. The primary theory is to hear what comes from the speakers before the room begins to affect the sound. Any subsequent sound that comes within ten milliseconds of the first sound is perceived as the same sound. Outside of ten milliseconds, the room reflections start to affect the sound. With sound travelling about 1.1 foot per millisecond, ideally, you don't want any reflecting surfaces within five feet of your monitors. This creates an initial sound gap, called a "reflection-free zone," where you will hear what comes out of the speakers *before* the room interferes with the sound. Careful monitor placement within the room, coupled with absorptive material around the speakers, achieves a reasonable reflection-free zone. Sometimes, moving a rack or other piece of furniture slightly can reflect the sound *away* from your ears, too. This further helps get rid of the close-order reflections that blur the sound coming from the monitors. The rest of the room should diffuse and disperse the sound with reasonable control of flutter echo and corner buildup.

Buy high-quality near-field monitors. This is not the place to save money. Put the monitor speakers on quality stands. There are some commercially available stands that minimize stand resonances while providing height adjustments. Place the monitors in the center of the shortest wall of the room. Avoid putting them directly against the wall, and stay away from corners, too. Keeping the speakers about eighteen inches away from walls is a good rule. Placing the speaker in a corner adds 6 to 8 dB to its bass response. Placing a speaker on a wall or flush-mounted increases its bass response by 3 to 6 dB. Rear-ported speakers can be adversely affected by certain placement, but most near-field monitors are front-ported. Also, don't place your monitors symmetrically within the room. If the ceiling is eight foot, avoid placing the monitors four feet up, because both the ceiling and floor would be equidistant, causing inaccuracies.

Start with the speakers about four to five feet apart. Make the speakers and your mixing position the three points of an equilateral triangle, with the speakers at ear level, pointing slightly in (and down, if necessary). Make sure nothing is between your ears and the speakers. Absorb broadband frequencies behind the monitors, over the mixing position, and along the rear wall. Place furniture or use diffusers in such a way to spread the sound around the room. Monitor at no more than 80 to 85 dB. It is at this level that the frequency response of the human ear is most flat. Make sure your monitors are in phase by checking the (+) and (-) terminals, too. Lastly, make sure you monitor critically in the near-field. It's no good to stand at the back of the room with this setup, because the room itself will affect your sound (maybe positively; maybe adversely). While it's fine to crank the speakers and listen outside of the near-field for fun, *never* make mixing decisions this way. Get your ears in the triangle before you diddle any knob.

Test the Room

The best way to test your room is to let your ears be the judge. Put on your favorite CDs, and move your setup around until it sounds good. Now, take those CDs to other listening environments, and take notes of how they sound. Bring the CDs back to your project studio and compare your notes. Make any necessary tweaks, letting your ears guide you. Also, test your mixes in a variety of listening environments, too. I find that once you get used to your room—and recognize its shortcomings—you will have no trouble mixing projects that sound good outside your environment.

Remind yourself of the sound of your room before you do any critical mixing. Compare your mix to favorite CDs, and emulate their sound. Many suggest listening first on headphones to hear any glaring mistakes that sometimes get missed through monitors. Next, do your initial balance at a low level. Once things sound tight, push up the volume, and check at that level. Continue mixing by alternating low levels and high levels. Check the final mix on headphones once again. Burn a test CD, and play it everywhere and listen critically. Take notes of these tests, and use it to remix the tracks, if necessary. Burn another test, and make the rounds again.

The Number One Monitor

We depend on our hearing for our livelihood. That means you not only need to take care of yours, you need to have it checked regularly. What good is investing in top-of-the-line speakers when your own ears are fooling you? If you don't know your own hearing shortcomings— if any—how can you expect to mix accurately?

Go to an audiologist, and have an audiogram made to test your hearing. You essentially wear headphones, while the audiologist plays frequencies starting at 250 Hz up to 8,000 Hz. The test starts at 40 dB and moves down in loudness. The test takes about fifteen to thirty minutes and costs between $80 and $175, depending on the audiologist you choose. What the test reveals is a plot of the frequency response of your hearing. Now, this test is designed to test the frequency range where human speech falls. Music and sound typically extends well below and far above this range. Still, the doctors I spoke with felt that examining this range for deficiencies could still give insight into your hearing's overall response. With an audiogram in hand, you can see where you might be compensating for hearing problems when you mix.

- You can find some interesting articles at *www.hearnet.com*, specifically aimed at musicians.

✘ Build an Isolation Booth

I used heavy moving blankets, acoustic foam, and bass traps to build my isolation booth (the tent idea mentioned earlier). I'm not so naive to think this design blocks sound completely. What I needed was a reasonably dead space that attenuated the sound escaping from and returning back to the booth, enough to not adversely affect my open-mic recordings. The levels are reduced sufficiently, so that the sound I'm recording effectively masks any ambient sound. Using the booth in conjunction with close miking and headphone monitoring works for me. This configuration enables me to get a clean, mostly dead sound for my microphone recordings. I can hear the sound of the instrument, mic, and preamp, and not the room. I also have a very live space for recording certain instruments, but overall, I prefer the isolation booth to get the clean signal that I can slice, dice, and sweeten later.

Harlan Hogan recalled that while recording a track, a landscaping crew came through his neighborhood. His client on the phone patch asked if what he was hearing was a leaf blower, to which Hogan, embarrassed, replied, "Yes." Rather than spend a fortune soundproofing his project studio, Hogan opted for a Whisper Room. This portable sound isolation enclosure, which looks much like a telephone booth, solved his problems relatively inexpensively, compared to traditional soundproofing. "I like the fact that the thing is portable. If I move from this house, I can take it with me. You can't do that with traditional soundproofing."

- Whisper Rooms (*www.whisperroom.com*) claim 27 dB reduction at 125 Hz, and as high as 44 dB at 4,000 Hz. That's not bad, but at a high price tag of about $3,000 for a 3.5' by 5' booth. Another source for all-in-one solutions is *www.vocalbooth.com*.

What if space is at a premium for you? Here is an ideal solution for one-room project studios. You can build a sound isolation booth for recording voice and single acoustic instruments that can be easily set up and disassembled and do it for under $125. This will not stop sound entirely. Its purpose is to deaden the space around the vocalist or instrumentalist and reduce the level of sound escaping from the booth, also attenuating the level of those escaping sounds when they return. Here's the list:

- Three (3) 36" bifold hollow core closet doors
- One (1) 54" x 54" x 2" acoustic foam
- One (1) 54" x 54" x 3" acoustic foam
- Foam adhesive

Cut each foam piece into three sections of eighteen inches each (six sections total). Attach the foam to each inside door panel, about four inches from the top, using the adhesive. (You can get more foam to fully cover the doors, but at additional cost.) Alternate the two-inch and the three-inch pieces, so that each bifold panel has a two-inch piece on one side and a three-inch on the other. Attach the hinge pins to the doors, and stand upright. Form a six-sided booth by folding the doors in slightly. Alternately, set the whole booth in a corner of your studio room. If you need more space, you can leave small gaps between doors. This is also useful if the artist needs to see out for cues. Reduce unwanted reflections by making sure there are no parallel panels. The different foam densities give you more broadband sound absorption. The luan panels absorb some frequencies, reflect others, and do nothing to the deep bass. Still, the mass is sufficient to reduce the sound levels enough for masking or for noise gating to be effective. To store, simply remove the hinge pins and break down the whole booth.

- Get the foam and adhesive from Markertek (*www.markertek.com*) and the doors at Home Depot or a similar store.

✖ Live Echo

Today, it is oh-so-easy to create reverberant spaces with your recording gear. Signal processing abounds with digital reverbs, plug-ins, and other digital models of spaces, ready for you to use. However, there is nothing better than real reverb. Most project studio owners do not have the luxury of a variable acoustic environment, such as those employed by commercial studios. This forces most recordings to be somewhat dead, with artificial "rooms" created electronically to house them. Many project studio owners get creative and press other rooms into service. There's nothing wrong with using your dining room to track drums. If it sounds good, go for it! Does your guitar amp sound good in the tub? Stick a mic in there and jam (make sure to turn the water off to prevent an accident).

Another possibility is a live-echo chamber. I know it sounds ridiculous, but you can do it rather easily. The echo chambers from yesteryear were simple affairs: a medium-sized reverberant room, a speaker tied to the mixer auxiliary send, and a microphone brought back to the mix. You essentially send the sound to the speaker, let it swirl around the room, and pick it up with the microphone, returning the natural reverb back to the mix.

First, find a suitable space. Concrete walls are the best, so look in the basement, crawl space, or stairwell. Paint the concrete walls with waterproofing paint to keep the moisture level low. Cover the concrete with Portland plaster, too. This stuff is hard and will keep a lot of sound energy spinning around the chamber. If necessary, build a door to close off the space. Place one speaker on the floor in the far corner, pointed toward the corner ceiling. A decent full-range speaker is fine. Place the mic in the near corner, about halfway up, pointed at the ceiling corner. Roll off sound going to the chamber at 200 Hz. This keeps the low bass out of the room. The speaker you choose can take care of this for you, too. Now, use a mixer channel to send some sound to the chamber, and pick up the mic signal on another. Combine the chamber reverb with the original sound, and bingo: live echo.

My live-echo chamber is a small, 8' x 10' x 4' crawl space off my basement. The room is tight and ringy, much like a bathroom, and sounds nice on a few things. I used it as described above, but recently retired it by sampling the acoustic response of this room using Sonic Fondry's Acoustic Mirror. Now, I just use the software plug-in when I want my live chamber sound.

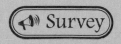

Where is your project studio located (home, office, other)?

The overwhelming majority—99 percent!—have their project studio in their home. One had a "dedicated studio on lot next to house," while another wrote, "currently, home/office, but I'm preparing a commercial location, too."

How many years have you had your project studio?

The average response from those surveyed was 3.75 years. The shortest was six months, while the longest was nine years. I myself have had a project studio for over fifteen years!

Describe the physical layout of your studio (size, studio/control room, etc.).

Virtually every project studio surveyed is a one-room combination control room/tracking room.

- My gear exists on the desk in my living room in my one-bedroom apartment. There is no separate control room.

- A room with two closets modified as iso rooms. My studio is essentially the control room. I can run a snake down to the living room or across the hall and use additional rooms as recording rooms.

- I take up approximately three hundred square feet of the basement. It is an open area.

- One-room studio in a spare room in my house, approximately 12' x 14'; all live tracking, I do in my living room.

- The single room comprising my studio is about 12' x 12'. All of my equipment is set up in a C-shaped configuration against one wall, with my digital, MIDI-controller piano facing a spill window into the cathedral-ceiling living room. Above the piano is a bookshelf with my studio monitors, software, and some scores. To the right of my piano is a PC workstation, stereo DAT, hard-disk recorder, printer, CD burner, and printing stock shelves. To the left of the piano is my rack mount stand, with sampler, CD drive, and operator manuals. A bookcase off against another wall holds most of my scores, blank software, office supplies. In the toe space of the bookshelf are two large totes with cables, electrical connectors, and electrical repair kit. In the closet of the room are my filing cabinets, marketing supplies, and more manuals and scores.

One corner of one of the bedrooms in my apartment. I transformed the closet into a recording (isolation) booth.

6

Transforming Your Gear and Career into a Moneymaking Machine

Building *your project studio business* and increasing its ability to generate ongoing income are your primary goals. You want to position yourself in ways that let you increase the value of the business and your personal net worth. That means getting involved in ventures that provide steady income, such as product sales and royalties. These income sources allow you to fund your business and personal lifestyle without worrying about bringing in more gigs. That kind of freedom can enable you to pursue specific projects for other reasons or to test the waters in areas where you currently do not swim. Knowing you've got the bills paid lets you take risks. Contrarily, if you are just surviving, you are forced to do work you do not want to do in order to meet your most basic life necessities. That leaves little time or energy for expanding your mind or your business.

One survey respondent felt that a project studio was *not* a great way to make money, because one person can only do so much. I agree that there are limits to the productivity of a single person working mostly alone. To *really* profit from your project studio, you must look beyond the simple eight-hour day and the typical gigs. The real key to profiting from your project studio is diversity. You need to expand your product and service line to offer a greater range, and also provide other add-ins that you can profit from quickly and easily. Meticulously evaluate your talents, and then determine how you can package and sell them. The more you can leverage your talents into separate income streams, the more money you can earn. You can choose to be multifaceted and diverse, or pick a narrow segment and work it hard. As Michael Carroll told me, "Diversify, work hard, and *never* give up!"

For example, you record songs for a band. It would also be prudent to offer duplication services for the finished CD. You send the master out for duplication, and charge the band your costs plus a commission (mark up the fee charged by the duplication house by 15 to 20 percent). You could go even further and really cater to your local music scene, where an artist or band could just walk into your project studio with their songs and you would record, mix, master, design, duplicate, and even help distribute and sell the CD. You'd become the one-stop indie shop.

A key component to your success is your ability to change fast. You can react quickly to new circumstances and carve out a niche in a lucrative area. By keeping up with the industry, you can spot trends and be ready for anything that comes your way. "I am starting over," James Utterback wrote in my survey. "I anticipate the video, visual, and Internet markets to overshadow the psychological preoccupation with just doing music and see more people gravitating toward the complete package. I hope to be there to usher them to new heights."

Whether you choose to work full- or part-time, you can tap into several moneymaking markets. You can:

- Record demos and album tracks for bands and songwriters
- Compose commercial soundtrack music and jingles
- Deliver sound production services, such as video soundtrack sweetening
- Master and duplicate CDs
- Run your own record label
- Provide many other music and sound production services

Outsource Your Way to Success

Because there is a finite time allocation available for billing, and therefore only so much a single person can accomplish, you should really concentrate on finding and building relationships with other people who bring added value to your project studio services. For instance, you could work with writers, voice talent, musicians, sound engineers, graphic designers, photographers, printers, duplicators, and more. This way when a prospective client calls about a project you can say you can write it, provide the narrator, record and edit the sound, compose the music, mix the master, design the package, and deliver the product with copies.

Focus on selling your solutions to the problems your prospects and clients face. And while your solution will be your doing the work from your project studio, the reality is, clients don't really care about that. They want the job done right, the way they want it, when they want it, and for the fee you agree upon. How you get it done is left up to you. Understanding this fundamental concept makes profiting from your music and sound project studio easier.

Personally, I rarely turn down a project, unless I know the client doesn't have a clue or it's way off base. If the project is beyond my skills or something I'd rather not do, I find others to help me out. Many corporate clients often prefer it when you handle whole projects, as opposed to just doing only the sound. For example, on a recent CD-ROM project, I not only obviously handled the music and sound, I created the graphics, assembled the master, designed the sleeve and CD artwork, and even oversaw the duplication. Aside from the music and sound and creating the final master in-house, *everything else for the CD was contracted to other companies and home-based professionals.* This allowed me to go from concept to finished product with my company, even though I only did a small portion of the actual work. Of course, I had to pay these other professionals to do their part, yet I was able to command a much higher overall fee than if I'd only handled the music and sound portion. I've even taken on projects where I did *none* of the work at all. I hired a contractor to do the work, marked up the fee, and billed my client when the project was completed. They never knew that I did this (nor did they care), and I was able to offer a service outside of my usual arena. I even made some cash (adding a 30 percent markup to the fee charged by the contractor) that I would not have otherwise received.

Music Production

Music is the mainstay for the vast majority of project studios created today. It would seem that the entire industry is built around making music. For instance, most of the gear filling the pages of the industry trades are musically oriented. Even if you use your equipment to produce other kinds of audio projects, chances are, you usually provide some kind of musical content, too. Whether you use your project studio to capture your own or others' music, this segment will remain an important contributor to your ongoing success and bank account.

The music industry is changing so rapidly that the route to success today means being independent. Gone are the days of the record company cultivating artists. Now, artists need to build their own fan base and sales track record before getting the support of bigger distribution. You can even be your own record label and bypass traditional record distribution entirely. This fact is, of course, why so many people start project studios in the first place: to work on their own material. For a gigging band, the personal project studio lets you create the products to sell at gigs, online, and through traditional brick-and-mortar distribution. You can keep the costs way down and build your business at the same time. For soundtrack and jingle composers, working from their own project studio lets them deliver complete scores, while keeping production costs low.

Many artists use their own project studio to record their original compositions. Sometimes, all the work is done in-house, while at other times they use commercial facilities in conjunction with their own project studio work. Typically, album tracking, overdubbing, mixing, mastering, and even duplication can all be done from the confines of a well-equipped project studio. Other artists just record demos, either to attract labels or for songwriting contracts. You can also make money composing and pitching your original songs for others to record. In addition to national acts, you can provide material for regional bands, small labels, and others. Another segment (one that I expect to be quite large) prefers to record their personal songs, rarely releasing their endeavors beyond the few copies they make for friends and family. Of course, renting time and providing your professional services to other artists is the oft-cited way many people make money from their project studios today. Using your equipment and talent to record other people's projects enables you to function as a small, inexpensive commercial or remote music production studio. It is important to note that the role of the producer has emerged as a formidable force in music production today. *Who* is producing an act is often as important as the act itself. You should strongly consider selling your expertise as a music producer, and not just as a studio or engineer.

The music production clients who record songs usually include bands and solo artists, songwriters, theater groups, schools, and churches. Typical music projects include producing demos and albums for bands and songwriters. You may even produce promotional demos for artists, such as a jingle singer looking to land commercial work. Many studios do the preproduction work necessary for projects, including composing, arranging, and orchestrating. Working out keys, tempos, and instrument parts before going into a commercial studio can save money for tight budgets. Several famous producers use their project studios this way. They listen to artist demos and work to pull together the critical information needed before actual production begins. Often, full-fledged production work for CDs, including tracking, mixing, and mastering, happens at project studios. Other situations include sweetening tracks by adding synth and sampler parts, and overdubbing vocals and instruments to backing tracks produced at a commercial studio.

It is also possible to take your project studio on the road to record live concerts. Personally, I've never quite understood why many local bands with great live acts sequester themselves and track a studio album. Their reputation and fans usually come from their live performances, so why not capture that and put it out instead? Many theater and church groups prefer to record on location, too. With a stereo pair of decent mics, some good mic preamps, and a portable recorder of some kind, you can go just about anywhere for music projects.

Commercial Music

Writing soundtracks and jingles is a well-paying business, made even more attractive when coupled to project studio production. You can make decent money composing and recording themes, jingles, and underscores for a variety of clients. Besides commercial soundtracks and jingles for radio and TV, there are dramatic scores for film, video, and TV; corporate audiovisual productions (sometimes erroneously called industrials); educational projects; documentaries; multimedia productions, including games, interactive media, CD-ROM, and the Internet; library music; other audiovisual presentations; and other markets.

Mark Snow, composer for *The X-Files*, works from his Synclavier-based backyard project studio. He told *Keyboard*, "I've always wanted to have my own self-contained environment, with all the gear and all

115

the stuff. To have the ultimate control has always been a dream of mine." With the Synclavier synched to a video of the show, Snow chooses a tempo, sets up a click track, and starts playing and recording into the Synclavier's internal sequencer. "What's happened is, I've turned into a first-rate improviser of film music. Sometimes, when I'm improvising, I'll fall upon something that is so great, I could never repeat it. And hopefully, that red [Record] light is on." Though most of his music comes from the Synclavier, Snow also uses a rack full of MIDI modules to expand his sonic palette. He mixes his completed scores in-house on a Mackie Digital 8-bus to a Tascam DA-88. The DA-88 format is often embraced by the film and TV industry as a mix-down format, because it can simultaneously handle a 5.1 surround and a stereo mix on its eight tracks and easily syncs to other gear.

Synching music-to-picture requires special equipment. There are several choices, but the emerging leader is hard-disk recording coupled to digital movies. David Conley gets all his film work on CD-ROM in Quicktime format. He imports these digital movies into his sequencer and composes to the screen action, with everything in perfect synchronization.

Clients for soundtrack and jingle music include producers and directors at audiovisual, video, and film production companies, cable companies, and radio and TV stations. Clients for jingles include advertising agencies, radio and TV stations, and sometimes the advertisers themselves.

- Use my other book, *How to Make Money Scoring Soundtracks and Jingles,* as your essential reference and guide to this lucrative area of the music industry.

Multimedia and Web Music

Composing music for interactive or other multimedia formats is another adjunct to the commercial music industry. Once again, there are specific technical requirements to work in this area. Your music is usually delivered in one of two formats: digital audio files (.wav or .aiff) or standard general MIDI files. In the case of games, the graphics always get the most processor time, with sound, including your music, relegated to whatever is left. This is a great challenge for the composer, as you are forced to write many short themes and loops.

To produce game music or music for interactive media, you need a simple MIDI setup (keyboard, sequencer, and general MIDI-compatible sound card) and a digital audio recording and editing setup. You'll be checking MIDI compositions with the sound card, to make sure your music will be compatible. You must understand that MIDI-based music will vary greatly from listener to listener, as it is entirely dependent upon the sound card used. Digital audio is, obviously, easier to control and plays back as intended. For digital audio files, you can produce the music full-quality. Ultimately, you will reduce the file size by downsampling it later and/or reducing the bit depth. For example, changing the sampling frequency from 44.1 kHz to 22 kHz cuts the file size in half. I would suggest using a mastering tool that lets you both convert and dither the audio. Dithering the audio adds some noise to it to help disguise quantization errors (the side effect of sampling the audio at a lower frequency or reducing the bit depth). You will probably deliver your final project as digital files via e-mail or CD-ROM.

Much like creating music for a film or video, game music requires a spotting session, where you sit down with the developers and decide where music will be played, what it should sound like, and other creative and technical decisions. Also, music is often created simultaneously with the game's development. This means that changes are inevitable, further increasing the composer's need to work well with the game's developers.

- Sources for information on this field include New Media (*www.newmedia.com*) and Interactivity (*www.eyemedia.com*).

Providing music for Web sites is another growing market. As with game music, you can create either MIDI files or digital audio files (in a variety of formats). This area is growing and changing rapidly, with new tools available regularly. For instance, if you want to or are called upon to create interactive audio for Web sites, you should check out the tools provided by Beatnik. According to their Web site, Beatnik is "the solution for high-quality, low-bandwidth interactive music and sound on any HTML, Shockwave, or Flash Web page."

- Beatnik (*www.beatnik.com*)

Library Music

This segment of the music industry is also growing exponentially. There are many people who rely on libraries for their music needs. These buyers are becoming increasingly sensitive to what constitutes good music. Composers must work hard to make their music sound better and be fresher and more original. Using only a simple MIDI rig doesn't cut it anymore. There is increasing competition, forcing most libraries to use real musicians and push the boundaries of production and composition. That said, there are a few really big houses out there, but there can be room for smaller independents as well.

There are several ways you can offer a music library. You can sell single tracks for a flat rate, offering nonexclusive rights to buyers. You can sell tracks, even entire CDs, to other music libraries. They buy your music, and then sell it under their name. You can also make some money selling other music libraries to your clients. This is best done in conjunction with music search services. For example, you have a corporate client who needs music for a sales video. You find the appropriate music on an existing library music CD. You make money from your search services and through a commission from the library music supplier (or by marking up your cost). Of course, you can profit from your own music library, too.

Most musicians have a backlog of unused music—some complete, others sketches and ideas. Why let this work go to waste? Pick it up, dust it off, and make some money from it. You can choose to either offer a diverse range of music or stick with a specific musical style. Offer the music on audio CDs and CD-ROM (.wav and .aiff files) for users to import directly into their digital audio workstations. Don't forget that your music library can also be the demo of your original music composition services. Sell the library CDs as a buyout, where the client pays one fee and can use the music nonexclusively in perpetuity. To keep costs down, burn your own CDs on demand or make short runs of twenty-five CDs at time. Print the booklets and CD labels in-house, too. This way you never have to make a CD until you get an order. This strategy clearly demonstrates the power of producing music in your own project studio. You have complete control and can minimize your production costs substantially.

Jan Cyrka works from his project studio to write music for the KPM music library. Using gear that he calls "state of the ark," he enjoys the freedom of this particular niche. "We can write whatever we want for the library music," he told *Home Recording* magazine. "In a sense, these [library CDs] have become our albums, because it's the music we want to do and enjoy doing." Cyrka explained the basic process of library music: "Generally, you produce a piece of music between two and four minutes long, and it needs to be fairly linear. Then, you do a thirty-second version . . . and finally, a 'sting,' which is usually between five and ten seconds."

The Internet is changing this industry, too. In the past, people would order demo CDs from library music suppliers and buy entire CDs based on a few snippets included on these demos. Today, you can preview every cut on a CD via the Internet. You can audition samples online, usually in low-quality formats such as Real Audio, then you can choose individual tracks, download them as MP3s, and pay for them online. The preferred method is still to ship entire CDs, though with online preview. A few clever music library producers are offering music products in hybrid formats, such as complete Pro Tools sessions or Acid projects. This method lets the music buyer remix the music to better suit their needs.

What do clients look for in their library music choices? First, they want quality music, faithful to specific musical styles and genres. They want to pay a fair price for the music and prefer buyouts, where they pay one fee to use the music nonexclusively. Lastly, they want the music tracks ready to use. Most library music users don't want to spend precious, expensive time fiddling with music. They want to choose a cut and go. Most libraries come on CD, either as audio or as digital files, to import into hard-disk audio recorders and nonlinear video editing systems. Most library music cuts come as full-length, sixty-, thirty-, and ten-second stingers. Some libraries offer alternative takes—rhythm only or different instrumentations, for instance.

- A few well-known library music suppliers include Video Helper (*www.videohelper.com*), Music Bakery (*www.musicbakery.com*), and Megatrax (*www.megatrax.com*). My *Melomania* music library comprises several old music tracks, along with new material developed specifically for the library in an eclectic blend of styles, (*www.jeffreypfisher.com*).

119

Sequences and Karaoke

A close relative to library music is selling MIDI sequences. If you have terrific keyboard chops and are willing to invest the time to carefully record popular music, you can make this a viable part of your project studio mix. Some bands and other musical acts prefer to purchase sequences, and often incorporate them into their stage show. It's rare not to find small combos playing and singing to MIDI backing tracks at lounge gigs. I'd like to believe that these performers sequenced their own versions, but I'm confident many just used their credit card to buy their act instead.

Alternately, you could produce backing tracks for the karaoke crowd. Look for clubs that already promote this wacky concept, and work to become their supplier for music. You might try DJs who do weddings, too. At some weddings, people like to sing songs, and you can provide the tracks. You might even go on-site to the wedding and record the amateur crooner for even bigger sales. Even better, perhaps you can get the person into the studio to record a top-notch version to play at the wedding—and hand out CDs at the reception (that you mastered and duplicated, of course).

Theater, Dance, Exercise, and Spas

Writing music for theater and dance companies can be another area in which you might expand. Many dance studios might be open to music for specific purposes (beat patterns, tempo, and so forth). You might create a cover version of a popular song at several tempos for the troupe to use when they practice or perform. Although many aerobics instructors prefer to use the current hits in their classes, you might find a few who would be open to original music produced by you. This can be another outlet for library music tracks. You produce a CD of specific high-energy dance numbers (aerobics) or low-key ambient pieces (yoga, Tai Chi) and sell them direct to these instructors.

Jeremy Spencer suggested another market for your instrumental music: "I heard that a local relaxation spa needed some new music, as the CDs they were using were becoming a touch monotonous for the clients. I found out the manager's name, mailed him your infamous sales letter [from my *How to Make Money Scoring Soundtracks and Jingles* book—JPF], and followed up with a phone call. Since my price was attractive, the spa said they would like a CD. This could open up a whole new avenue of hot clients, as there are literally hundreds of places like this around. I suggest putting together library CDs specifically with an hour's worth of New Age/ambient music, and pitch them to spas and other relaxation places."

Audio Production

Audio production encompasses a wide range of activities, including voice-overs of announcers and narrators; spoken-word projects, such as audio books, radio spots and on-hold messages; sound recording and design for multimedia (radio, TV, video, Web, games, etc.), including sound effects, Foley, Automatic Dialogue Replacement (ADR), and more. You will find far more opportunities in this market than music alone. Therefore, the savvy project studio owner will pursue clients who need a bevy of straightforward audio production. Although recording simple narrations are not the most creative projects to come into my office, they are better-paying, with more reliable clients.

Spoken Word

Corporate clients are always looking for better ways to deliver information to staff, clients, and the media. You can help them by producing their audio projects, including on-hold messages, cassettes and CDs, videos and CD-ROMs, and more.

Clients include corporate communications departments, government agencies, radio and TV stations, multimedia production companies (video producers, animation houses, and graphic design firms), audiobook publishers, and even individuals. For example, you might record a speaker delivering a speech at an association conference, for distribution to its members.

Voice artist Harlan Hogan (*www.harlanhogan.com*) likens his work to telecommuting. "I still do the majority of my work at commercial facilities, as I enjoy going to studios and working directly with producers. But for nonbroadcast work and short spots, I use my studio." Hogan has a very modest setup, comprising a CD-burner-equipped PC running Syntrillium Software's Cool Edit Pro (*www.syntrillium.com*), a Mackie mixer, and two expensive mics (a Neuman U-47 and a Sennheiser 416 shotgun). A little-known secret to spoken voice recording is that many voice artists prefer to use a shotgun microphone. The 416 has a tight pickup pattern that zeroes in on the voice, and its proximity effect (the bass boost created by being too close to the microphone) can thicken a thin voice and help create that prototypical announcer voice quality. "I love the 416," confessed Hogan. "It seems to cut better, with a sort of built-in compression that sounds smooth to my ears." He also uses a DAT deck for session backup. "As soon as a session starts, I put the DAT into 'record' and let it run until the session's over. The real tracking takes place in the PC, but if something happens, I have the DAT backup just in case." Hogan's DAT is connected to the PC through the S/PDIF port. Often, what happens is, the voice talent does an initial run-through that is just great, but doesn't get recorded. "With the DAT running, you can capture moments that might otherwise get lost," he explained.

Nonbroadcast clients typically do their own soundtrack editing and sweetening and just need the raw narration from Hogan. He can quickly cut his tracks, encode an MP3, and e-mail it to the client soon after. "I try to stay away from full-fledged work and concentrate on capturing my performance clean." If the client needs more comprehensive services, he always suggests they go to a commercial studio, where they can get full service. However, Hogan will occasionally handle entire spots with voice, sound effects, and music, mix the finished track, burn a CD, and messenger or overnight the disk to the client. "I start at 11:00 A.M., and by 3:00 P.M., the client has the finished tracks in hand. This is really a great way to work. I love it."

Though Hogan often records without client oversight, some prefer to listen in on the sessions. For these situations, he uses a phone patch that lets the client provide suggestions and direction, and then, they instantly hear him record the result. Oddly, Hogan sometimes never actually meets his clients. "I worked with a guy for twenty-two years and never met! When we finally did get together, he told me that I'd ruined our story!" Hogan's advice for up-and-coming voice talent? "Don't just take acting classes. Take some basic audio engineering classes. You will need it."

Commercial Spots for Radio and TV

Radio stations need a lot of spots to round out their format. This can be a boon for the smart project studio owner. Local radio needs music, sound effects, sound design for ad spots, stingers, and music beds. While they won't pay top dollar for original compositions (unless they have a big advertiser that needs a jingle), they are good prospects for library tracks, sound effects CDs, and non-buyout music. They also farm out production duties. Knowing that you have the chops to deliver spots for them can put you in an enviable position.

Most commercials are either sixty, thirty, or ten seconds in length. Station IDs are usually short pieces used to identify the radio station. Some promo spots, on the other hand, often vary in length and usually promote some station-sponsored event or other shows on the station. Automated stations are very conscious of spot timings. They get a network feed that lets them drop in local commercials in two-minute blocks. If the commercials run short, there is silence or dead air before returning to the network feed. If the commercials run long, they will get chopped off when the network audio returns. Radio stations that run live, with real people, are a little less concerned with spot timings, because the DJs don't need to hit specific events or time. TV is, of course, more carefully timed. TV commercial production falls under the film/video postproduction section later in this chapter.

You must realize that radio stations love to do ad spots in-house, because it is cheap. They almost never charge their advertisers for production. What they *really* sell is air time. So, they'll go to an advertiser and say, "You buy fifty spots, and we'll do your commercials *free!*" This sales approach makes it very hard for independent spot producers to compete. What I would suggest is bypassing the radio stations and going *directly* to the advertisers. Though you'll face some tough obstacles, you must work to convince them that your production will make their ad stand out and be more memorable. Most ads produced by radio stations start to sound alike. If an advertiser really wants to be heard above the din, you must give them the tools. That means good writing, good talent, good music, great production values—exactly what you do, right?

For example, prepare a generic jingle or radio ad that you can relyric/rewrite easily. Visit a radio advertiser who is *not* using a jingle, collect some of their promotional material, then return to the studio and write/record a "demo" jingle or ad spot that uses their promotional message, name, etc. Next, approach the advertiser, and play them your demo. They will be impressed that you took the time to make a "custom" spot for them. If you don't make the sale, choose another prospect, relyric the same jingle or rewrite the ad, and start again.

Using a software multitrack is the way to go for radio spot production. Its random access nature and visual feedback make it a fast, efficient tool. EQ facilities and other effects can make cleaning up audio tracks a snap, while enabling a myriad of creative options, too. Time compression is another useful tool. This essentially lets you expand or reduce the spot's timing without changing its pitch. The typical spot would have a couple of tracks for voice-overs (VO), a couple of tracks for sound effects and backgrounds, and a couple of tracks for music. Delivery may be as digital audio files, CD, or DAT. Having access to sound effects and music libraries can make producing radio spots easier, too. It is rare that original music gets composed (unless a jingle is used or the advertiser has a bigger budget). Producing a good voice-over is critical. As you read above, some VO artists have their own studio and can ship the files to you. You may also record them in your studio. A good quality microphone and microphone preamp is all you really need. Most radio stations use the Electro-Voice RE20 or RE27, though other mics work fine. A good pop filter is also a necessary component. Mixing final spots with light, gentle compression is a good idea, too.

Slow builds are anathema in radio. A half-second start before the announcer kicks in is usually all that's needed. Many spots start right on the downbeat! Nearly every spot has wall-to-wall sound, with the VO comprising 80 to 90 percent of it. Music and sound effects complete the illusion. If you need to use multiple music tracks, try making your edits at musically appropriate places, such as just before a downbeat, or use short cross-fades to hide the edits.

Audiobooks

Michael Moss, owner of Soundscape, explained how his project studio is suited for the audiobooks industry in an article in *Mix*. "A regular studio couldn't provide the kind of comprehensive services that audiobooks require. It's not a matter of just studio time; it's a matter of being able to do all of the things that each project requires." Audiobooks have become increasingly sophisticated. There's music to write and produce, sound effects to find, create, and produce, and, of course, narration to record. These elements need to be assembled and mixed into the final product. Your project studio can be a cost-effective alternative to traditional commercial venues by providing the one-stop-shop services that audiobook makers need.

On-Hold

It's so rare not to be placed on hold when you call a business nowadays. A survey by Premier Technologies, provider of digital on-hold equipment, showed that 94 percent of those businesses with on-hold message capabilities use a customized message to provide entertainment and useful information and to promote their products and services. Of those surveyed, 97 percent said their on-hold presence improved their company image, and 67 percent said it increased their sales. You can make good money producing these on-hold messages. Much akin to radio spots, on-hold messages typically combine short VOs with music. What is important to note about producing on-hold messages is that, according to Premier's survey, 40 percent report changing their messages quarterly, and 17 percent change them monthly. That means the majority of your work will bring in repeat business. Nearly any business with a telephone can use on-hold. That creates a huge demand for your services. Just doing one or two sessions a month can pay your overhead and free up time for other more creative (but lower-paying) gigs.

Film/Video Post

Bringing together all the sound elements—narration, dialogue, sound effects, and music—to create the final theatrical, television, video/DVD, or CD-ROM release falls under the general umbrella of film and video postproduction. You may use your project studio to do one or many parts of the project. This industry, which used to be dominated by a few high-profile companies, is now segmented into many smaller production houses.

Music and Sound Editing
for TV, Video, and Film

Nick Carr, award-winning music editor for Nickelodeon's *SpongeBob SquarePants,* has the humblest of home project studios—it fits into one corner of his living room! Using only a four-track hard-disk editing system, some sound modules and effects processors, a video deck and TV, and stacks of music library CDs, Carr arranges music cues that define this animated series. He told *Electronic Musician* that he works from the spotting notes provided by the show's director. Although this show uses mostly library music, Carr does sporadically compose and play some music himself. His greatest challenge is matching the pre-recorded tracks to fit the on-screen action. He solves this problem through careful editing coupled to tempo, pitch-shifting, and other time compression techniques. After Carr completes the music, the show's director comes in for a screening. There are usually changes to be made before the director gives final approval. Carr then dumps the software-recorded tracks to a Tascam DA-88. At the final mix, the dialogue, sound effects, and music are combined into the final show. One last chore for Carr is to prepare the music cue sheet that details the music used on the show. The performing rights societies use this information to collect and distribute royalties to the composers of the music actually used.

Travis Powers, sound effects master for *The Simpsons*, told *Keyboard* about his work on the series. Working from a copy of the show with picture and dialogue only, he notes all the events that need effects. He then gathers the material he needs, often creating and recording much of the sound effects himself. His main ax is a Synclavier synched to the video. "Sometimes, I'll play the events in real time, while watching the picture. Other times, I use the Synclavier's sequencer." The show averages eight tracks of hard effects and another eight tracks of background noises.

Sound Design for Movies and TV

Sound designers are called upon to produce the onscreen sounds and other ear candy that enhance the motion picture and TV viewing experience. Most sound design involves less of the recording itself and more of how the sound is manipulated. Gathering real-world sounds (footsteps, doors closing, and such) is one obvious need, but creating new sounds and hyperreal sounds is where the real action is. Many sound designers enjoy the challenge of coming up with these distinct and unique sounds. There are synched sound elements, called hard effects, such as footsteps, crashes, explosions, etc. These are sometimes created from individual sound effects or through a process called Foley, where artists recreate and record these sound effects "live" while watching the movie. Also, there are individual background ambient sound elements—bird chirps and traffic noises, for example. Another task falling to sound designers is fixing and replacing production sound, called Automatic Dialogue Replacement (ADR) or by its old "looping" designation. Instead of relying on library sound effects, many designers build their own personal libraries of sounds. Once they go through a project, they'll determine what they have already and what they must get. Then, out to the field to record the sounds and back to the studio to make them better.

For *The Phantom Menace*, the sound designers mapped their effects across the keyboards of their Synclavier workstations. Then, while watching the film on a monitor, they "played" the sound effects in real time, usually in multiple tracking passes. This kind of high-tech Foley is employed more often than not. The sound designer not only creates the evocative aural palette, he lends his performing talent to the show as well.

Sound Design for Games and Interactive Media

The game market is another opportunity for your project studio. The typical project has background ambience, interactive elements, object and interface sounds, and music. A game could have as few as 1,000 sound files, with a large-scale project upwards of 5,000 individual sound elements (music, backgrounds, sound effects, and voice). One of the most difficult challenges in this industry is managing resources. Many elements compete for CPU processing and related technical considerations. The music and sound usually gets the least access to resources. That means that planning out audio components and executing them requires some very specialized knowledge.

Unlike creating sound effects and music for a film or video, where the work is done after the project is edited and nearly complete, sound design for interactive media is often done in conjunction with the software production. That means that significant changes are often made during the production. What this really means is that the interactive media sound designer is an important part of the software development team.

Interface sounds, as the name suggests, are the sounds that accompany the project, such as button clicks. These sounds usually provide information or cues to the user. Object sounds are more up-front sound effects that match screen action, such as a door opening. Music can be of two varieties: general underscore and specific cue. The underscore is akin to incidental soundtrack music in movies. The specific cue music relates to some onscreen event and can be somewhat similar to interface sounds.

127

Juggling these elements with enough variation to be interesting and still use the minimal amount of resources is the sound designer's challenge. Creating the mix is often harder. The best approach here is to use the product—play the game or follow the training—and get a feel for how to juggle the sound elements. Another issue is that some projects are released in multiple, incompatible formats. The sound designer is then faced with making the necessary conversions and alterations to ensure complete cross-platform compatibility.

Sound Design for Sample Libraries

Another related industry for sound designers is the burgeoning sample and synth patch libraries. If you can design sounds for a variety of synths and/or create samples of real and imagined sounds, you have another profitable venture for your project studio. Flip through any *Keyboard* issue, and you'll see pages and pages of ads from companies selling samples, loop libraries, MIDI tracks, and more. This market is similar to music libraries, except you market the raw sounds for musicians and other sound designers to use for their work. You could also just specifically design sounds and program for production houses and other project studios. This area is somewhat similar to sample selling, but targeted at a different market. Here, you design the sounds effects and such used by these various audiovisual producers. Occasionally, another composer might need your skills to develop sounds for their synths and samplers.

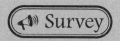

What kinds of projects do you handle with your project studio?

♪ This is just my personal studio, which won't be for just anyone's use.

♪ Songwriting, backing tracks, CD burning.

♪ I now work full-time from my home producing song demos for nonperforming songwriters, album tracks for performing songwriters, and radio commercial production. I rely entirely on word-of-mouth referrals to fill the room. As a multi-instrumentalist and vocalist proficient in many musical styles, I'm looking to compose for film and interactive multimedia.

♪ Recording individual instruments or vocalists, demos, eight-track digital audio to be synched at pro facility.

♪ We have done a number of CD projects, a couple of music videos, several TV commercials, some voice-overs, and a couple of animations.

♪ Recording my own material to send to music publishers, the odd corporate video, and theater projects. I also record original relaxation music, which I solicit around town.

♪ Song demos for nonperforming songwriters, album tracks for performing songwriters, and radio commercial production.

♪ I produce records, as well as radio production.

♪ Full album recording and production, custom music tracks, voice-overs, commercials, karaoke recordings, mobile recording, and audio program editing and mastering

♪ Eighty percent bands making albums, usually local bands for local and regional release. Ten percent multimedia, sound f/x, and soundtracks for CD-ROMs and videos. Ten percent jingles and radio/TV ads. We also offer limited-run CD and cassette duplication.

♪ I am in the process of making demo for submission to a label . . . hopefully.

♩ I started out recording demos for my band, then demos for other bands, then I recorded and released a solo album. Now, I'm composing and recording background music, etc.

♩ CD mastering, soundtrack work for video games, voice-over, audio for Internet, live recording, etc.

♩ Radio and TV, advertising jingles, scores for television, movies and multimedia, classical music concert pieces.

♪ I was producing rap music mainly.

♪ So far, archiving old analog tapes to CD and Web sound design.

What kinds of projects would you like to have, but don't yet?

♪ Major label singer/songwriters or bands hiring me to produce rather than engineer.

♪ I'd like to continue doing exactly what I'm doing now.

♪ Writing and producing scores for television, film, and radio.

♪ My dream is to compose for film and interactive multimedia.

♪ Advertising [for] TV/film/radio.

♪ Label-funded projects with bigger budgets and more promotion.

♪ Major label album projects with an actual BUDGET to get things done right.

♪ More of the same: commercials, corporate presentations, TV scores, film scores, etc.

♩ I will be seeking projects that evolve through the recording process toward packaging, promotion, and widespread recognition. My services will include music and graphic production for Internet, broadcast, and other communications avenues.

♪ Singer-songwriters, producing and arranging artists, scoring soundtracks.

7

More Ways to Transform Your Gear and Career into a Moneymaking Machine

T*he previous chapter* profiled several typical ways people earn money with their project studios. This chapter looks at those sometimes-overlooked income-producing ideas. Most make ideal add-ins to complement your other services. However, you may one day find yourself moving in an entirely different direction with your project studio. You begin offering these ancillary products and services, and they wind up becoming greater contributors to your overall success. Never give up your successful ventures to concentrate on untested ideas, though. To lessen your risk, devote only a portion of your resources toward exploring these other possibilities.

Audio /Video Duplication

Since music and sound are often the last steps for many projects, the next logical area for you to expand into is offering mastering, duplication, and format conversion services.

Mastering

Mastering is the final step before duplicating a project. It's main function is to ensure a uniform level and sound to a music or sound mix, with no distortion. Often, mixes get the final tweak to make them shine. Mastering can often make or break a CD, and those professionals who excel at this production step are often highly sought after: Bob Ludwig, Bernie Grundman, and others.

Mastering is usually done at specific facilities and almost always outside of the regular recording and mixing phase and environment. A mastering engineer usually brings fresh ears and experience to a project. This can be a terrific way to expand your project studio offerings. Once you've completed the mixes, schedule time for mastering. Never do it the same day as a final mix, unless you are forced to because of a deadline or other pressure. You can also offer to master projects created outside your facility. It's quite easy to promote this service. Play for a prospective client a section of music before mastering and after you sweeten the same track. The difference your prospect hears will make the sale.

Most mastering facilities use some special equipment: EQ, compressors, limiters, and noise reduction processors. They also have high-quality playback devices and top-of-the-line monitors. There are some mastering processors out there that purport to emulate some of this gear. Specifically, there is the Waves L2 Ultramaximizer and the T-Racks Mastering software. Armed with one of these mastering processors, you can sweeten final mixes for a variety of projects.

- Waves (*www.waves.com*)
- T-Racks (*www.t-racks.com*)

Internet Mastering and Encoding (MP3)

The digital distribution of audiovisual material will overtake traditional means. This creates still another moneymaking opportunity for you. Mastering music for MP3 or other online music formats is different than creating an audio CD. Mastering online music is a two-step process. First, you master final mixes specifically for online delivery. There are certain undesirable artifacts of Internet compression processes that can be reduced with proper mastering techniques (refer to chapter 8 for details). Second, you encode these special audio mixes into the online format needed. You can now generate revenues for mastering audio CDs, creating separate masters for Internet-based encoding, and also providing the actual encoding.

Surround Sound Encoding

One of the largest areas for growth in the past few years has been home theater sound. Most new projects are produced in 5.1 surround, but there is also a growing trend of taking old material and remixing it to surround sound, such as the DVD release of the Beatles' *Yellow Submarine*. This trend is expected to continue, and that could mean a possible market for your project studio. As surround sound continues to penetrate the home market, two formats will compete in this growing arena. DVD Audio is a 24-bit, 96 kHz format designed specifically for 5.1 surround. The Sony/Phillips Super Audio Compact Disc is a two-layer CD with 16-bit, 44.1 kHz on one layer and the 24-bit, 96 kHz 5.1 surround on another layer of the same disc. The need for remixing old material and new material to these new formats will keep many project studios busy for years to come.

Audio Restoration Services

Cleaning up music tracks and restoring old recordings is another niche for the project studio. Many people have old recordings that they'd love to hear on CD. Although this is very easy for the do-it-yourselfer, many don't have the time or inclination to do it themselves. That's where you step in and save the day. You can offer to do CD transfers, clean-up, and mastering. Closely related to this field is finding, restoring, remastering, and rereleasing out-of-print recordings.

Duplication

You can provide both duplication and packaging services to those who use your project studio. You need to create working arrangements with duplicators and perhaps a graphic design firm (for covers and booklet liner notes). The well-known duplication firm, Disc Makers, offers a Studio Partner Program, where you recommend them to your clients and give them a package of sales material. If the client chooses Disc Makers to handle their duplication, your project studio gets a commission. What could be easier? If you choose to do it yourself, you can get quotes from firms and mark it up to your clients, earning a commission.

- Disc Makers (*www.discmakers.com*)

You can also duplicate short runs in-house. Beyond making a dozen or so, though, you'll either want to farm it out or expand your gear list. There is CD replication equipment available that can produce ten CDs at a time. These turnkey packages often come with printers for basic printing on the disk. Add a decent color printer for the booklet/tray card, and you can be a one-stop shop for short- to medium-run duplication.

In addition to duplication, you can also help your clients distribute their finished masters. Provide lists of distributors, contacts at local music stores, details about online distribution sources, and more. Also, many companies look for special gifts to give away or use as premiums and incentives. Music comprises over 25 percent of *all* premium and incentive purchases. What you need to do is find a match between the music and a company or professional association.

- There is an annual Premium Incentive Show (*www.piexpo.com*). The premium and incentive industry's online buyer supplier connection (*www.supplierfinder*). Also check out *Incentive* magazine (*www.incentivemag.com*).

Record Label

Some project studio owners operate a record label, using their studio for production. Success in the music industry no longer starts or ends with a major label deal. Online distribution enables you to easily start and run your own record label, comprised of just one artist (you) or any number of others.

How do you define a record label? It's simple. The label finds, cultivates, markets, and promotes musical talent. That usually means that you front the production, recording, and duplicating costs, help sell and distribute the finished products, and give the artists a royalty on each sale. You keep a substantial portion of the profits for yourself.

Dave Davies explained how he runs his GSC Records label: "I search out local bands whom I think have large market potential, record two of their tunes at no cost-no obligation (to them), then make an offer if I feel I can add something to their sound. I'm very picky, as I don't have unlimited resources, and can only speculate on a couple of artists at a time. The deals I sign with artists vary between 50/50 down to $1.50 per CD for the artist. Essentially, I act just like a large label—just on a different scale."

How does a basement record company work? You use your project studio to record the music, edit, mix to stereo, master, design the artwork, make the CDs, and sell the finished products (at gigs, Web, etc.). Award-winning engineer Roger Nichols explained this process in an *EQ* article several years ago: "In the span of a week, I was the record producer, the mastering engineer, the CD plant, the record company president, and the entire art department. It showed me that if you play with your high-tech toys enough and learn how they work, they can help you create things that give you just a little edge on the next guy." Nichols essentially took some music mixes, transferred them to a computer editing program, cleaned them up, sweetened them, arranged the CD, created the master CD in software, burned a few dozen CDs, used an art program to design the booklet and tray card, printed that at Kinko's, and then assembled the whole package, ready to release, sell, use as a demo, etc.

Talking to the *Chicago Tribune*, Bob Salerno, who runs Bobsled Records out of a basement studio in Aurora, Illinois, said he learned firsthand how the current record industry works. "Major labels would rank bands according to commercial potential, instead of artistic worth; great bands would get dropped, because they wouldn't make enough money soon enough. They talked about artistic development, but if a band didn't sell at least three to five hundred thousand copies of their first record, they were done." Salerno is running his label differently, grabbing bands that "write great songs that reflect our times." He gives his artists freedom to create and doesn't focus on the money. He believes that good music will find its audience with a reasonable amount of promotion behind it. "We're setting out to change the industry, and doing it from Aurora is a way of saying that you can do it from anywhere."

✕ Mechanical Rights

Don't forget, if you record copyrighted material, you must pay mechanical royalties to the music publisher. These are the rights to reproduce copyrighted music onto tape, CD, videotape, or film. The Statutory Mechanical Rate is 7.55 cents per song per unit (rising to 8 cents in 2002). In other words, if you used one copyrighted song for a CD and manufactured a hundred copies, you'd pay $7.55 for the mechanical rights to that single song. Money earned from mechanical rights is split 50-50 between the artist and publisher. Securing mechanical rights is quite easy with the compulsory license. Instead of asking permission to use a song, you essentially inform the publisher that you intend to record the song and will pay the mechanical royalty. You can use the compulsory license if: the song has been recorded already, you do not change the melody or other song basics, you complete a "Notice of Intention to Obtain Compulsory License" at least thirty days before the song is released, and you pay the mechanical royalty of 7.55 cents per song, per copy.

- To secure mechanical rights, use the Harry Fox Agency (*www.harryfox.com*). Download the "Application for New Licensing Account" and the "Mechanical License Request Form." You must complete the application if this is your first time doing business with Harry Fox.

Other Project Studio Services

Desktop Video Production

Here's another area where many sound professionals are landing work. Sound is one-half of all audiovisual presentations. Why make only half the money when you can make 100 percent? Start doing the visual portion of multimedia and digital video projects, and you become part of a burgeoning industry. Many clients prefer one-stop shops, where they can get their whole project completed. Concentrating only on the sound can sometimes keep you from landing the whole project when another competitor promises the whole shebang. Today, you can digitize video with ease, perform all kinds of visual and audio miracles, and master the video to DVD, CD-ROM, Internet streaming, and even good ol' VHS. This market will emerge as an ideal gig for certain project studio owners. Armed with a capture card, nonlinear editing (NLE) software, and your imagination, you, too, can be part of this industry segment. If your skills fall short, team up with a graphics design firm or other video production house, and work together to provide CD-ROM, Internet, and digital video services.

This is the direction I'm taking with my company, Fisher Creative Group. While traditional video production has always been a small part of my business plan, we naturally progressed to computer-based presentations exclusively. Now, producing promotional and instructional CD-ROMs, Web sites, and videos is a significant proportion of FCG's work. I hire out much of the graphics work to independent contractors and handle the sound and basic programming myself from my project studio. After creating the masters, they get sent for duplication and final delivery to the client.

Web Site Content

As broadband Internet access becomes even more commonplace, streaming video and audio will be much more solid and reliable. That means somebody is going to need to encode all that material. Isn't it right that you should get a piece of the encoding pie? Using some special software tools, you can create and encode audio and video for the Web. You might offer complete Web services to your clients by partnering with a Web design firm, where you handle the audio and video and they handle the site programming, and so forth. If you are so inclined and skilled in the ways of the Web, do the work yourself. Get your own server, high-speed Internet access, and create your own online community—all from the comfort of your project studio. You could even record bands at night and manage their Web sites during the day, for example.

Lessons

Many people tell me that teaching music lessons is easy money. Charge $10 to $20 an hour for a few students, and you can easily bring in over $300 a month ($20 x 4 students x 4 weeks = $320). While it is typical to teach the young Eddie Van Halen wanna-bes, you might be wise to consider the senior community. There will be a lot of baby boomers, with money to burn, who always wanted to learn the guitar or piano. You should provide their instruction. Posting a notice at your local senior community center should do the trick. There's a senior community down the street where my mother lives that I'm sure could keep me up to my ears in lessons. If I only had more time . . . .

Teaching lessons from your project studio base is also a way to introduce up-and-coming talent to recording. Once they master their instrument, get them to record in your studio and make even more money. Alternately, instead of music lessons, you can offer recording lessons and other seminars. Get people to your studio to learn about digital audio, for instance, and convince a few to come back another time to record as paying customers. Alternately, give a free hour to a band or songwriter. This gets them into the studio, hopefully wanting more and paying for more studio time.

Consult

If you possess certain skills needed by the music and sound industry, you may parlay them into income producers. If you know how to install and troubleshoot MIDI and recording equipment, you can provide those services to other project studio owners. Stop giving away your experience; get paid for your advice.

Live Sound Engineering

Several project studio owners rent PA equipment and include their services along with the gear. Schools and churches often need help in this area. Many bands would welcome a good mixer for their gigs. This can be steady work or perhaps a one-time consulting session, where you hook up the gear for the church or other organization and provide a basic setup and operating instructions. Pitch this kind of service to the same bands who record at your studio, if that applies.

Home Theater

As people spend more and more time at home, the trend for setting up extensive media rooms continues. The technology available can frighten some people off, and that's why many turn to professionals to design and install their home theater/media rooms. That could be you.

Software

Writing software for the music and sound industry is another way to capitalize on your particular strength. Do you write code? Write some for the rest of us. You could develop the next music or sound industry killer application, or at least a cool plug-in or two. I'd love to see an integrated accounting, database, contact management, word processing package that is specifically for music and sound industry professionals, especially those who run a project studio.

Writing

Writing about your projects serves two purposes. One, you get paid to write about what you know. Two, you secure certain promotion for your project studio and other professional services. Having written over five books and countless magazine and online articles, I know full well the benefits of making writing part of your overall business plan. What can you write about? Solutions and entertainment are the two best subjects. If you've solved problems or know some inside information about music and sound topics, you have possible subjects for your articles. You could write about gear acquisitions, the details of a recent

141

project, tips and tricks for using a piece of equipment, etc. I started out writing reviews of music gear, progressing into music business topics, where I've concentrated ever since. Writing a book is a formidable task, but writing a series of articles that you ultimately string together into a book is often a better approach. You can use the individual articles at first, and when you've authored enough material, create a small book or booklet.

Gigging

I include this as a way to make money because it is often a primary way artists acquire income: project studio by day, band thang by night. I'll leave off the details, only because they go beyond the purpose of this book. You must realize that playing is a fine way to diversify your business and wring just that much more money from your talents. I've always felt that as a player, you can have multiple personalities. You can be an all-original band, you can play covers and grab the lucrative wedding receptions and other parties market, and you can play solo gigs (lounge piano, coffee houses, etc.). You can also be a session player-for-hire, either at your project studio or elsewhere, including commercial studio gigs.

Your Project Studio Store

First and foremost, you will sell your studio time and/or professional expertise to those who use your project studio. You can also provide a myriad of other products and services. Always sell supplies (strings, tapes, CD-Rs, even some gear) to the clients at your project studio. For example, a songwriter currently using your studio for demos mentions she wants to do them at her own home. Since you are probably going to lose her as a customer anyway, help her create her studio, and profit from that help accordingly. Sell her a four-track studio (cassette multitrack, microphone, and headphones, or the software equivalent). Either establish a deal with a nearby music store or provide links from your Web site that pay you commissions on the sales you originate. Now, you just need to drive traffic to your Web site and encourage people to buy the resources you recommend and endorse.

Consider selling books and music that can help the people who use your project studio improve their career. Is there a new band that needs help managing their career? Sell a book on the subject. Sell music CDs or copies of other productions done in your studio. Did you just finish the soundtrack for a children's program? Sell copies to other clients who have children. Of course, you'll also want to sell your CDs and other products that you create yourself. My books and CDs are prominently displayed at my project studio, and although I often give them away as a premium for good clients, I sell a good number to others, too.

You may want to establish an independent dealer or join an affiliate program. You can set up deals with others to sell your stuff in exchange for a piece of the profits. You can have any number of people out there peddling your wares, with you giving them a commission on the sales they make. This concept doesn't need to be limited to product sales. You can implement a similar program for services. When people recommend you or your project studio, they earn a percentage of the sale.

Amazon.com's affiliate program gives a commission for products (books, CDs, software, etc.) sold through your Web site. You essentially link your site to theirs. If a person clicks through and orders something, you make some money. Alternately, you can often contact suppliers directly and make deals to distribute their products. You can usually get 40 to 50 percent off any product you buy directly from its producer. For a few products, this is easily manageable, but it can get rather difficult working with multiple vendors.

Catalog

A catalog that you keep both on the Web and in print can help you promote all the products and services you offer. You could even combine a newsletter with the catalog and make it your main promotional piece. Provide reviews of products you endorse, profiles of clients and their projects, new equipment acquisitions, upcoming events, discount offers for studio time, new products and services, and more. If you set up a simple format, you can update it easily and send it out regularly. I feel the print and Web versions work together quite well. The print version drives people to your Web site and is handy when you send out a promotional piece or when someone is in the studio. The Web site is great for people who find you on the Web and who inquire via e-mail (send them to your site, don't mail a catalog).

143

Sell Your Gear

There's no reason not to make some money from your old gear once it's lived its useful life or been replaced by the next BIG thing. Sell the gear on consignment at the local music emporium. Make sure you have a contract with the music store and that the store is reputable. Or instead of selling the gear, trade it in. Though you probably won't realize a great sum in this case, it can often be the down payment on an expensive purchase. Again, you are probably forced to dealing with the music store, so make sure the deal is equitable. Sell the gear online, either at an online auction or from your own Web site. Of course, you can take out classified ads (online or paper) and post flyers to sell your gear. Lastly, you can give the gear away. Donate old gear to charity, or even give it to a client, employee, or the kid down the street.

8

Your Project Studio and the Internet

T*he Internet embodies the digital revolution* that has created the project studio explosion. Once connected, you have a powerful resource and ally that lets you research critical information, expand your project studio, collaborate with other people from around the world, and so much more. As a project studio owner myself, I use the Internet every day to handle e-mail correspondence, send and receive audio and video files, prepare my *Moneymaking Music Tip of the Week* e-mail newsletter, update my Web site, process orders, follow industry news, research information about the industry, new products, or for projects I'm working on, prospect for new clients, service existing clients, promote all aspects of my business, write and post articles and columns, and any number of other tasks. The Internet, my computer, and a telephone together form my primary means of communication with the outside world. For many project studio owners, the Internet is the main way they conduct business each day.

Get Connected

Using the Internet in conjunction with your project studio may be a little different than simply signing up with an online service and surfing. You need a computer and modem as the most basic equipment for your Internet use. You obviously also need access to the Internet. You should consider a local Internet Service Provider (ISP), where you can get a basic dial-up account. It may also be wise to have a fallback connection through one of the big online services in case your local ISP folds, leaving you in the lurch. Alternately, you may decide you need high-speed access to the Internet, so you will need to choose an ISP who offers DSL, ISDN, or cable modems.

Usually included with your ISP account is an e-mail address. Choose the name carefully. Try to keep it short and simple, and avoid cryptic words and odd spellings. If you register your domain name (see below), you'll want to use it as your e-mail address. Encourage your clients and prospects to contact you via e-mail. It's a very efficient and convenient way to communicate. Check your mail a few times each day, and make sure you respond to all e-mail inquiries promptly. Develop some standard replies to cover your most asked questions. These generic replies will save you time, and they are easy to personalize by simply slipping in a custom line or two.

Also, create an e-mail signature that accompanies all your outgoing e-mail. Include your contact information (e-mail address and phone number) along with the address to your Web site. Consider featuring a short benefit to accompany your address, instead of just the URL itself. For example: *Shift your music career into high gear at the Moneymaking Music Web site: http://www.jeffreypfisher.com.* Make sure you use the entire "http" address in this case, as most e-mail programs will automatically make it a hot link that people can click and be taken to your Web site immediately.

To get your own custom Web site address or URL, register your domain name at *www.networksolutions.com* for about $35 a year. Register either the name of your project studio or your personal name: *www.yourname.com,* for example. You will want to keep this domain for a long time, so make sure you select a name that stands the test of time. You'll also want to select an e-mail address to go along with your name, such as *info@yourname.com.*

Get space on a server to hold your Web site. If you sign up with a local ISP, chances are they include a certain amount of space with your account. Remember, audio and video clips can eat up a lot of server space quite quickly. Make sure you have enough room to meet your needs. The only problem you will find with a local ISP is that your Web URL will have a funny name, such as *http://www.mcs.net/~fishercg/.* You can have them use your virtual domain name after you register it. Discuss what you want from your ISP before you sign up. They may offer package deals to a small business such as yours. At this point, you can surf the Web, send and receive e-mail, and have a place to host your Web site.

Promotional and e-Commerce Web Site

You need a Web site for your project studio. This Web site is your own store that contains your promotional message and delivers it to the world 24-7-365. Let it include online equivalents of your brochures, flyers, detailed product and service sheets, articles, newsletters, audio and video samples, pictures, and more. You can even sell your project studio products and services directly from your site, or just use it to generate and qualify sales leads. Most importantly, you should use your site to service your clients by providing upload/download areas for your work and providing other value, such as information, samples, useful tips, links to other important locations, and more. However you decide to use your Web site, make sure it presents your best company image in a pleasing and entertaining way.

Think of your Web site as a virtual community and meeting place for people interested in you and what you provide. It can be *the* place to connect with other people to promote and sell your project studio products and services. While promotion will be your main focus, there is nothing standing in your way of also making your site informative and entertaining in ways that people rely on. If you provide real value, people will come back to visit (and buy more), and hopefully tell others about you, too.

Design your Web site to be simple and straightforward. Make it easy to navigate, well constructed, and totally content driven. Content rules; the rest is just bells and whistles. Concentrate on content before anything else. Organize your thoughts. Organize the delivery of information logically. Decide what is most important first, second, and so forth. What is the real reason people come to your site? Is it to see a huge in-line graphic—y'know, the ones that take forever to download? Or are people coming to your site to get something? They need a reason or several reasons to visit, stay, and come back. Include compelling offers that get people to return to your site, buy your project studio products and services, and get people to identify themselves to you, so that you can deliver other content and promotional material. I feel the best start page for any site is a table of contents to the rest of the site. Pictures, logos, and other such material should be secondary and placed lower down the page. Because problem-solving is the central concept to good promotion, you should make your start page a series of problems and their associated solutions that you provide through your project studio.

Putting together a Web site is something you may choose to do on your own or hire someone else to do. In either case, you first need to develop an Internet strategy. Are you going to use your site just for promotion? Or are you going to make sales? Your answers will dictate the basic structure of your site. For example, a composer with a project studio may have the following pages:

- A home page that serves as an introduction to the person and the site.
- A page with the full description of the composing services.
- A page with audio and video sample clips (may be integrated with the above page).
- A page featuring products available from the composer (soundtrack albums, demo, etc.) and an order form.
- Other pages to support the main information as needed (bio, FAQ, testimonials, etc.).
- The composer may also have a section just for current clients, for uploading and downloading files. This may be a password-protected, private part of the Web site, or you can just password-protect the files themselves.

Keep your Web site simple. It's always tempting to use the latest advances, but I caution you that you may create more problems than they are worth. No one will ever complain that your pages load too fast or that information is too easy to find. Choose a clean, uncluttered design with easy navigation. Avoid huge graphics and background audio. Provide links to large graphics and audio instead. If you include sample audio and video, encode in several popular formats, and provide links to these formats on your site, letting people choose for themselves. Tell the people how big the files are, too.

Make sure all your printed material—letterhead, business cards, invoices, CDs, etc.—leaving your project studio carries complete contact information, including your e-mail address and Web site URL. Include that information with all your promotions and ads. Prepare a small flyer or postcard that promotes your Web site and the benefits of visiting it. You can stuff this in with all kinds of packages and letters leaving your office, leave them on tables, pin them to bulletin boards, and more.

When your site is ready, register it with the main search engines. Make sure the titles you use on your Web site pages describe what the pages and site are about. Also, use META tags to accurately describe your Web pages. These META tags are part of the HTML programming language used to create Web pages. They let you include a description and several key words to describe your site. People coming to your site do not see this META information. It is used by the search engines to categorize your site effectively. When you submit your Web site to the popular search engines, a Webot visits your site and indexes it. The META tags help you control that indexing. Needless to say, make sure you include a good description and several keywords that people would typically type at search engines to find information about what you do.

Take advantage of free or low-cost classified ads to promote your project studio Web site. Don't feel you have to use an ad to sell directly; use it to convince people to visit your Web site. Buying banner advertising for your Web site probably doesn't make sense. However, partnering with others to cross-link your sites is a good idea. Another idea is to provide content for other Web sites, and trade a promotional message for the content. Personally, I write lots of articles for a variety of online resources. I provide this material in exchange for letting me promote my products and services at the article's conclusion. This keeps my name and promotions in regular circulation at the popular music and sound Web sites and e-zines. Also, don't neglect the traditional means of promotion, including news releases, magazine and newspaper articles, advertising, etc.

Also, find and participate in newsgroups and mailing lists that feature potential buyers of your project studio products and services. You can answer questions and refer people to your Web site for additional information. When someone posts a question you can answer, post a reply to the newsgroup or mailing list (and also send the author an e-mail message with your reply). Usually, it's best to provide direct answers free of blatant promotion or ads, and instead, rely on your signature to promote your site. Occasionally, you can promote your products and services directly, but always try to be subtle.

Since people can surf the Web anonymously, you might want to create ways to have them identify themselves to you. This way, you can capture some contact information and send additional informative or promotional messages to the person. You can have people sign your guest book or some other banal tactic. Or get a little more creative and have people complete a survey or sign up for a free demo, newsletter, e-zine, or other such device.

Use the Internet for Research

The vast information source that is the Internet is invaluable to the project studio owner. On the Web, you can find information on just about anything, including prospective clients. You can keep up with the latest industry news, find out about the newest gear, and discover just about anything you would need to know to make your business better. You can use the Internet to find collaborators, partners, independent contractors, and clients. You can even take courses or lessons. Start at the major search engines. The keywords you type affect the results you get. Usually, the more narrow your choices, the better your results. However, it can often pay to be a little general, because you may get information and access to sites that your more-narrow search eliminates. Also, make it a point to visit the online sites promoted by the industry magazines; there, you'll find news and other useful tidbits. Web sites run by equipment manufacturers and dealers can provide useful information, too.

You can also use the Internet to find information about projects you are working on or to get help overcoming a problem. You can search for and research people, keep track of what your competitors are doing, pick up recording ideas, and just follow the news in general. When I needed to choose an encoding format for a video project, the Web provided the information, along with samples of the quality offered by different software codecs. Also, the Internet played a vital role in the preparation for this book. I logged many hours online researching the topics. I spied on my competition, looked at Web sites of other project studio owners, and found other books, articles, and Web sites on the subject. Finally, through e-mail, I sent and received the project studio survey that comprises some of the information in these pages.

For the computer-based project studio, the Internet is a terrific place to find software, freeware, shareware, and evaluation demos. Are you contemplating buying a new software multitrack? Download the demo, and give it a long, hard look before investing your hard-earned cash. Not many people would use a new piece of software on a gig, but I once did. After seeing Sonic Foundry's Vegas multitrack software at a music store, I downloaded the demo and chose an on-hold session to use for my seven-day free trial. I had actually only worked with the program for about thirty minutes before using it for the session. Is that nuts, or what? It's a real tribute to Sonic Foundry that you can actually *use* Vegas out of the box. No need to plow through manuals or endless dialog boxes. Now, I'm no novice—I know Windows and multitrack recording—so, not having to jump those hurdles gave me a distinct advantage. Nevertheless, new software is potentially hell on earth. I'm happy everything went smoothly. I was so happy with this product that I bought it before my seven days expired. The same was true for the RBC Voice Tweaker. I downloaded the demo and used it on a scratch vocal track. The result was amazing. It didn't take long for me to decide to buy that product, too.

At artistPRO.com (*www.artistpro.com*), you can get free, Web-based professional audio training that teaches and tests your knowledge on critical areas of the recording process. Courses include understanding the mixer, essential EQ theory, dynamics processors, effects processing, microphones, digital recording, hard-disk recording, and instrument recording, including drums, guitar, and vocals.

Need to improve your keyboard chops? OnlineConservatory.com (*www.onlineconservatory.com*) provides live, one-on-one keyboard and piano music lessons over the Internet. Using their own Melodus propriety software in conjunction with Microsoft NetMeeting, you can learn online.

A terrific place for novices is the Center for Electronic and Computer Music provided by Indiana University (*www.indiana.edu/~emusic*). There, you'll find an overview of electronic music in the twentieth century, information about microphones and mixers, a digital audio primer, facts about analog synthesis, and more.

Internet Shopping

Shopping on the Internet is great for several reasons. It's oh-so-easy. You can find a bevy of information about the products and services you are considering before you buy. And you can price-shop quickly, ensuring you get the best deal. Shop around and look for bargains. There is always going to be a Web store selling it for less than anybody else. A few clicks can save you big bucks. When I bought one software product, most vendors had the same price, until I discovered one site selling the same product for far less than the others. You know who got the sale. Extra time invested? Ten minutes. Money saved? $100. Also, read a lot of reviews before you buy any gear. If it's software, always download the demos and try before you buy. Don't forget about the many auction sites that keep springing up. They are great for finding and buying good used gear and for helping you sell your old gear, too. Last year's gear can still do some amazing things, and often for less money. You don't always need the latest, greatest.

- The best auction site for professional audio and music gear is at *www.digibid.com.*
- There are several online merchants for gear. My favs are *www.americanmusical.com, www.samash.com, www.musiciansfriend.com,* and *www.doctoraudio.com.*

Prospect for Clients

David Conley told me he landed his last two films via Internet solicitation. Your Web site is only one way to promote to prospects and clients. Used in conjunction with other promotions, it can be the main way you get leads and make sales. Even if you talk with prospects by phone or in person, you can send them to your Web site for additional information. I've even used my Web site in sales situations while a prospect was sitting in my own studio next to me.

In addition to having people come to you, you can actively search out prospects and clients through the Web, too. You can look for notices in the newsgroups where people need services that you offer. You can visit Web sites of people, bands, and companies who can benefit from your project studio. Get creative, and start hunting down possible sales leads right away. Through e-mail and other promotions, you can contact the people you find and let them know how you can help them. Don't get this confused with mass marketing or spam. You will research carefully and only target promotions to specific people and companies. The Internet makes this kind of one-to-one promotion and sales a snap.

Collaborate via the Internet

The typical scenario for finding and working with other musicians was to post a flyer at a music store or other bulletin board read by your fellow players. Consequently, you were usually forced to work only with local talent. The Internet gives you the opportunity for connecting with and collaborating with both clients and talent from around the world—often in real time! You can collaborate on many levels, from simple e-mail correspondence to file sharing and even virtual studio sessions.

One way to collaborate on audio files over long distances is by using MP3 files. You and your collaborator both need recording software that imports MP3s, supports overdubbing new audio in sync with the MP3 audio, and mixes to new MP3s. To maintain sync, provide a clear count-in, using a sharp attack sound on each track. For example, record a drum part prefaced by the count-in. Encode this track to an MP3, and e-mail your partner (or upload it to your site for download by your partner). Your partner imports the MP3 drum track into his software. He copies the count-in from the drum track to a new track. He records a bass part and sends an MP3 mix of the bass track back to you. You open the bass track up in your software and align its count-in with your original drum track. The two parts will play in sync. You can once again copy the count-in to the next track and overdub again, continuing back and forth until the project is done. You partner then burns a CD with the high-quality versions of all the parts he did and sends the CD to you. You replace the MP3 files with the higher-quality files for the final mix.

You can also collaborate using one of the new online virtual studios. The Rocket Network was the first Internet recording studio. Using proprietary software in conjunction with certain compatible host programs, you can collaborate on music and sound projects with other people from around the world via the Internet. It can be a fine complement to your project studio, providing access to people in other areas and allowing you to work from your studio on projects in other cities. This can dramatically cut production expenses, while opening up new avenues of creativity. This kind of peer-to-peer networking is the wave of the future for collaboration via the Internet.

According to their promotional literature, the "Rocket Network includes two key elements: Internet Recording Studios and Studio Centers. An Internet Recording Studio is a virtual workplace where audio professionals meet and collaborate on projects. Rocket Network Studio Centers allow partners and online resellers to offer custom-branded Internet Recording Studios to their existing communities of audio professionals."

To use the Rocket Network, you need their RocketControl software and a computer-based host application with RocketPower. As of this writing, Steinberg's Cubase VST and Emagic's LogicAudio support the system. Several manufacturers, including Pro Tools, have plans to implement RocketPower into their software. I'm sure other software will begin to implement the necessary protocols in the near future.

- For more information on Rocket Network, go to
  www.rocketnetwork.com.

Emagic Logic Audio Platinum 4.6 or higher users can use the Emagic Pro Studio Center as "an online virtual studio complex [to] co-operatively create new music with other musicians via the Internet twenty-four hours a day, seven days a week."

- Visit Emagic and find out the details at
  www.emagicstudios.com.

Using Ednet with ISDN lines and specialized modems and codecs, you can run sessions anywhere in the world. For instance, a singer could be in New York, while your project studio is in California. According to their Web site, "Ednet's audio products give you full production-quality stereo audio transmission via high-speed data circuits between the studios, in real time. Hardware audio codecs digitize, encode, transmit, and then decode the audio signal on the remote end, [providing] full-quality audio over commonly available ISDN data circuits." Having the ISDN system can be rather expensive for most project studios, unless you plan on a great need for long distance production and collaboration.

- Ednet (*www.ednet.net*)

You don't always need the Internet to work with people at other locations. You can, of course, collaborate from your studio over a regular phone line. You can use your phone to approve a session in another place, or your client can listen in on your session. The inexpensive solution is a simple phone patch. Basically, you listen in on a session at another studio from your telephone. For example, you need a voice-over recorded with talent in another city. Using the phone patch, you can interact with the talent and remote engineers as they record your project. They then ship the tapes or files to you overnight or via e-mail. Alternately, your client can listen in on your session as you produce their audio. You hear your client through your monitoring system, and they hear the session on their telephone. You can interact with one another just as if you were in the room together. You can play back audio examples and they can make suggestions or give their approval over the phone. The phone patch can really speed up approvals and let you work across distances with a minimum of fuss.

- You need a telephone handset audio tap, such as the THAT-1 provided by JK Audio, Inc. You can get it through Markertek (*www.markertek.com*).

Electronic Musician reported another unique way to collaborate via the Internet. There is a biannual Recording Fest held in the city of Olomouc in the Czech Republic. "The Recording Fest features the Moravian Philharmonic Orchestra ... and [your] recording could be done by an experienced, professional engineer in a concert hall." The article explained that this orchestra is not hired by the hour, but rather paid per finished minute of the final recording. *EM* claimed to get twenty-eight minutes of music recorded by a live orchestra for only $4200.

- Symphonic Workshops (*www.symphonicworkshops.com*)

Provide Client Services

The Internet helps you provide superior service to all your clients. Sending files via the Internet is a terrific way to keep connected with your clients and secure quicker approvals. Why get in the car to drop off a CD when you can e-mail the files instead? David Conley explained how he used the Internet to send evolving music tracks to his client. "For my last film, I sent music to the director via e-mail using MP3 compression. Later, I began posting Quicktime movies to my Web site, so he could see how the music synched with the action."

"I used to make DATs, and then burn CDs and overnight them to clients," recalled Harlan Hogan. "Now, about 80 to 85 percent of the work going out my door is MP3. I record my tracks, encode them to MP3, and e-mail them to the client. For larger files, I upload password-protected files to my Web site, and the client downloads them later. I then overnight the CD to the client as a backup. I have recorded a ten-minute narration, encoded it, and posted it to my Web site, and my client has their tracks less than thirty minutes after I finished them." Hogan says even radio stations are preferring to get spots in MP3.

Home Recording magazine recently reported this tidbit about Rich Tozzoli completing the sound design work for NBC Interactive with Bob Costas: "That project's audio was done over the Internet by uploading sound effects from his Iomega JAZ drive via computer to NBC's web server. 'It was great,' said Tozzoli, 'definitely the wave of the future.'

As a project studio owner, you can even provide Web hosting and other e-commerce features to your clients. Studiowerkz is a unique site sponsored by ByteAudio. Through Studiowerkz, you function as a small e-label, providing promotion and distribution to the music artists who use your studio. Studiowerkz pays you a commission on the sales (Web site, online sales generated, etc.). This is an easy way to support acts and earn some additional money by providing a related service that requires little intervention on your part. I'm confident other such opportunities will pop up after this book is printed.

- Studiowerkz (*www.studiowerkz.com)*

✂ Easier File Transfers

You can, of course, easily send a sound file to anyone else by simply attaching it to an e-mail message. This is fine for most projects, as long as the file sizes remain relatively small. However, there are some other alternatives to the e-mail attachment. Full-sized audio files, about 10 Mb per minute in stereo, can take a long time to up- and download on slow dial-up connections, so this strategy is best employed by people with high-speed Internet connections. Rather than sending audio files as e-mail attachments, you can use File Transfer Protocol (FTP) as a viable alternative. What you essentially do is upload your files via FTP to an FTP server, and the other person downloads the files from the FTP server using an FTP client. Most Internet Service Providers provide space on their servers for Web pages and often throw in an FTP server, too. Using FTP software, you would connect to the server and upload your files. Your client would then connect to the same server and download the files to their computer. What is especially nice about this situation is that you can upload files one at a time and your client can download them the same way. It's convenient for both parties and relatively easy to do. Alternately, you can post your files to your Web site for downloading. Just upload your files and tell your client where to find them. You might want to create subdirectories to discourage casual hackers from finding your work, or just password-protect the files to handle the security issue.

Most FTP servers such as these are public, which means anyone can connect and download files. In many cases, this would not be a problem, but you may have the need for security. You could look for a secure FTP site that requires login and password verification. An easier method would be to zip or compress your files and require a password to unzip them. Audio files do not compress very much into password-protected zipped files, but the point is to secure the files, not make them smaller. This way, if someone steals your files, he won't be able to open them without the proper password.

- You can turn your computer into an FTP server by using special software. Check out *www.wftpd.com* for a possible solution.

Sell Direct

One obvious alliance between the Internet and the project studio is distribution. You can sell your music and sound projects from your own Web site and through affiliations with other online sellers. Artists can sell their CDs, a sound designer can sell sound effects and sample CDs, a composer can sell soundtrack CDs, and so on. All those little add-ons discussed in previous chapters can find their way to your Web site, too. If you are just promoting your room via the Web, you can still offer package deals and other such arrangements at your Web store. Use your imagination, and carefully examine your goals to decide on the right e-commerce presence for your project studio endeavors.

Good-Ink Records set up its own Web site and claims 20 to 25 percent of sales come from there (the remaining sales through traditional distribution channels). Good-Ink sees the Web site as a way to "foster a community for the fans." In addition to MP3s, news, tour dates, and other information, Good-Ink runs discussion lists and encourages its artists to participate regularly. Deanna Knudsen, Web master for Good-Ink Records, told *Fast Forward*, "MP3 sales are dependent on availability. If the track is on a CD . . . [people] just buy the CD instead. If the track is exclusive to digital format, those normally sell pretty well."

One of the great benefits of the Internet is how it levels the field for all the players. The smallest indie label can compete right alongside a major, and many people will not know the difference. That said, I don't see the Internet as a substitute for traditional music marketing and promotion; it's just another means to reach and connect with people. For the aggressive, it can be a wonderful way to provide extra value to fans. For example, a band needs to get people to their site, where all the real information and entertainment can be found. The Web site is the band's store and a community for like-minded people to gather. It should be interactive and personal, and the band should take a very active role in the site's content. The Internet used this way becomes a niche market instead of a mass market. Once people realize that they can address their fans on a personal level, they will move away from mass marketing and concentrate on "preaching to the converted." There is already evidence of this: Todd Rundgren uses his site to personally connect with fans, as does Joe Satriani. Sonic Foundry started *www.acidplanet.com* specifically for users of their Acid software. There will continue to be more little communities of people gathering to exchange ideas, hopes and aspirations, and yes, products and services.

If you prefer, you can team up with other sites to promote and sell your wares online. MP3.com is the most well-known site that provides services to musicians. It is free to sign up, and there are no ongoing fees. You get Web space to promote your music that can include pictures, artist information, events and gig calendar, and MP3 music clips. From this Web site, you can sell your own CDs and track your site's activity (visitors and sales). What's especially attractive about MP3.com is its nonexclusivity, which means you can sign up with other similar sites to expand your promotions and sales around.

- MP3.com *(www.mp3.com)*

The Amazon.com Advantage program is another similar service. It's key difference is that it's open to book publishers, musicians, and video producers. According to Amazon.com, their Advantage program is "a complete promotion and distribution system for independent musicians. When you join Amazon.com Advantage, you're putting your CD in the Internet's busiest music store, right next to CDs from major label bands. It's completely free, and there are no exclusive contracts, so you're not limited in how you promote and sell your music." Amazon.com provides a Web page for promotion and clips, extensive reporting, and fast payment. They even stock your product and ship for you. This kind of situation lets you put your product distribution on automatic. You can just concentrate on getting people to your site and getting them to order.

- Amazon.com *(www.amazon.com)*

If you decide to sell your project studio products and services online, you will need to accept credit card orders. Credit card processing can also be useful in-house, depending on your clients. Some people may want to charge the services you provide. Visit the bank that holds your business checking account for information about getting a merchant account. Frankly, unless you do a good volume, you will have a hard time securing a merchant account. The fees alone can hurt your profits substantially. Instead, you can choose a third-party provider to handle your online payments. There are two well-known firms: Kagi and CCNow. These firms provide custom, secure online order forms that your buyers access from your Web site. Your clients choose the products they want, enter their address and credit card payment information, and Kagi or CCNow processes the order. They even send an order confirmation e-mail to the buyer and another one to you. You then ship the products yourself. Best of all, there is no setup fee or minimum monthly fee. Instead, both Kagi and CCNow take a percentage of each sale (under 11 percent). They pay you the remaining amounts regularly. Kagi is great for single products, while CCNow supports a shopping basket system. Make sure you carefully read and understand their agreements before signing up with either service.

- Kagi (*www.kagi.com*)
- CCNow (*www.ccnow.com*)

Internet Music Encoding Tips

Whether you need to send a file to a partner or client or provide a sample on your Web site, you need to encode your high-quality audio into smaller, Internet-friendly files. There are several formats from which to choose, the most popular being MP3 and Real Audio. A decent-quality monaural recording of your music or sound is fine for most Internet delivery formats. Here's how to do it right.

Digitize your audio to the computer (or use whatever software you choose to create the final mix). Mix your completed take to a mono file (.wav or .aiff). Import this file to an audio editor, such as Sonic Foundry's Sound Forge XP. Run the DC offset utility on the mono waveform. (DC current is applied when recording and sometimes doesn't align the zero point in the waveform correctly. This utility compensates for that fact and makes the waveform ready for further processing.)

Filter out the really low bass, everything below 40 Hz, with a steep high-pass filter. Some people also suggest adding a little 2 to 4 dB EQ kick between 3 to 4 kHz. This is the frequency range in which most compression encoders are most sensitive. It is also the range of frequencies that makes human speech intelligible. And it is also the range of frequency the ear structure itself enhances the most (for the reason mentioned in the previous sentence—ain't evolution clever?). I prefer adding a little 2 to 4 dB boost at 80 to 100 Hz, 3 to 4 kHz, and again at 10 kHz, with a graphic or parametric EQ.

After the EQ, compress the mono waveform with a 4:1 medium attack and slow, long release. Adjust the threshold carefully to about 2
to 6 dB below the loudest peak level. (You're probably peaking at -1, so
set the threshold at -3 to -7.) Experimentation may be necessary here.
Next, normalize the volume to 95 to 98 percent. You are left with a
big, fat mono audio file with reduced dynamic range and a very in-
your-face sound. Now, save the music file to your Internet format of
choice (Real Audio, MP3, etc.) with the highest quality playback, even
though the encoding process may take some additional time.

✖ Quick and Dirty
Real Audio Streaming

If you choose to encode to Real Audio for your Web site, you must take an extra step to make the audio stream for people visiting your site. First, encode the audio to the Real Audio format. If you encode as described above, you can choose their 28.8 mono audio only selection. This is fine for most demos and should be playable for almost any connection. Save the encoded file following this convention: file_name.rm. Next, create a simple text file with only one line that indicates the exact URL of the audio file, for example, *http://www.your-name.com/file_name.rm*. Save this text file as file_name.ram. Now, place a hyperlink on your Web page that accesses the file_name.ram file. The browser will read that file and automatically locate the *http://www.yourname.com/file_name.rm* and play the sound file. When a person clicks on the link, the Real Media player will launch and begin streaming the sound file.

Burning CDs

Even though you may use the Internet for sending files to clients and for collaborating with others, there may be times when it's easier to burn a CD and overnight it. Here are my tips for successful CD making. Defragment your hard drive after you've mastered your project and before you cut the master CD. This puts the files together and can reduce CD burning problems. If you are just burning a track or two, you can skip the defrag routine. Make sure you have enough memory and hard-disk space before recording your CDs. You need headroom for the process to work satisfactorily. Disconnect from your network, disconnect from the Internet, shut down any other programs (including screen savers, antivirus, and other background tasks), and concentrate just on burning the CD. Use silver or gold blank media, and avoid the "dark green" discs. Never touch the bottom of a disc. Keep it stored in its original container until just before you drop it in the CD-RW drive. Don't use paper labels on masters, as they can increase error rates. Write on the disc with a Sharpie, outside the data area if possible. Always burn using Disc-At-Once when making masters. Record your discs at lower data settings, 4X maximum. Alternately, record the CD image to your hard drive, and then burn the discs from the image file. This takes up space on the hard drive, but can often make CD burning faster and less error-prone.

Computer Secrets

It would be wonderful if you could dedicate one computer just for your project studio and use it for nothing else. But many of us are forced to use our computer for everything: music and sound production, paying bills, writing letters (and books!), and surfing the Net. Because a computer in this situation is the vital partner of your business—in fact *it is your business*—you need to treat it well.

The computer world changes so rapidly that the very act of writing it down in this book renders the information obsolete. So, I've chosen to offer more general, universal information that can stand the test of time. Buy the most robust computer you can afford. Get the biggest hard drive, most RAM, and fastest speed you can purchase with your available money. Don't scrimp in any way. However, plan for your computer system to last about three to five years. I almost got five out of my last system; I hope to do nearly as well with this current hardware. Do you go with a Mac or Windows system? Choose the software you like, and *then* buy the platform it runs on. The same is true for operating systems. If your favorite music or sound software only runs under Windows NT, that is all you need to know to choose.

I highly recommend an antivirus program that you keep up-to-date regularly. Add a personal firewall to your system if you use it on the Net. This will block all kinds of horrible things that try to worm their way onto your hard drive. I've been attacked several times, and the software has saved my butt each time. I am also suspicious of all e-mail attachments, especially programs and other things that can infect Windows (.exe, .com, .dll, and .vbs). There is a downside to having the firewall and antivirus software running; it can really hurt your computer's sound performance. I always turn all these programs off before starting a recording session. Since I use Windows, I recommend you CTRL+ALT+DELETE once to call up the task manager, and hunt down and "end task" on all the other background programs running (my calendar program, bill reminder, CD-RW, and so forth). Freeing up all these resources can improve performance substantially.

Tweaking the Computer Performance

Most professionals agree that having one computer dedicated to audio production is the ideal solution. You can keep all the junk off of it and tweak it for audio alone. Alternately, you can either partition the hard drive or install separate hard drives, one for audio and the other for business tasks. Some people prefer to keep their software and data on two separate drives. This lets you perform overhauls on your program drive without affecting your data. Others use partitions to separate data and programs, but this isn't a good idea if you need to reformat the hard drive, because the partition will be lost, too.

For many of us, the computer is the benefactor of a thousand and one tweaks and refinements. Over time, you upgrade software, grab new software, update the OS, install new drivers, and make a myriad of changes to the underlying guts. The problem is, we often forget to record what we did or why. I've downloaded software patches, installed them, and then deleted the files, only to discover I needed them again after some other failure. When you have to reinstall programs, you may need the patches. You could waste valuable time searching for all the little pieces. If I download a program update, after

165

installing the program, I move the installation software to a folder that I back up periodically to CD. Now, I keep a CD-RW filled with all the patches, driver updates, and text files with my notes that I accumulate during the course of a computer's lifetime. This material can save you in the event of a major problem, and it can save some time when little problems arise, too.

If you can, have your computer made especially for music. You can then control precisely what goes on the hard drive and keep the junk (and its associated problems) away. If you buy off the street, take some time to hunt down and destroy the junk yourself. Remove all the applications from your Startup folder. This will keep these programs from loading each time you boot. Get rid of the other background programs. Common culprits include virus protection, calendar reminders, utilities, and so forth. Turn off power management features, or your system might go to standby when you don't want it to. Dump fonts and other memory hogs that you no longer need. I prefer to boot up simply and add tasks as I need them (my antivirus and firewall software do not boot; I start them before I connect to the Net). Reboot often. Nothing like dumping the garbage and starting over to prevent crashes during critical times. Always reboot your system after installing any new software, too. Run diagnostic utilities to monitor your system for errors that can be fixed. Make sure you keep all your program disks. Make sure you back up all your files regularly, too (see below).

Data Backup

One of the most critical duties of operating your project studio is backing up your work. Unlike an accountant, who can print a copy of her spreadsheet, sound files are large and unwieldy (and they don't print well either!). They require a specific approach. Probably the best all-around solution for most project studio owners is a CD burner. Each CD holds up to 650 Mb, which is usually enough for most projects. Other options include JAZ drives, Data DAT backup, swappable hard drives like those offered by Glyph, and recordable DVDs. For heavy session work, DVDs, with their 5.2 Gb data capacity, are the clear choice.

Establish a routine for backing up, such as at the end of every working session. Your backup strategy should include your computer files, including system files, programs, tweaks, patches, and so forth. Back up these files before any major change to the computer (new software,

OS update/patch, etc.). Also, back up your personal files (word processing documents, bookkeeping files, etc.). I usually burn a single CD backup of these files once a month, backing up new files to floppies in the interim. Don't forget to back up your audio files, project files, and session notes. Back up the raw files after a session concludes. This way, no matter what happens next, you can always return to the originals. Make periodic backups as the project progresses. For audio projects, I back up the computer files (wav, aiff, etc.) to a *data* CD and also burn an *audio* CD of the mixed finals. Since I'm not convinced of the reliability of CD-Rs, I usually make multiple backups of final projects and store one set off-site.

Make sure you clearly identify your backups. For example, if you back up to CD-ROM, put a face label on the CD itself and on the face and spine of the CD box. Record what's on the backup in the blank CD booklets. Make sure you print your contact information (name, address, phone, e-mail) on every CD and box, too. You should also create a database (even if it's just a text or word processing file) that records what is on your backups and other archived data files. Use carefully chosen keywords when you list a CD's contents to make searching the database easier. You might also want to keep other databases to hold your session notes and for all your sound and sample CDs. Again, use keywords to make finding what you need easier. File these backups and archived data discs logically, such as by date and alphabetical order by client or project. Alternately, create aliases (MAC) or shortcuts (WIN) to your CDs. Simply create a new folder to correspond to the CD (backup, archive, sample disc, etc.), put shortcuts to the CD's files in the folder, and then file the CD. Now, you can search the folder for what you need and know where it is. You'll need to find the CD manually, of course.

Keeping Organized on the Computer

Keep copious notes on your projects on your computer. The ideal tactic is to create individual folders for all projects and keep all the related material in the folder (or subfolders of the main, if needed). Save the software project, its underlying files, and a simple text document with the production notes. Title the folder the same as the project (the song's title, if that applies). I often do alternative mixes/arrangements and save them in the same folder under different names. Since I'm constantly tweaking tracks and balancing a mix, I came up with this handy naming and organizing convention. When naming a file, put a number in the first position, e.g., 1ROCK. As you regularly save subsequent versions, name them 2ROCK, 3ROCK, etc. You won't keep deleting the old versions, but rather saving different versions that reflect your progress. This way, you can easily return to earlier ideas. When you do finally complete the final version, give it a final name, and save it. And don't forget to make a backup of this final song, too.

Manage all that disparate information with a nifty little computer program called Info Select. Instead of following precise database guidelines, you just enter your thoughts into windows—the equivalent of a computer note card. When you need to find something, just type in a few letters or keywords, and Info Select locates what you need immediately. This flexibility is ideal for us creative types, who often lack the discipline required by traditional databases. This productivity tool could be a whole new way for you to work and think. Check it out at *www.miclog.com*. Also, a much less robust but far cheaper software entry with a similar metaphor is Jot+ Notes from *www.kingstairs.com*.

Computer Use and Repetitive Stress Injuries

You will spend a lot of time at the computer. Though it can be hard to tear yourself away from an intensive session, this is something you must do or risk the consequences. Sitting at your computer (or playing your instrument) *is* your livelihood. You can't risk losing your source of income when it is far simpler to prevent Repetitive Stress Injuries (RSI). Wouldn't it be a shame to not be able to do the work you love to do because you can no longer sit at the computer and accomplish the most simple tasks? This is a dire scenario, robbing you of your ability to make money. Unfortunately, as more and more people spend countless hours keyboarding, mousing, sitting still, and straining to see glowing screens in low light, this scenario will be repeated up and down the street. It is so simple to take precautions to protect your health. These issues should be vitally important to you, as your future livelihood depends on your ability to do certain tasks.

Your back can hurt, your neck, shoulders, and wrists, too. These annoying pains can really interfere with your work. If the pain lingers for more than a few days (or hours), you should get help. A good, comfortable, supportive chair is essential, as is proper keyboard and mouse technique, breaks and rest, and exercising, especially stretching. I can't believe how much time I spend at the computer. Between writing, managing the Web site and Tip of the Week, surfing the Net, handling e-mail, and of course, running my project studio, it is rare that I don't do some computer-related task. That makes me painfully aware of the potential problems associated with using the computer.

What remedies should you take? Reduce your overall computer use, and make sure your computer workstation is set up properly. The monitor should be in front of you, slightly lower, so that the screen top is at eye level. The keyboard and mouse should be at the right height that lets you relax your arms and shoulders. Sit up straight, and use a chair with adequate spine support. Don't rest your wrists on armrests, pad, or desk while keyboarding or mousing. Reduce mousing when you can, and use keystrokes (or voice commands) instead. Take frequent breaks—at least three times an hour. Get some vigorous exercise (aerobics, brisk walking, etc.) during the day. Stretch frequently (do stretches at your desk, practice Tai Chi, etc.). Do something else if you feel pain while at the computer.

- Here are several helpful resources for preventing RSI: *www.tifaq.org*, *www.engr.unl.edu/ee/eeshop/rsi.html*, and *www.rsihelp.com*.

Don't forget to protect your ears, too. Play too loud for too long, and you will suffer hearing loss. Turn it down. Watch out for eye strain, too. When I switched screen resolutions from 640 x 480 to 800 x 600, I started getting headaches. A trip to the eye doctor revealed an increase in my prescription. Coincidence?

Some business experts say you should only focus on activities that let you build your business and make more money. They suggest that you delegate all the other tasks, or simply don't do them. At the same time, health professionals urge us to take breaks to avoid physical problems, such as RSI, and to avoid mental problems, such as burnout. While I agree focusing your energy on building and sustaining your project studio should be your main goal, you need to balance that with other activities. Personally, after a long session, I enjoy running to the bank, post office, and so forth. I don't see this as a waste of time or energy at all. It is a way to refresh, distract the mind, and reenergize. It's good for my mental and physical health, which directly affects my business success.

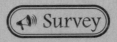

Survey

In what ways do you use the Internet with your project studio (collaborate, prospect, promotion, etc.)?

Research, a little prospecting, and e-mail were the main uses for the Internet by the respondents. Here are some typical responses:

- I use the Internet to research and evaluate all purchases I make for the studio. I only buy what I think I need, and I make sure to get the best of it.

- I am fond of the Internet and can see it will be the new marketplace.

- Right now, just contact with clients via e-mail.

- Collaborate with other artists and a little promotion and networking.

- We use it mainly as a way for people to check us out before they come in.

- To promote our band.

- Mainly promotion.

- I have used it to collaborate, to advertise, to market for guitar lessons, etc. I've also used it to jam online.

- Currently, just for e-mail communication. Plan to have my Web site posted soon.

- Information gathering on products. Will eventually have a demo site to generate sales.

- Promotion and prospecting.

9
Preparing to Promote

If *you don't convince people* to buy and *keep* buying what you sell, your project studio is doomed. There is only one way to make sure you have a steady stream of new business coming to your door. You must make ruthless self-promotion a permanent part of your project studio life. Unfortunately, promotion and sales are always the last things you want to do. As J. Dennis Onopa told me, "I tend to spend more time than I should behind some instrument or console, rather than 'beating the bushes' looking for new clients." This is a common theme for many music and sound professionals. Let's face it, we would *all* rather be doing our creative work than drumming up new business. Sadly, there will be no creative work to do if you don't find anyone to buy your project studio products and services.

What are the basic tenets of ruthless self-promotion? First, decide what you are going to sell. Create complementary products and services (or different service levels and product prices) that give people choices. Second, identify the people who want what you sell. Third, find out how you can contact them. Fourth, promote directly to them and work to make sales. Fifth, build relationships with clients to make additional repeat sales. Sixth, repeat these steps throughout your project studio business career. To use these self-promotion techniques effectively, you must also:

- Understand why promotion is so crucial
- Master certain fundamental skills

- Create an image and clarify your message about what you are about
- Gather information about your market
- Commit to success and plan how and what you will do
- Produce the promotional material you need
- Use many promotional tactics, including advertising, publicity, Internet, relationships, events, and sales
- Maintain your efforts

If you've committed yourself to running your career and project studio as a business, you are mentally ready to jump into the promotional arena. Also, commit yourself to working hard at bringing in more business. Decide on clients and projects you want to get, and do the necessary research that allows you to promote yourself and land the gigs. Don't stop until you get what you want. You are the rainmaker who must promote regularly and make every promotional opportunity count.

Think how you will promote and sell your project studio products and services before you actually create them. Knowing what you will sell and how you plan to promote these products and services helps you focus clearly. Otherwise, it's far too easy to get lost in production, instead of worrying about how you will sell what you make.

Identify your target market. If you have multiple products and services, you will also have multiple markets of possible buyers. For every single thing that you sell, take the time to research the buyers, who they are, where they are, and how you'll reach them and convince them to buy. You will always be more successful when you target your promotions to groups of like-minded people. For example, the approach you take to get bands to use your studio will be far different than when you try to land a corporate music or sound gig.

With this information carefully organized, you can move to the next step and establish an image and central message for your business and career. This image should appeal to the broadest range of buyers in the markets you've researched. This image and message should permeate your promotions and be directly represented by your promotional materials.

Now, you can begin to develop the promotional material you need that shows your intended markets what you can do for them. Precisely what kind of promotional material you prepare depends both on what project studio products and services you sell and how you plan on selling them. Once you complete this material, you can begin promoting your business. You will use advertising techniques (space and classified ads, coupons, mailers, direct mail, online, etc.), publicity (news releases, public relations, articles, books, booklets, and more), and direct sales techniques (on phone, in person, demos, people, etc.).

Since the purpose of your promotions is to find possible prospects, narrow that list down to only the most promising leads, then work this smaller segment until they become your clients. At the same time, use your promotions to appeal to current and past clients, with the sole intention of urging them to buy something again. As your promotions begin to generate steady business, you must still continue to find new clients. You never stop promoting. Instead, put about 65 percent of your time, money, and energy into promoting to your existing clients. Put 35 percent of your resources toward getting new prospects. If you are just starting out, you'll have to flip the percentages (65 percent to new, 35 percent to existing) until you get rolling.

Appealing to Clients

From a promotional standpoint, most clients could care less about the equipment in your project studio. They are mostly concerned about the final result. Therefore, solving problems should be the main focus of all your promotional efforts. People don't care about microphones, plug-ins, or other technical matters. They simply want to realize their visions. For many, *how* you do what you do is superfluous. Your clients ultimately *buy only you*, not your gear, not your room, and not your credentials. You will be far more successful if you focus your promotions and sales on your client's wants, needs, desires, and aspirations and, for the most part, ignore the features of your project studio. Put simply, promote the benefit of using you with your project studio and *not* the project studio itself. David Conley summed this up best: "People come to me with a problem, and it is my job to formulate a solution and actualize it, whether it be a film producer who needs a score, a singer who needs music, a guitar player who needs that certain sound, or a radio station that needs a program."

David Peacock of Cutting Edge Productions told *Mix,* "I started as a musician, and that's how I still market myself, even as a studio owner." Film composer Gary Chang, who has a sophisticated project studio, concurred when he also told *Mix* that his studio doesn't really exist. "It's transparent to the client. I don't charge for the studio; I charge for my time and talent." Most successful project studio owners agree: "The client hires ME, not my studio!" Because of this, you can build your studio around your personal preferences and not have to worry about promoting your gear. "Sorry, we only record on SSL consoles" is something a commercial studio might face as an objection; the project studio owner rarely will. However, a client might insist on a certain piece of gear or format—surround sound, for example—and the savvy project studio owner needs to make sure her client knows she has the necessary ability.

Find Your Market(s)

Do you know what you will sell? Do you know to whom you plan to sell? Have you established an image and central message for your project studio business? Do you have some ideas on how best to promote yourself? To answer these questions, carefully analyze your market and determine what approaches work best for the work you want to do. Not everything works in all situations. Something as simple as hanging out "after hours" at the right location can generate the business you need. Other times, you must pursue more conventional promotional ideas.

Defining, finding, and reaching the people who buy your project studio products and services is fundamental to ruthless self-promotion success. Answer these questions to get the market information you need: Who exactly comprises your market? What problems, needs, wants, and desires face these people? How do your project studio products and services meet those needs? What ways will you promote these benefits to your market? Where will you place your promotions? When will you promote?

There are several ways you can get reliable information about the people who buy project studio products and services. Open your eyes and look, and listen carefully with your ears. The information you need may be right in front of you, coming from current clients and prospects. Find out precisely why a client chose you. Use what you learn to find more, similar clients. Next, ask others, especially past buyers, for their insight. Check out your competition by collecting their promotional material. Where do they fall short? Use what you learn to carve out a niche or a bigger piece of the pie. Check out the local music club scene. Listen to the radio, watch TV, and go to the movies. Go to the record store and do your research; ditto the video game or software stores. Surf the Web. Read local newspapers and larger metropolitan media. Scour the national media, such as *Time*, *Wall Street Journal*, and the music and sound industry trade press. Join and participate in trade associations, or become a union member. Go to the major music and sound industry trade shows, and attend smaller trade shows that reach your specific audience, too. Through this research, you will gather a lot of information about your prospects and clients. Use this information to determine and implement the best promotional strategies that appeal to them.

For example, you want to attract singer-songwriters to record at your project studio. Where do you find such candidates? You can post flyers at music shops and hope somebody calls. A better tactic might be to find local songwriter organizations. Join these groups, and show them how you can help them record their songs better. Another example might be a composer looking to score video games. To find game developers, look on the credits of current games or other interactive media for basic information about who makes them. Get their contact information (start online at the company Web site), and then initiate your promotions with a sales letter and demo reel. You might offer to compete for the next gig by doing some speculative work.

Finding Specific People

With a broader idea of the prospects for your project studio products and services, turn your attention to uncovering the *specific* contact information you need. For example, if you decide to pitch your services to multimedia production companies, you need to find these companies and secure the contact information (names, addresses, e-mail addresses, and telephone numbers) of the possible buyers. You can get industry contacts from a variety of sources. First, start locally, and then look nationally. Try various trade magazines, independent creative directories, and chambers of commerce (including those run by state government agencies). Here are a few places to start:

- Start at RR Bowker (*www.bowker.com*) to find their *A/V Marketplace*. Some of their directories are expensive, so check with a good reference librarian first.
- *Mix Master Directory: Resources for the Professional Audio Industry (www.mixonline.com)*

175

- *Recording Industry Sourcebook (www.artistpro.com)*
- *Record Company A&R, Music Publisher,* and *Film/TV Music Guide (www.musicregistry.com)*
- The MIT List of Radio Stations (*http://wmbr.mit.edu/stations/list.html*)
- Resources about the film industry at *www.filmbiz.com* or *www.filmmusicmag.com*

You can also find new clients through your partnerships with other independent contractors. By teaming up with others (graphic artists, video producers, etc.), you can instantly expand your market by "sharing" clients. Another often-overlooked way to drum up new business is from within the same company. You may work for one department of a larger corporation; other departments within that same company may also need your services. However, these people may not know about you (and how you've helped their colleagues). When you've finished a project for one department, ask if there would be other people/departments who may need similar help. Simply ask your current client for a recommendation, and ask permission to use his or her name when you call the other department. Better still, have the current client call on your behalf. Getting recommended to another department or division from within puts you at a distinct advantage. You essentially get networked into the new gig.

What you essentially need to do is create a list of contacts and work it ruthlessly. Tim Butler compiled his own list of prospects in his market area. "I've been mailing sales letters and brochures and following them up with phone calls every few months." Harlan Hogan claims that a mailing list of 5,000 nationwide keeps him busy. He produces a new demo reel about every two years and stays in touch with an annual calendar mailed to his list.

Establish Your Image

The best image for you to convey is that of a problem solver or dream spinner. You need to be accessible, both easy to get in contact with and personable enough to work with effectively. You need to be sympathetic to your clients' problems and concerns. You need to master techniques that let you work smoothly with knowledgeable people, novices, and the wholly misinformed. Most importantly, you need to be technically proficient with the services you offer. People prefer to work with people with whom they are familiar. That requires you to make tiny image and attitude adjustments to become a little more like your clients. Putting yourself in their shoes enables you to put people at ease. You clearly show that you identify with your clients and that you fully understand their needs. These messages are what you must convey to prospects and clients. Make sure all your promotional materials and your room physically support these images. Also, be sure you demonstrate a successful, take-charge, can-do, and enthusiastic attitude. Finally, make sure you look the part by dressing appropriately.

Clients for Life

Today, business is more relationship centered than ever before. It's no longer about impersonal sellers and nearly anonymous buyers. You can't rely on making single or even high-volume sales anymore. You must, instead, concentrate on cultivating clients for the life of your business. You must institute promotional plans and customer care programs that allow you to build and maintain strong commercial relationships with every person who brings you business.

As the saying goes, you'll probably get 80 percent of your business from 20 percent of your client base. That 20 percent is crucial to the success of your project studio venture. Finding and keeping these clients should be your major focus. They pay the bills and, therefore, provide you with the freedom to pursue other ventures. I cultivate major anchor clients in all my ventures and urge you to do the same. If a moneymaking idea doesn't lend itself to a major client, then I caution you not to pursue it. Making it up in volume often taxes your resources. If you have to work just as hard to bring in teeny-weeny amounts of money, it may not be worth it. Instead, concentrate on bigger clients and landing better-paying gigs.

Most sales promotions are ideal for *starting* contact with new business, but once people begin to know and trust you, that's when you will truly prosper. Build relationships, and you will profit comfortably from long-term client loyalty. Don't go for the quick sale. Instead, focus on creating mutually beneficial relationships that can better sustain your career. You may find that most of your business will come from a small cadre of loyal clients. These people are crucial to your existence. Do everything you can to make them happy and keep them coming back for

177

more. Steve Horelick, owner of Oasis, has PBS as an anchor client. He told *Mix,* "When someone gives you forty episodes, you've got work for twenty-four months, so you tend not to think about adding more work."

The more you find out about people (clients or prospects), the easier it is to sell them more of your project studio products and services. You'll easily spot needs and desires, and then can pitch your help accordingly. Learn about your clients; it can often help you have more productive sessions and can also help you to make additional sales. I find the best customers for my on-hold services are those clients who use my services for another unrelated project. Invariably, I call their businesses and discover no phone-hold messaging. After I complete the current project, I pitch the phone-hold service as a helpful suggestion.

Don't be shy when asking for work. While I don't believe calling up and saying, "Do you have anything for me to do?" is the right tactic, calling up and pitching ideas is advisable. Say you just finished some radio spots for one client. Ask that client when he needs you to start on the next round of spots. Also, call another client or prospect and tell her how you just finished this project, and show her how easy it is to produce a great spot and get it on the air selling *her* products and services. They might say "no." That's okay, because you demonstrated your willingness to look out for their interests. Of course, they might say "yes," and you've made a virtually effortless sale.

The way to build these relationships is by going the extra mile for your best clients. If a client or prospect says something about his business or personal life, write it down and keep this with your files. This way, you can reintroduce this tidbit during a sales call or other meeting. "Last time you recorded here, you were gearing up for a West Coast gig. Did the bass player I recommended work out?" Sometimes, paying attention is all you need. On your visit to your client, you notice an office filled with golf paraphernalia. Chances are, you have a golf nut on your client list. Now, use that information to your best advantage. Go golfing one afternoon to do business. Give the client tickets to the local tournament. Have some personalized golf balls made, and deliver that as a gift after a successful project. You want to be remembered when you call and your ideas to be considered. Recalling and using information about your clients can help you better tailor the products, services, promotions, premiums, incentives, and gifts you provide.

So, get personal. The very nature of your project studio lets you focus on individuals. You will not be opening the doors to just anyone, so take the extra time to choose and work closely with the people you want to work with. These cliques are important to your longevity. Why do many people choose to work with the same people? It comes down to one thing: trust. David Lynch trusts Angelo Badalamenti to deliver the best musical score for his movies; he doesn't hire any other composers. I work with the same voice talent, because I know what they can do and I can depend on their work. I'm busy enough without having to find and audition new talent. In a way, it's a form of simplifying your business life. Your clients will feel the same way. If they know what you can do with the minimum of fuss, they will bring you their continued business. If you are difficult and fail to meet their expectations, they will walk. You should prefer having a steady stream of known quantities. Anchor clients give you certain freedoms, so you are not forced to constantly go after meager, unsatisfying gigs. They provide the money to keep your business going and, in turn, give you the impetus to find new projects and explore new creative expressions without worrying about the bills.

Master Promotional Writing

What do your clients buy? Your project studio offers specific services provided by a professional—YOU! To reiterate what I said earlier: *your clients buy you personally*. They buy your experience, knowledge, and creativity. They buy the opportunity to learn your techniques. They buy your fresh perspective, opinion, and candid advice. They buy change (because they are tired of an old supplier). Most importantly, they buy the results you can help them achieve.

Let's face it, people only want two things: to get rid of pain and/or to acquire some gain. All your promotions should focus on these two fundamental concepts. You can help people remove a pain when you say something such as, "Stop paying too much for studio time." Alternatively, you can promote a gain when you say, "Make money releasing your independent music CD."

As you begin to prepare the promotional material you need, always focus on your clients' perspective. What precisely do people get when they buy from you? You don't provide solutions, your clients get solutions for themselves (from you). Do you feel the difference this subtle shift makes? Also, make sure you talk directly to people, one-to-one, with all your promotions. Address them as "you," and appeal to their own self-interest.

Closely related to this point is focusing on the benefits clients get when choosing you. Always downplay your product and service features. Features are the specific attributes of something, while benefits are what you get by using it. Using a feature in a promotion would be something such as: "Record your CD using our state-of-the-art equipment." The better promotion would be to use a benefit instead: "Get the professional sound you need to grab a label's ear."

Always make sure your promotions include an offer of some kind and a call to action. Offers can be hard or soft. A soft offer would be inviting your prospect to ask for a demo, call for more information, or other similar deal. Soft offers invariably just let you solicit a lead. That is, you try to find out if someone is really interested in what you offer. This helps you separate real prospects from the chaff. With a lead in hand, you may need additional promotional material, even a meeting, to close the sale. A hard offer is usually of the "buy now" variety. Always use a combination of lead-generating and direct-sales offers with your promotions. The call to action is where you tell people to take the next step to get the specific benefits they need, such as: *"Call now!"* Don't forget to include your complete contact information with all your promotions. You want to make it oh-so-easy for prospects and clients to get the benefits they want fast.

When you approach someone cold, you can bet they will be somewhat suspicious of your motives. One proven method for reducing that suspicion is through testimonials and endorsements. When other clients and the media say good things about you, use this material to ease a new prospect's fear. How do you get this material? Your publicity efforts will yield the media quotes you need. If a client provides a testimonial, ask permission to quote it in promotional material. Alternatively, you can actively solicit testimonials by asking your best clients to write a few words and securing their permission to use them. With these blurbs in hand, sprinkle them liberally in your promotional material.

Dealing with Features

After you have promoted all the benefits your clients can get and made offers that either move to the next step in the sales process or make the sale immediately, then—and only then—provide some of the features of your products and services. Clients require some indication of what you have, lest they think all you have is a cassette portastudio and a cheap microphone. However, these descriptions can be very brief and simple: 24+ track, all-digital studio.

Some clients will be very concerned about your gear. Often, this predisposition originates in a general naiveté about our industry. Still, you should have a basic equipment list available for these requests. Draft a single-page flyer with an indication of the gear you have available. On this same page, put a profile of the people at your project studio, to demonstrate that your mastery of gear is more important than the gear itself. Also, recognize that this demand by clients for your gear list usually boils down to these issues. First, are you professional? Prospects and clients are inherently skeptical. You don't buy unknowns, and you can't expect them to either. They want to know exactly what (and who) they are getting for their money. Your promotions must persuade them that you are the best choice. Second, they want to know that you have the latest, greatest toys that will make their project special. A client reads that so-and-so used the new Fazzmagorical 3000 on their album and it went on to sell 17 million copies, so the client figures his company should use the Fazz 3K on its corporate video, too. This, of course, is ludicrous, so you just need to reassure the client that you have all the tools necessary to complete the project. Lastly, the request may be a format issue. Clients may need guarantees that the work you perform will be compatible with their systems. Thankfully, most audio formats are portable and platform-independent (or easily converted).

Crafting Your Promotional Kit

You can start with these basic promotional pieces: an introductory sales letter, a generic flyer or small brochure about your project studio products and services, and a demo reel that shows your mastery of what you sell. If you offer multiple products and services and/or appeal to wildly different prospects, consider preparing separate promotional pieces for each product, service, and market segment. It's completely legitimate to have more than one business card, brochure, and demo CD. This way you always have the appropriate promotional material targeted at the specific business you are pursuing. Additionally, you may prefer to prepare an all-encompassing promotional kit and use it as your main way to contact prospects, clients, and the media. Here are the key ingredients that go into a successful promotional kit.

Cover Letter

Use this both to introduce your project studio products and services and to reference the other pieces in the promotional package. Always address this letter to a specific person, and customize it accordingly. Indicate other contact you've had, for example, "I enjoyed meeting you at your Club gig Friday night. Here is additional information about my production studio . . ." Make sure you prominently include your contact information on this letter and on all the pieces included with your promotional kit.

Brochure or Flyer

Never expect clients or prospects to know what you do. Clearly spell out all your products and services in your promotional material. Don't neglect the ancillary services that you offer, such as duplication. You can use a single-page flyer to list everything you provide, or prepare a simple brochure. The #10 or "slim-jim" brochure is a good tactic. Take a piece of 8.5" x 11" paper and fold it into thirds. This fits neatly in a standard #10 business envelope and gives you a cover, an address panel (this can be a self-mailer), and four inside panels to promote your project studio. Put a picture on the cover, along with a strong benefit headline. Use the first inside panel for testimonials from satisfied customers. The three inside sections profile your music and sound products and services. This section can also include your prices. Let the back panel contain your contact information.

Biography or Basic FAQ

A short biography can help you explain what you are about, where you came from, and what is happening now. By carefully constructing this document, you can provide background material, company and personal history, and your key philosophy.

Alternatively, use a basic question and answer, or FAQ, format to present and answer the fundamental questions prospects ask about your project studio products and services. First, you recognize the problems your market wants to solve and/or the gains they wish to acquire. Second, you solve those problems or introduce those gains through your project studio products or services. Third, you address every sales objection in a clear, focused, benefit-filled way. Your buyers should be fully informed about what you offer and, more importantly, precisely how you can help them. Finally, you give clear instructions on how the prospect can get your project studio products and services and realize the benefits you've presented in the promotion for themselves. What's especially useful about this format is its versatility. It can be a sales letter, brochure, proposal, and a Web FAQ with little modification on your part. If you place such a FAQ on your Web site, make sure to provide links to audio samples, so people can hear examples of what you offer. You can find a real-world example of this suggested format on my Web site at *www.jeffreypfisher.com/melo.html.*

Past Media/Client Coverage

If you have media interviews, reviews, and other such material, include copies with your kit. Also, include a page with several testimonials from happy clients, or just include entire letters of recommendation. You should also consider other success documents that clearly demonstrate your experience, such as case studies, where you show how you solved a particular client's problems (the results you achieved). Client lists, project credits, and awards you've earned are also useful here, especially if your credentials are impressive—Grammy, Oscar, Emmy, for example.

What do you do if you are a beginner? Chances are, you have some credits to get you started. If you did some work for a current or past employer, use that. Fresh from school? List the projects you did for school. Best advice? Get up, get out, and earn some credits as fast as you can. Start accumulating them and adding them to your list of credentials ASAP.

Demos

Your demos are the calling cards of your project studio. As their name implies, they demonstrate what you can do. And since prospects are skeptical, you need to clearly show you are experienced and reliable. Also, you'll notice I said demos, plural. You should consider having multiple demos that feature the various work you do. For example, you might have separate demos for music recording, commercial jingles and soundtracks, and on-hold and radio spots. You might even have a video demo to highlight and sell your sound-for-picture expertise.

Whatever demo you decide you need, keep it short and to the point. My experience shows that you have about thirty seconds to make the sale, often less. You must grab your listeners right away and hold their attention for half a minute. If you get past that initial hurdle, you can usually keep them listening for a couple of minutes more. Just understand that the prospect or client is going to make her decision in a few seconds.

The montage is the format to choose. Edit together snippets from a bunch of projects into one seamless commercial, and do it in two minutes. Think of your demo as your personal late-night commercial, like those that sell "Hits of the Hair Bands." Using quick music and sound hooks and narration, just like those commercials, is the way to go here. After that initial presentation, feel free to expand the demo with a few other full-length tracks. Leading with the montage and following with four songs or other sound material would be ideal. Let the other demo tracks reinforce your abilities showcased in those opening two minutes. It's the first track that tells and sells; the rest of your demo usually just reassures the already-sold prospect that he or she made the right decision.

Make sure you master your demos with consistent levels and tone, with just the right amount of polish. Package it nicely, too. Use labels, tray cards, and booklet inserts, and be sure your contact information is on every part, especially the CD itself. Since most people stack CD cases, print big and bold on the case spine (too many homespun CDs are blank here).

One great way to promote your project studio is through samples. Your demo CD serves this purpose, as do clips on your Web site. The "free sample" is an ideal way to sell just about anything. Your objective? To get people to buy from you. How? Through promotional techniques that enable people to hear what you do (and buy if they like it). Strategy? Give away a little music, sound, or time for free. Why? You hope that people will like what they hear and want to buy more. You offer a sample, just as the cookie store lets you try its latest culinary delight. The proprietor hopes you'll like the cookie and buy a dozen or so to take home. You hope people love your sample track and buy the whole CD, commercial composition services, recording services, etc. People are inherently cautious, but if they try something first—and like it—those free samples will help you close more sales faster.

What if you don't have any material for your demo CD? As mentioned before, dig up whatever you can at first, and work to replace old experience with new credits quickly. Also, you can fake some gigs. For example, you write a jingle for a brand name product or put together a soundtrack for a commercial spot (featuring a prominent product/service). You then include this mock-up with your demo. Make sure you don't claim that you actually did this spot. Include a simple disclaimer saying your demo represents the kind of work that you do and your abilities. Don't write a fake McDonald's jingle and then say they were a client.

Photo

Pictures are useful promotional tools. A shot of you working in your project studio can function as a publicity shot or be used as part of a flyer or brochure. Take photos of clients at your studio. Post them on walls, include them with your newsletter and Web pages, and use them for publicity. Make sure you ask for permission. If you send out press releases accompanied by pictures, there is more of a chance that a paper or magazine will run or feature your story. The shot of you standing next to your famous client, coupled to a short news release ("Famous client records at [your studio name here]") can usually get coverage in many magazines and newspapers. Write your own caption for the photo on paper, and tape the paper to the back of the photo before sending it to the editors at local and national presses.

Other Goodies

You can include all kinds of doodads with your promotional kit or as separate promotions. Called "ad specialties" by the firms who sell and manufacture them, these can be a way to keep your name in front of prospects and clients. No mug, notepad, calendar, or other such imprinted item should ever take the place of true prospecting and customer service. You will be far more successful if you just pick up the phone regularly and use other surefire promotions. Still, these items can have value and serve as a useful, albeit small, part of your overall promotional effort. What you select should be useful to prospective clients—at the place from which they would order your service. Appeal to corporate clients? Don't provide an item that gets used in the home.

Also, the item should relate to your business in some way and be consistent with your image. It should feature your contact information prominently. Select good quality merchandise that has longevity (which means food is out; once eaten it's gone . . . and you are forgotten). For example, serve beverages in customized mugs at your studio, and then tell the client to keep the mug after the session is over.

One terrific promotional item is an annual, customized calendar. Use it to keep your name in front of your best prospects and clients 24-7-365. Fill your calendar with industry trivia, history, tips, words of wisdom, or other information related to the specific project studio products and services you promote and sell. Also, include some regular offers, such as specific discount coupons sprinkled through the year.

Important Production Notes

Prepare all your promotional material (letters, flyers, brochures, pictures, and demos) in two formats. One format must be physically reproduced, so that it can be printed, duplicated, and mailed or delivered in person. The other format is virtual, so that it can be sent via e-mail and posted to your Web site. For the paper-based material, have letterhead, envelopes, business cards, and mailing labels designed. You will use these business stationery forms the most. Letterhead is particularly versatile for everything—correspondence, promotions, invoices, etc.

Put everything that comprises your promotional kit into a folder with your company name on it. I prefer tabbed file folders, with your company name printed on both the folder's face and tab. Alternatively, print your name on the folder face and a main benefit on the tab. Send the folder in a padded envelope, or use the post office's priority mail envelopes and pay for the better service (even if the cost is slightly higher).

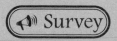

Who are your clients? Where do they come from?

♪ Clients are mostly ad agencies.

♪ Bands and individuals, usually from references of other bands/individuals.

♪ Creative directors for theater.

♪ Songwriters mostly, and some small/home businesses. Entirely word-of-mouth referrals.

♪ Usually vocalists.

♪ Mostly young local bands, but I have done corporate and commercial work.

♪ Mostly local bands who hear albums by other local bands and like the way they sound.

♪ Production companies.

♪ They can find me on the Internet, or word of mouth— the best way to advertise.

♪ Advertising firms, larger video and multimedia production houses.

♪ Musicians and Web developers.

♪ Mostly advertising agencies, film supervisors, production companies.

♪ I'm looking for clients!

10
Unleashing Your Promotions

When it comes to successfully promoting your project studio, you have only four goals. First, to find people who want or need what you offer. Second, to contact them in some way. Third, to get these people to contact you. Fourth, to convince these people to buy. That means you need promotions that both generate leads and that follow up those leads to close sales. There are several ways to generate leads, including ads, flyers, sales letters (e-mail and postal), publicity, Web site, and networking. There are many ways that you can respond to the leads you do get, including a sales letter, small brochure, FAQ sheet, product or service sample (e.g., a CD or an MP3). There are four ways you can convince the buyer to open his or her wallet: another letter, telephone sales, face-to-face meetings, and Web site or other store setting, such as back-of-room sales. Maintaining long-term relationships with past buyers is another key to continued success. To keep in touch, send promotions when people buy from you and ask them to buy again, use publicity to remind them, and stay in touch with a small newsletter (postal and/or e-mail).

There are many ways you can promote your project studio products and services. You will probably use most, if not all, of the ideas explained here. What you will find is that certain promotions work better than others in particular situations. You will also discover that you are good at making sales in some situations and abysmal in others. Work your strengths when contemplating which promotions to use. If you present well in front of people, pick up the phone and/or meet prospects and clients in person. If you are somewhat shy, use mail (postal and e-mail) and other lead generators to contact prospects and clients.

Many people erroneously confuse promotion and advertising. Advertising is only one small slice of the entire promotional pie. What makes ads so attractive is their promise of instant new business. That is usually a deceptive lure, especially in the project studio business. Building your credentials through client success and sharing that success with subsequent prospects and clients is the best way to promote your business. Sometimes, you will advertise your success, and other times others will promote these successes through publicity. You control your advertising completely—its look, placement, frequency, etc. However, you have little control over publicity. You never know if something will appear or, if it does, what form it will take. A one-page news release can often be reduced to a single sentence buried in the back of a magazine. What is especially important to note is that people are inherently skeptical of advertising and dangerously respectful of publicity. If you take out an ad that tells how good you are, people will be suspicious. If a media source tells these people how good you are, it will be believed.

Advertising Your Project Studio

Advertising takes many forms, not just the full-page color ads you see in your favorite magazines. It's rare that you will be taking out such ad space to sell your project studio, mainly because there are so few appropriate places. The trade publications are too national and virtually useless for targeting local or regional prospects. (If you are fortunate enough to have some local music paper or other trade press, they make ideal places for your ads.) Instead, you should advertise one-to-one by sending promotional messages to prospects and clients in the form of sales letters, postcards, and promotional kits. If you do, however, decide to place ads for your business, running many smaller ads is better than one big ad. The best tactic is to use one larger ad followed by several smaller ads repeated regularly, and then reusing the one big ad periodically. Make sure your ad includes strong benefits, offers, and contact information.

Many project studio owners tell me that yellow page ads work fine. If you are selling studio time only, this may be the way to go. For others who sell professional services instead of the project studio room itself, the yellow pages are a waste of money. Instead, look for professional directories that reach your prospects. Guides to area businesses, perhaps one dedicated to the audiovisual industry, are the best places to look for possible clients and to promote your services, too.

Writing directly to a client, on your letterhead or via e-mail, to promote your project studio is really the proven method to secure new business. These sales letters can be easily created and carefully worded to appeal to a prospect's interests. You can include a small flyer or brochure, and mail this to your contacts. You might hold back your demo, using it as the offer in the sales letter. This gives people a reason to contact you, furthering the promotional process. If you promote electronically, you can still draft a solid sales e-mail letter, and provide links to your brochure and demo on your Web site. Occasionally, you may send your entire promotional kit to a prospect, but usually only after some other initial contact, such as a cold telephone call or in response to another promotional offer. Mailing promotions regularly can increase your chance of getting noticed. Don't let them stand on their own, though. Follow up these mailings with phone calls!

Postcards are inexpensive ways to put your capabilities in front of prospects and past clients. They can function as a mini-ad, billboard, reminder, and more. They don't need to be opened and are inexpensive to create, design, print, and mail. Use postcards to promote successes and to indicate the services you offer. Including a discount or other special offer can entice a better response. For example, a voice artist could send a postcard along these lines: *"The City Council was presented a video promoting XYZ for a new park project. XYZ was awarded the bid! Tess Adams was the voice on the video. You hear, a great voice gets great results. Call today, and let Tess help you."*

Publicity

Publicity lets you tell your market about each success and remind them that they, too, can experience your benefits. You first need to find the right targets for your news—the media that your prospects and clients read. Ask your clients, and look for copies of appropriate newspapers, newsletters, and magazines around their offices. Also, search the Gebbie Press *All-In-One Media Directory* at *www.gebbieinc.com* for the information you need.

While you can submit the usual publicity fare to your media contacts, such as new clients, projects completed, and equipment and personnel acquisitions, you should really work to have more specific coverage on your area of expertise. Provide case studies in ready-to-run article format that show how you completed a recent project. Alternatively, suggest articles on topics that feature your experience. Again, the focus should be on what you did for clients. Emphasize the human aspect, not the technology, and leave the gear lists at home, unless you used something to solve a problem.

Follow this format as you submit your news releases. On your letterhead, type *News Release* centered at the top. Below that, justified to the right hand side of the page, put *For immediate release,* and under that, your contact information (name and phone number). Space down a little, and center your headline. Write the body of your release under that, making sure to provide the who, what, when, where, why, and how information in the first paragraph. Your sentences should be short and simple, written as a journalist would report the news. At the end of the release center the characters "###." If you include a photo with the news release, write your caption on paper, and tape the paper to the back of the photo.

One proven way to get a news release printed is to offer some kind of free item, such as a free tip sheet, newsletter subscription, or other related item. Writing a tip sheet that solves problems for potential clients, such as "What You Need to Know Before You Go to the Studio," gives you the hook to hang a promotional message on in a news release. Here's a real-word example:

NEWS RELEASE

For immediate release
Contact: Jeffrey P. Fisher, (630) 378-4109

FREE Moneymaking Music Tips

If you need help promoting and selling your music and sound products and services, you can get a free subscription to Jeffrey P. Fisher's **Moneymaking Music Tip of the Week** delivered via e-mail to subscribers. According to Fisher, each issue provides several short tips to help music and sound professionals make their careers more successful. To get on the list, send an e-mail message to *jpf@jeffreypfisher.com* with *subscribe tip* in the subject or body.

###

The real power of publicity comes by using it several ways. Publish it in a trade or local media outlet, mail it as a reprint to clients and prospects, post it to your Web site, hang it on your studio wall, and give it out to new prospects as part of your general promotional kit.

Promotional Newsletter

Preparing your own newsletter is an ideal way to stay in touch with past clients and to connect with possible prospects. You can choose to send your newsletter via postal mail, deliver it via e-mail, or both. Whatever delivery format you choose, make sure to keep the newsletter consistent in content and timing. Once each quarter is fine for most promotional campaigns, but once each month can be better, if a little more work. Use your newsletter to profile recent projects, deliver important news, discuss gear acquisitions (how you used the gear to solve a problem is more important), provide tips and techniques appropriate to your client base, reprint letters and testimonials from satisfied clients, share some industry insight, announce new products and services, introduce new employees, sell ancillary products and services, and anything else you feel is right for your newsletter.

One project studio and small label used a regular newsletter to great success. Each issue always led with an article about the company's latest news. There were also articles on songwriting technique; various tidbits, such as inspiring quotes, music picks, and so forth; a coupon for a discount off studio time; updates on artists; networking opportunities; a listing of recent projects completed in the studio; advertisements for specific services; and a catalog of merchandise, including music CDs, T-shirts, songbooks, instructional packages, and so forth. The format was a twelve-page self-mailer (three 8.5" x 11" pages folded in half to form a booklet), stapled at the spine, sealed with a sticker, and sent first class to the studio's mailing list.

While this example is somewhat ambitious, you can get by with much less. Print your newsletter on your letterhead, with just a few short paragraphs. Create some generic "departments," and fill them in with the appropriate information. Have at least one strong offer with each newsletter, such as a discount, special deal, or whatever. You might print a catalog of products and services and include that with your newsletter, too. This catalog need be nothing fancy; just make it a flyer with details about what you offer on both sides of a sheet of paper. Include an order form at the bottom of page two. This flyer can be designed just once and used over and over. I suggest using the same catalog with each newsletter mailing, updating it when you add new products and services. To make it look different, print it on different color paper for each mailing. Use your letterhead for the main newsletter. You can, of course, choose to e-mail the newsletter and/or post it to your Web site. For example, my e-mail *Moneymaking Music Tip of the Week* includes one basic tip, a bonus tip, a threads area for ongoing communication within the list subscribers, profile of a resource (usually a book, CD, or something else for sale), and a list of additional regular resources all found on my Web site through clickable links.

Telephone

Your telephone will continue to be the main method that lets you connect with both prospects and clients. For current and past clients, pick up the phone and call often to check on past work and to solicit new jobs. For new prospects, you can place cold calls or use other promotions to warm up some calls. Eric B. Thompson felt that "cold calling or mailing a sales package with a follow-up phone call are probably the best ways to go, especially if it's a local call. It's warmer, more friendly, and you establish voice recognition, can introduce a person, the character behind the business. A cold call I made a year ago to the proprietor of a prominent ad firm led to the establishment of an immediate and strong rapport (didn't hurt that the proprietor is an avid guitarist himself). I'm now at the top of his list for jingle scoring referrals."

Preparing for cold calls is simple. Create a sales script that you follow. Don't read it word for word. Instead, prepare an outline to guide your call. Alternatively, create a FAQ to help you field common objections. Also, listen carefully to the person on the other end, and tailor your message accordingly. Follow the tips outlined below in the in-person sales section, too. Pick up the phone and call. What do you have to lose? You don't have the gig now, do you? If the prospect says "no," you still won't have the gig. If the prospect says "yes," however, it could be the start of a profitable relationship.

Sell in Person

One of the best ways to promote and sell is to take your work and meet people face-to-face. Even better is to get them to come down to the studio to see and hear what you have to offer. In either case, you can play your demo in person and customize your sales presentation to the situation. When on your own turf, you can dazzle people with your command of your technological domain. You can also choose tracks that better fit with their demands, too. Believe me, people are impressed by project studios. Even those people who follow the industry are still awestruck at times. Make sure you have a comfortable space and that everything is working. Consider doing A/B comparisons if you have a before-and-after project example. Play the original A track, and quickly follow it up with your sweetened and mastered track B. These are the things that close sales! If you take your stuff on the road, make sure you have a battery-powered portable boom box to play your demo. Don't expect the prospect to have something to play it on.

Practice and master these basic sales techniques. Greet any prospect or client with a firm handshake, a warm smile, a kind word, and a positive attitude. Use active listening, where you focus on what the prospect and client tells you. Listen 70 percent of the time; speak under 30 percent. When you listen, people will tell you what they want. Once you know that, then you can show them how you can give them what they need. Pay particular attention to a person's speech and mannerism tendencies. You can mirror these tendencies to build instant rapport. Ask questions, and show your interest by nodding, agreeing verbally, and so forth. Focus on them, not you (no sob stories or name dropping). Try to appear as if you are rather busy, but don't rush matters. You want to create a sense of success and urgency. Be prepared, and bring demos and other promotional material, but only offer them when asked! Don't give away the store. You need to help these people, but don't tell them *everything*, because there will be nothing left to sell. The most important point in a sales situation is to ask for the order. Act as if you already have the gig. Instead of saying, "I hope you consider recording here," take a more positive approach, such as, "Let me look at my schedule to see when we can get started on your radio spots. Next Tuesday looks good. Shall I book the voice talent, too?" Lastly, follow up all sales meetings promptly with a thank you note and anything else you promised to send.

Networking

Networking means leveraging casual contact into leads, referrals, and sometimes even work. Almost any situation can be a networking opportunity. First, prepare an elevator pitch or sound bite about your work that lets you describe what you do in twenty-five words or less. Second, always have business cards and a few brochures with you. With this prepared, you can start conversations with people. After the usual pleasantries, ask them what they do. After they finish, provide your pitch and a card, if it makes sense. You might prefer getting the other person's contact information and following up later. Networking is a win-win situation for all parties. Your aim is to get possible leads to people who might need your services and to help the other person if you can.

Become part of the scene, and you can network more effectively. Trade shows and other industry events, along with association meetings, are ideal places for your networking endeavors. You can pay for a booth, set up your promotional material, and grab leads by appealing to people who wander past your booth. Alternatively, you can go to trade shows that feature your clients and prospects, and promote to them at *their* booths. Similar to this idea is to go to a club to listen to a new band, then introduce yourself and your services to the band during a break.

Word of Mouth

Many people who completed my Project Studio Survey cited "word of mouth" as their main promotional strategy. When you do consistently good, quality work, people will start seeking you out. Word-of-mouth promotion needs a little coaxing to get your message out effectively. Always let people know you are looking for gigs. Try to get more work from the same client. When you complete a project, ask for another. Ask for referrals to other clients, or ask them to recommend you to a friend. Getting a specific referral is best. Ask if you can use the client's name when you contact the referral. Encourage happy clients to tell their peers. They can provide names for you, as above, or offer to call on your behalf. Provide business cards, brochures, and other promotional material, and invite your clients to pass the material on to others who might need your services. Offer incentives (discounts, commissions, etc.) for clients to provide other work. Thank everyone for their business, and really thank those people who send business to you. Thank your clients publicly for their business in news releases, newsletters, Web, etc. Make sure your complete contact information is on everything leaving your studio. For example, have your project studio name and contact information preprinted on blank CDs. That way, every CD leaving your studio has your credits on it. Don't dominate the disk; leave room for your clients to add their information. Another important component to word-of-mouth promotion is to get credits. Insist on being fully credited on every project you do. Finishing the sound for a video? Ask for a screen credit. Recording an indie release? Ask for credit in the liner notes. Better still, ask to put in complete contact information in the liner notes, and trade that with the indie band in exchange for a discount off your services. Other prospects may see these credits and bring business to you because they liked what you did.

Internet

Chapter 8 already addressed this topic substantially. Let me reiterate here that your Web site can be the base for all your promotions, because it combines advertising, publicity, networking, and sales in one neat little package.

Welcome Letters and Thank You Notes

When you land a new contract, drop a short note to the new client welcoming him to your business. If you have specific requirements, use this contact to explain them. One of the simplest promotional tools you can use is a "thank you." Thank your clients in person, and also send them thank you letters, cards, even small gifts. Also, send a thank you note to the media who give you coverage after it appears.

Holiday Time

Giving tokens of appreciation at holiday time is a traditional business function. Don't think too narrowly about the gift, though. It has two purposes: to thank your best clients and show how much you appreciate their continued support and to encourage your clients to buy from you again. What makes the ideal business gift? Give them a discount coupon (percentage or dollar amount) toward your project studio products and services. This strategy both thanks and rewards your

197

clients simultaneously. Since your coupon is only good for your business, you also encourage them to buy from you again. Of course, you can use coupons, discounts, and sales at other times of the year, too.

Fax, Voice Mail, and On-Hold

If you communicate with prospects and clients via fax, place your promotional message on the cover sheets. Also, make sure your voice mail message presents your image well and that it promotes your project studio, too. If you place people on hold regularly, consider getting your own on-hold messaging system and promoting to people while they wait.

Open House

You can often expand your client list by getting people to your door. While you can host an informal open house, you might be better off to host seminars that appeal to your targeted prospects. For example, hold a recording and mixing session to show possible prospects how to get their projects to sound good. You can even charge a token fee for the instruction and use it to generate new business, too. Make sure you have plenty of promotional material on hand when you host either situation. Put together a goodie bag with your promotional kit inside for everyone to take home.

Niceties

When people come to your studio, be the consummate professional, and also be the gracious host or hostess. Keep your space neat, clean, and organized. If you waste precious minutes accomplishing the most mundane tasks, your clients will not be happy. Provide food, drink, comfortable seating, and a work space for them. Worried about drink spills? Provide a separate lounge or reception area. Corporate types usually need a telephone nearby, too. If you're home-based, first-time visitors may feel uncomfortable working in your home. Don't say, "Help yourself to whatever is in the fridge." Get the food yourself instead. Do show people where the bathroom is, and make sure it's clean, stocked with TP, fresh towels, and such. One project studio peer keeps a play area for kids, stocked with coloring books, crayons, books, and some videos. The parents who are forced to bring their little groupies along for a session appreciate such attention to their needs.

Follow Up and Follow Through

No matter how flashy your promotions, they will die a certain death if you don't follow up regularly. Get on the phone, send e-mail, and reconnect by letter and postcard with all the leads, prospects, and clients your promotions bring your way. "Dig in with both feet at the beginning," advised Jimmy Graham. "Do the best you can for each client, and if you can't, say so. Charge a fair price! If you are running a professional project studio, step into the clients' shoes, not their wallets, and give them something that you can be proud of."

Working with Clients

You should spend a great deal of effort getting new clients. Once you get them, make sure you invest even more resources toward making sure they are satisfied and, therefore, bring you additional business either themselves or by recommending you to others. Always remember that you work for clients, and it is your sole purpose to help them realize their visions and make them look good in front of their bosses, friends, peers, etc. "I try to go the extra mile and deliver more than I promise," said one project studio owner. "Also, if there's a problem, I will take responsibility for it (whether it's directly my fault or not) and deal with it up front. Clients don't want excuses; they want results. I always try to salvage the relationship, even if I take a loss on one job. When people know that they can always expect a certain attitude and level of service, then they're comfortable and always come back. Consistency has been the key for me, because I rely on repeat business and referrals."

Music and sound production, like many creative endeavors, is a collaborative art. You need to build solid, mutually trustful relationships with all the people who use your project studio. Have the right attitude, and be supportive, offer praise, provide constructive criticism, and stay neutral. Don't demean clients, especially in front of others. Always respect their privacy. Listen, and take their suggestions, too. Some of their ideas may be outlandish, but it is your job to realize *their* visions. Keep your mind open to possibilities. Another survey respondent said her greatest challenge was "reconciling creativity and artistic expression with commerce. Often, I'm in the position of helping to realize someone else's vision for money, when I would rather make decisions based on my own taste. It's hard to help create something you think isn't great, when your client wants it that way."

Some clients may have their own ideas about how to approach an issue. You may have a better solution. How to introduce your idea without stepping on toes is a skill you must master. Rather than discussing these ideas ad nauseam, it can often be better to just demonstrate what you mean. There is nothing wrong with doing two takes: "Let's try it this way, and then that way, and compare the two." One client had a specific way he wanted to open a video project. It wasn't working. Rather than waste time explaining why we should change it, I quickly threw together an alternate version and A/B'd them for the client. He immediately saw what I meant, and we went with the second take. (By the way, this was done via the Internet. I quickly made tiny, low-res Real Video copies and e-mailed them to the client. We discussed the videos by phone as he watched them on his laptop.)

One of your first important tasks when meeting prospects or new clients is to uncover the decision maker. Often, this may appear a simple task. If one person walks into the room, that's the one. Unfortunately, that is rarely the case. This person may be the point person, but not the real decision maker. There may be higher-ups with whom you may never have contact. Alternatively, you may have a group of people in the room. Again, you must find out who is going to actually place their stamp of approval on your work. You need to make sure that this person is happy.

When meeting clients on *their* turf, follow these guidelines. Be on time. If you will be late for a scheduled meeting, call ahead and explain your delay. Dress appropriately; think business casual. Bring additional promotional material with you—even if you've already sent some. If I know what the project is, I often bring suitable material to show the client that I have already done what they need. One caveat though: don't push your promotional material on people. Wait to be asked. What you really should do is focus on what the client has to say, and demonstrate how you can best meet her needs. Avoid the jargon of the trade; keep the conversation simple. Take notes during your meeting. Even if you have a good memory, you show your interest and attention to detail by writing down important points. Set deadlines for the work you will do. There's nothing worse than the vague notion of "sometime." Make sure you can deliver what you promise and in the time frame allowed. Try not to burst their bubbles. Many client ideas are eccentric. Your job is not to rip them, but rather to find ways to make them work.

When meeting clients on *your* turf, use these ideas. Make the clients comfortable. Greet them warmly with a firm handshake. Invite them in. Show them where to put their coats, where the bathroom is, where the phone is, and offer them a beverage. Get started right away. It is best to be set up before the client arrives. For example, for a voice session, set up the mic, and check to make sure it's working properly. Leave headphones nearby, and check their operation, too. Place a music stand near the mic, and supply a red pen to make copy changes. Have the lights on. Provide a stool or chair (though many voice artists prefer to stand). Have the multitrack loaded with fresh tape (or create folders on the hard drive) for the project. Take care of possible interruptions before the session begins. For example, I usually crank the AC for an hour before a session, because I'm forced to turn it off during recording.

Take charge of sessions and explain as you go along. Avoid becoming dictator of the project studio, though. Ask for ideas and suggestions and try to implement them. Each session should be a collaborative effort. Don't diddle knobs quietly without offering a running narration of what's going on. I know sometimes you just need to A/B something for clients, but be courteous and acknowledge their ignorance (or erudition). If you have a problem, don't get flustered. Have everyone take a short break, while you hunt down and fix the gremlins.

Always try to make your clients feel special. Have copyright forms on hand for songwriters and bands. Have compulsory mechanical license copies on hand for bands who cover material. Have a tip sheet available that explains copyright law, trademark law, and how to obtain the mechanical license legally. Write a "how to prepare for a recording session" tip sheet or provide a checklist to all new clients. Surprise them with a discount of some kind (free hour). Give them a gift of some kind (your latest CD, perhaps). Send a thank you note after they give you new business. Stay in touch regularly, and concentrate on how you can help them again.

Deal with Client Problems

Sometimes, a client demands too much. Your best way to avoid this problem is to work out project details in advance. Carefully word your promotional material and contract, so there are no surprises. If the client complains or has a problem, work hard to satisfy their requests. I was once bumped from studio time by another band who needed a demo fast. I was angry, because I'd booked in advance and getting the lads together was no easy task. Reluctantly, I rescheduled. When our new time came, the studio owner/engineer played the tape of the other band for me. He also informed me that the band landed a record contract because of this demo. In other words, he made me feel as if I was partially responsible for this band's success. I didn't really believe it totally, but it did defuse my anger somewhat. He then gave me two free hours recording time, too.

Manage Your Promotion

Even when you are busy, you can't neglect your need to promote, or you may turn around one day and have nothing to do. Instead of sending out mass mailings, concentrate on a few prospects and customers from week to week. This should take very little time and cost little (phone calls, printing, and postage). Plus, it's an easily manageable schedule that allows you to promote regularly without overwhelming your time. Even if you still mass-promote, as when you send out a regular newsletter, you would still follow the tips provided below. Also, keeping track of all this information is vital. Consider getting sales automation management software, such as Act!, to manage your data, or set up your own database instead.

Set aside thirty minutes each week to work your promotions. Use this time to promote to five new or past prospects, reconnect with five past clients, and follow up with the five potential new clients you contacted the previous week. Mail promotions (sales letter, flyer, postcard, etc.) to five prospects. These prospects can also include the media where you are seeking publicity or other promotional opportunities (articles by and about you, for instance). Contact five past clients (by either e-mail, postal, or telephone). Contact the previous week's five prospects by phone to follow up the promotional mailing. Because timing often plays a critical role as to whether you get an assignment or not, this strategy helps you connect and reconnect with prospects and clients regularly. By pitching a variety of your project studio products and services with these promotions, you let prospects and clients know precisely how you can help them. When there is a need for your services, you want to be the first person they think of to call.

Last Promotional Message

Promotion is crucial to sustaining your project studio. This chapter provides a solid introduction to the subject. However, if you feel you need additional help in this area, I urge you to read my other book, *Ruthless Self-Promotion in the Music Industry*. That resource contains even more detail and numerous creative promotional strategies, including extensive chapters on advertising, publicity, Internet, networking, closing sales, and more.

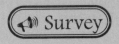

Survey

How do you promote your project studio? What promotions are the most successful? Why? About how much money and time do you spend on promotion in a given month?

This was a three part question, condensed for easier understanding.

♪ Word of mouth and a promo pack, one day a week.

♪ This is only a personal-use studio, so no promotion.

♩ Word of mouth. People usually leave so happy with their project they wind up telling someone about it. About $50 to $250 per month.

♪ Telephone calls and info kits, which contain a demo CD. $20 and about ten hours.

♪ I get referrals from current clients and general word-of-mouth.

♪ Mostly long-distance and postage, about $40 to $100 per month.

♩ Word of mouth. because most of the time, people come recommended, which is good, since the studio is located in my home.

♩ Yellow pages, flyers, compilation CD's, newsletters. They get noticed by the people that want to buy my services. Approximately $100 to $150 a month.

♩ Word of mouth. Yellow pages. Concerts that we put on. Occasionally, some radio. The best are the ones that offer a lot for a low price, 'cause musicians are either broke or poor money managers (myself included).

♩ Sales letters and brochures. About twenty hours preparing and mailing materials, $50 in postage and paper.

♩ E-mail, newsletters. Two-for-one deals, 10 percent off. Limited time promotions are great. It gives a sense of urgency.

♩ Cold calls, direct marketing, Word of mouth, networking. Hard to say—maybe twelve hours, $50 per month.

♩ I will be doing video for cable, brochures, press kits, handouts, word of mouth, and the Internet. I will be spending about twenty-five hours a month on promotional activities, including videos, Internet development, and promotional materials.

♪ Mailings, phone calls, Web site, demo CDs. Usually three to four days a month and $50.

♪ Web site, local music papers, word of mouth.

11
Starting and Managing Your Project Studio

T*oo many music and sound production professionals* start their project studios ad hoc and run them by the seat of their pants. You must understand that there are tremendous benefits to getting serious and operating your project studio as a legitimate business. This chapter, along with the next, combine into the proven project studio road map you need to be successful.

Startup Ideas

Don't feel you need to be full-time with your project studio to find satisfaction. There's nothing wrong with pursuing your project studio career part-time. You can find balance and fulfillment in your spare time. If you need a day job to pay your bills, be proud of your commitment. Just over half of the survey replies came from part-time project studio owners. Most surprising was the fact that only one of the part-timers worked in the music and sound industry. The remaining part-timers worked at mostly unrelated jobs.

You can also use your part-time work as a springboard to full-time business. A common thread that ran through the responses was for the project studio to eventually become their only way to make money. Eric Thompson summed it up this way: "My plan for the short term is to build up a substantial enough business, carve out a large enough niche that allows me to work out of my project studio full-time." With nearly half the respondents already living that dream, I feel the part-time owners can look forward to reaching their goals.

If you work full-time at a day job, consider moonlighting. Work to land some gigs off-hours, and build your business this way. Work part-time at a day job and part-time from your project studio. Save a financial cushion that lets you stop working and concentrate on the studio. Hopefully, you'll earn enough money quickly enough to protect that little nest egg. Let your spouse work to pay your expenses, while you start the project studio business. Turn your current employer into a client. In other words, get into a situation where you can continue to work, not as an employee, but as an independent contractor. Whether you are beginning from scratch or launching a new venture, start small, and try to do your best with what you already have.

Legal Structure

There are five ways you can set up your project studio business: sole proprietorship, partnership, C corporation, S corporation, and limited liability company. The form you choose depends on your particular situation. There are financial and legal advantages and disadvantages to all the business structures, detailed below. Consider discussing this issue with your accountant and a legal adviser. The accountant can fully explain the financial impact of these business forms, while your lawyer can explain the liability issue.

A sole proprietorship is wholly owned and operated by one person; the owner is self-employed. It is the most-used business form, and you need do very little to begin. Beyond getting a business license and filing a fictitious name statement, you can start immediately. Sole proprietorships are often called Schedule C businesses, so named for the tax form required by the IRS. All business income and expenses are part of the owner's individual, personal tax return. Sole proprietors take on all liability for the business, and this liability extends to the owner's personal assets. This means that someone can sue you and, if he wins, can receive a monetary award paid from your *personal* savings and from the business. The project studio survey indicated that the vast majority of project studio owners are sole proprietors.

A partnership is defined by the Uniform Partnership Act as the "association of two or more persons to carry on as co-owners of a business for profit." Income and expenses flow to the partners' individual tax returns, just as a sole proprietorship, in percentages agreed upon initially. I highly recommend you have a formal, clearly defined partnership agreement that includes a dissolution or buyout clause. As with the sole proprietorship, partners take on unlimited personal liability.

The C corporation is a distinct legal being that is separate from the individuals who own it. There is specific paperwork that must be filed and strict guidelines to be followed when choosing the corporate form. As a separate entity, the corporation can shield its owners from personal liability. Lawsuits only affect the corporate assets, not the owner's' personal savings. The Subchapter S corporation is essentially the same as the C, except the corporate profits flow to the owners as dividends, with taxes paid personally instead of by the corporation. There are special requirements for setting up a Subchapter S Corporation with the IRS. A Limited Liability Company (LLC) is a hybrid business form sharing some traits with the corporate form and functioning somewhat like a partnership.

One of the best ways to get additional business help is through the Small Business Administration. They have a variety of programs ready to help you. Specifically, check out their Service Corps of Retired Executives (SCORE), comprised of volunteers prepared to help you on a variety of business topics from accounting to marketing and a little of everything in between. The SBA also sponsors regional Small Business Development Centers, which can also provide help in several areas. Stop by the SBA's comprehensive Web site (*www.sbaonline.sba.gov*) for the details.

Select a Name

Choosing a name for your business is one of the most difficult decisions you may have to make. You need to choose a name that accurately reflects the work that you do. Keep in mind that from a promotional standpoint, selling yourself is most important. That is why most professionals use their legal name for their business: Joe Pro Music and Sound. If you plan to operate your project studio business using a name other than your legal name, you will need to file a fictitious name statement, or "doing business as" (dba), with your local government. Contact your county municipality for the specific requirements.

You may also need to secure a tax ID for your business. In most cases, your social security number is all you need, especially if you are a sole proprietor. A corporation gets its own tax ID. Also, states with a sales tax may require a separate sales tax ID number. Contact your state's department of commerce and industry for specific information.

Zoning and Other Local Regulations

Find out and be sure to meet the specific regulations that pertain to operating your project studio in your town. For example, you may need to obtain a business license from your local municipality. Also, there may be other regulations that affect your business. For instance, though local zoning lets me operate a home-based business, it forbids having clients regularly visiting the home for business purposes. Therefore, I either visit client offices or conduct business via telephone and modem, so this strict regulation has not been an issue for me. If you are constantly recording clients at your home, you would not meet the regulations in my town. Go to your local clerk's office, and ask them what you need to do to legally start a business from your home.

Protect Your Assets

As a functioning business, you need to protect your investment. The equipment filling your room is an obvious asset. The other most important asset is you personally. Since you will do the lion's share of the work, you need to take steps to protect yourself. Buying insurance is the way to protect all your assets. There are several types of insurance that you must have, such as health insurance and property insurance. You may elect to have life insurance, disability insurance, and liability insurance. You should talk with your insurance agent to determine what coverage is right for your particular situation.

Homeowner's or Renter's Policy

You need to be aware that these policies often don't cover equipment used for business. This doesn't affect you if you consider your gear personal property. However, if you are using your gear for business (and hopefully exploiting the tax advantages of this strategy), you need to check with your insurance carrier. Your project studio might not be covered or the amount may be far too low. You may need a rider to your personal policy or even a separate policy altogether. Also, if you have people visiting your studio, you may also need to consider liability insurance to cover accidents. The same rule applies: If the people are there for business reasons, make sure your policy covers it. Go visit your insurance agent in person, and explain your situation fully and accurately.

Write down an inventory of all your gear, including name, model number, serial number, original purchase price, and purchase date. Don't forget all the software on your computer, too. Keep this off-site, and also give a copy to your insurance agent to keep with your file. This is the evidence you would need in the event of a loss. For certain items, you may want to have regular appraisals. For example, you have a vintage Fairchild compressor that you can't replace. Have the item appraised periodically, and file the appraisal with your insurance agent. This way, you get the right dollar amount should you suffer a loss. Take photographs of your gear, and attach the specifics about each piece to the photo. Keep a set for yourself, and file one set with your insurance agent. Alternatively, videotape all your gear. This need be nothing fancy. Just run around your project studio with a camcorder. and focus on every piece of gear for a few seconds. Describe what you are seeing. and give an indication of what you paid for it and when. Store this videotape off-site. Put it in a safety deposit box at a bank or in a fireproof safe at a friend's or relative's house.

Health Insurance

Do you have health insurance? "Sadly, no" was the refrain expressed by the clear majority of self-employed project studio owners. This is a problem. Health insurance protects your main asset: YOU! Though you should work hard to protect your health by living a healthy lifestyle, without health insurance, you put your other savings at risk. It is also one of the largest expenses incurred by small business owners and, therefore, the most disregarded. Health insurance should be part of your project studio overhead. The health insurance premiums that you pay are fully deductible business expenses for corporations and prorated for the self-employed. A comprehensive policy, called major medical, usually covers most medical and hospital bills. If you can't afford its higher premiums, choose a basic health care policy to cover emergencies and hospitalization, including surgery (often called a catastrophic policy). With basic coverage, you are prepared for major incidents, but are forced to pay for everyday health needs (sickness, well care, etc.). The savings over a full policy can far outweigh the downside. Alternatively, you can try to join a group policy to save on medical insurance costs. Look to trade associations, musician's or other unions, and other such avenues for possible group insurance rates. Also, you may be fortunate to join the policy of a working spouse. Finally, some countries provide universal health coverage for its citizens, such as our Canadian neighbors.

The key elements of health insurance policies are premium, deductible, percentage paid, out-of-pocket totals, and exclusions. The premium is the amount you pay for certain coverage. The deductible is the money you pay before the insurance kicks in. The higher your deductible, the lower your premium. The percentage paid is what your insurance carrier pays after you meet the deductible, usually 80 percent. You pay the remaining 20 percent of your incurred medical costs. The total out-of-pocket is the maximum amount you pay in any given year. All covered medical costs beyond this dollar figure will be paid 100 percent by the insurance carrier. Exclusions are procedures not covered by the policy—maternity coverage usually costs more, for example.

- To find the right coverage you need at a price you can afford, check out *www.ehealthinsurance.com,* where you can compare policies easily and with no obligation.

After reading the results of the project studio survey, Frank Wyatt wrote, "I was made aware of the health insurance problem via this survey and realize that this is a great problem not only for us, but for many Americans. I have found that by taking courses in media technology at a local community college that I am able to get a reasonable health insurance coverage, as long as I take at least six credit hours per quarter. This is a great benefit for those of us in this industry who need to stay on top of the technology. We gain the state-of-the-art knowledge and can get a reduced rate on medical coverage simply by being part of the college system."

Liability, Disability, and Life Insurance

Umbrella liability insurance protects you in the event you are sued. You can buy a specific dollar amount to protect you in such a situation. Disability insurance provides a portion of your lost income if you are disabled long-term or permanently. While Social Security also pays for permanent disabilities, the amount you receive will not come close to your lost wages. Disability policies pay a percentage of your income once you become disabled and after a certain amount of time has elapsed, such as six months (called the elimination period). This insurance is really expensive, but if you lose your capacity to work, how will you support your family? The erroneously named life insurance leaves your beneficiaries a substantial cash settlement upon your demise. The premium you pay is based on the coverage (amount of money) you want. If you have minors who depend on you, then life insurance is another necessity.

Copyright, Trademarks, and Patents

The final assets you need to protect are your intellectual property—what you create in your project studio. Thankfully, copyrights, trademarks, and patents are low-cost methods that ensure you benefit from the long-term use and reuse of your creative properties. Copyrights cover literary, artistic, and musical works. Trademarks are brand names and/or designs that are applied to products or used in connection with services, including business names and logos. Patents protect inventions and improvements to existing inventions.

✖ Copyright

The meaning of the term "copyright" is found in the root of its name. You, as the copyright owner, gain control over copying. You must authorize (and presumably get paid for) reproductions, derivative works, public performances, and sales of copies of the work. With respect to sales of copies, you only get the right of first sale, meaning the initial sale of the item. You have *no rights* to second or subsequent sales—garage sales, auctions, etc. When someone makes a copy of work you created and own the copyright in and sells it as his own, this is copyright infringement at its simplest.

Creative professionals, especially musicians, are perpetually worried that someone, somewhere, will steal their creative work. Contrary to popular misconception, there is no great mystery on how to copyright your original material. *Copyright protection is automatic.* As soon as you affix your material (e.g., music and lyrics) in a tangible medium (write it down, record it, etc.), it is afforded *full* copyright protection. Ideas are not protected, regardless of the form the idea takes. Only the exact way the idea is conveyed, like the words on this page, is given copyright protection. A principle of operation (how something works), such as a copy machine or pharmaceutical drug, is not given copyright protection, but it may be patented. A band name and logo, or the title of a book or motion picture, may not be copyrighted, but can be trademarked.

You do not need to include the copyright symbol, but it is always a good idea to do so. The symbol © and the word "copyright" are interchangeable. The correct format is: © 2001 Jeffrey P. Fisher, or Copyright 2001 Jeffrey P. Fisher. Also, registration of a copyrighted work is not mandatory. No publication, registration, or any other action in the Copyright Office is required to secure copyright. A common misconception is that a work is not copyrighted until it is registered. This is wrong! The work is copyrighted the moment it is fixed in a tangible medium. Another misconception is that by registering the work, you prove authorship. This is also quite misleading. Registration allows the author to "stake a claim" to the work in question. The Copyright Office does not determine the validity of submitted work. The copyright law provides several inducements or advantages to encourage copyright owners to register. Registration establishes a public record of the copyright claim, and registration is ordinarily necessary before any infringement suits may be filed in court.

Get all the information you need from the U.S. Copyright Office at *www.loc.gov/copyright/* or check out this book by Lee Wilson: *The Copyright Guide: A Friendly Guide to Protecting and Profiting from Copyrights, Revised Edition* (Allworth Press, 2000).

✖ Trademark

The U.S. Patent and Trademark Office defines a trademark as "any word, name, symbol, device, or any combination, used, or intended to be used, in commerce to identify and distinguish the goods of one manufacturer or seller from goods manufactured or sold by others. In short, a trademark is a brand name," e.g., Krispy Kreme. The USPTO defines a service mark as "any word, name, symbol, device, or any combination, used, or intended to be used, in commerce, to identify and distinguish the services of one provider from services provided by others." Service marks are often slogans.

Get trademark information at the U.S. Patent and Trademark Office Web site, and use their online search to see if there are any registered, pending, or previously used marks similar to yours before filing a trademark application (*www.uspto.gov/web/menu/tm.html*).

Retirement Planning

One final component to protecting your assets is saving for your retirement. As the survey showed, too many self-employed individuals neglect this area. You may be pulling down a nice income, but if you aren't contributing to you and your family's future, you're not as successful as you should be. You will find additional information on this subject in chapter 13.

Employee Issues

If you have employees, make sure you know and follow all the regulations that pertain to them. If you use independent contractors and pay an individual (nonemployee) over $600 in a year, you need to file a 1099 form with the IRS showing the compensation you paid out. The other person needs to claim the money on their own tax return and pay any taxes due on this money by themselves. Other than reporting the money you paid, you have no further responsibilities.

Basic Money Issues

Being in business requires you to keep track of its financials. You need to set up your bookkeeping system, collect your income, pay your expenses, pay your income taxes, and feed your retirement. First, determine your start-up costs. These expenses would be the initial money you would need to open the doors: gear, furniture, professional services, business forms, deposits, licenses, and so forth. You don't need a huge infusion of cash to begin, unless you are starting entirely from scratch. Chances are, you already have some things in place, and you just need some start-up money to take care of some legal and promotional matters. Also, find out what it is going to cost to run your project studio. Called overhead, these costs might include rent, utilities, promotional expenses, professional dues, taxes, supplies, insurance, loan payments, etc.

Next, start a business checking account. Deposit all your project studio income into that account, and pay all your business-related expenses using checks drawn on that same account. Additionally, use a credit card for business purchases only, and pay it off on time from the business checking account. Also, make sure you understand all the tax consequences and how they affect your project studio business. You have to make regular tax payments along with the usual year-end tax preparation. Meet with your tax advisor or accountant to make sure you handle this issue satisfactorily. The next chapter deals specifically with these issues in greater detail.

Organizing Your Business

While most project studio owners tend to handle all the tasks themselves, as you get more successful and busier, you may want to farm out more and more of the mundane tasks to other professionals. What usually happens for project studio owners is, they begin to lose time to administrative duties (bookkeeping, promotion, client schmoozing, etc.) and have less time for actually working on projects. In this situation, hiring a helper can free up the time necessary to get the real work done. "I have a secretary, some part-time writers and performers, and two salespeople," explained J. Dennis Onopa. "My function as the business owner is accountant, composer, producer, and peacekeeper."

Personally, I find handling these other business matters somewhat therapeutic. After sitting at the computer all day working on tracks, it's refreshing for me to run some errands, clean up the studio, write a few checks, and make a few promotional phone calls. You may decide otherwise. You can hire independent contractors to relieve the strain of your day-to-day activities and provide ancillary services to your studio. You may need a lawyer, accountant, bookkeeper, and so forth to regularly handle certain business tasks. You might also consider a sales rep or similar person to do the promotion and selling of your project studio for you. You certainly may need musicians to play instruments that you currently don't or other artists who provide needed services—voice talent, for example. Follow the advice on building a team in chapter 3.

Hiring a manager or an agent as an adviser is the strategy most employed by project studio owners. An agent takes a percentage of your sales in exchange for helping you land gigs. A good agent has contacts and believes in what you do. Sometimes, agents put together package deals, where one client does the video and the other client (you) does the audio. Having a manager can help you focus on your creative side, leaving the business and promotion to another. It's a good idea, even if that manager is more a part-time helper than a full-fledged agent. Many project studio artists prefer to use an engineer. This way, the artist can concentrate on the creative content, while the engineer worries about getting it down on "tape." This helper can be a partner, an independent contractor whom you hire occasionally, or a full-fledged employee.

Adding People

There can be a certain comfort and safety in numbers. The volume of work you may need to sustain your project studio business may force you to bring in a partner just to handle the load. The key here is to find a partner who complements your skills, not one who duplicates them. If you just want to concentrate on the creative side of your project studio, you might consider adding a partner to handle the business. This person can do the bookkeeping, bill collections, and most of the promotion. This person can be the "heavy" when it comes to slow-paying clients, too. As one half of a successful partnership described their relationship, "He networks and brings in the business, while I stay at the studio to take care of things like writing checks." Having an extra pair of hands, feet, and another car can be most helpful, too. The general gofer can often take care of many mundane tasks, such as running out for supplies, dropping off packages at the post office, backing up files, cleaning, and so forth.

Successful partnerships have this one trait in common: clearly defined roles. If each person knows his or her precise duties, there can be little room for argument. Create some formal contract or agreement. Include all the details of the partnership, such as lines of authority, business purpose, and so forth. One typical mistake is that partners record how they will start the deal, but neglect to include the opt-out information. What if one partner wants out? Give some thought to the partnership dissolution before you sign on. I suggest hiring a lawyer to help draft the partnership agreement.

Because you and your partner will be spending a lot of time together, you must make sure you are compatible. Many have commented that a good partnership is akin to a good marriage. With a 50 percent divorce rate in the marriage corner, it's easy to see why so few partnerships make it either. Make sure you define your goals and that you work toward these goals steadily. There are bound to be problems and conflicts along the way, but focusing on the long term can keep it in perspective for all partners. Meet and review regularly to keep the communication lines open and to make sure that you are not working at cross purposes.

You know your partnership is working when you utilize each partner's talent to the fullest, get more done faster and it's better, trust

219

each other with each other's projects, finish each other's sentences, and when you suffer and celebrate together. Your partnership is not working when you spend more time arguing than doing, are absolutely sick of seeing each other, neither of you has any fresh ideas, and when the business starts suffering. Composer Martin O'Donnell told *Screen* that "the best thing you can do is go golfing together and beat up on the ball. Because if you look at the other partner and all he represents is the drudgery—you're in trouble."

If you add employees to your payroll, create guidelines for them to follow when performing the work you require. Respect them, and trust them. If you don't trust them to do the job you hired them to do, train them! It's that simple. Compliment the positive, and work together toward your common goals. If they make a mistake, let them learn from it. As Tom Peters says, "When managing people, let them run their own little corner of the world as they see fit. And leave them to it. Give them the information they need to make informed decisions. Give them the tools to get their jobs done right. Encourage them to seek constant education and to grow as people and as business professionals. Make your organization a creative, nurturing environment . . . where people can develop and mature."

If you choose independent contractors instead of partners as suggested earlier, you can expand your business and handle additional tasks simply and easily. More importantly, subcontracting some work lets you concentrate on several projects at the same time. You can increase your earnings substantially without facing the problems that often come with partnerships. The real key is to select the right subcontractors and let them work in their own way around your stringent guidelines. And the best part is, if someone messes up, fire him and get another helper. You don't even have to fire him, really, you can just stop giving him your business.

To Union or Not?

The choice to become a member of a union is up to you. The specific benefits of joining the American Federation of Musicians are outlined below. You must understand that once you join the union, there is no going back. You will be prevented from doing nonunion work, and that can affect the projects you work on. You will also be required to hire only union help. That usually translates into higher costs for your production services, which can mean your price is too high compared to the nonunion shop down the street.

What does the AFM have to offer? According to its literature:

- Pension. The money collected for the pension plan comes out of the employer's pocket, not the musician's (yours!).
- Insurance. You can choose the group plan and usually get a better rate for you and your family than trying to set up a plan on your own.
- Auditions. You'll get regular notices of possible gigs and how to apply for them.
- Referral service. The union keeps lists of all "available" members.
- Wage scales. Union musicians are paid specific fees for specific work.
- Contracts. There are specific contracts approved by the union for musicians to use.
- Working conditions. The union sets limits to working conditions for its members.
- Negotiations and adjudication. The union is there to negotiate wage scales and to act on behalf of its members.
- Career assistance, seminars, and other information. The union provides many services to its members to help them better manage their professional career.
- Rehearsal space. Many local unions have places that members can use to rehearse.
- Regular meetings. Members can network with their peers and keep up with the latest news and information affecting the professional musician.
- Death benefit. 'Nuff said.
- *www.afm.org*

Telephone

Get a separate business line with voice mail that answers when you are on the line. Get another line for modem connections (or get a cable modem, DSL, or whatever gets invented after I write this book) if you plan to use the Internet significantly. It can be helpful to have a cell phone, too. My graphic designer wears an earpiece/microphone head-set connected to a portable clipped to her belt. Whether she's at her desk or taking care of domestic duties, the phone is just a button push away. This configuration gives her lots of freedom without worrying about missing calls. It also lets her talk hands-free, so she can continue working. Consider a wireless phone if you'll be away from your desk significantly. This is probably the best bet for a part-time venture. You can have your "business phone" with you wherever you go. Use the wireless as your only business line, and take it everywhere. If your project studio is part-time, you can even have the phone at your day job to field calls. Your clients may never know you only work part-time, because you'll always take their calls.

Office Forms and Automation

You don't need a bunch of business forms for your project studio. Just get a nice stationery set, comprising letterhead and matching envelopes. Use this for all your communications, including promotions, contracts, invoices, and so forth. A computer running certain business software can really make managing your project studio routine easier. You need software that helps you do your work (virtual studio, MIDI, etc.), keeps track of prospects and clients (mailing list), reminds you of appointments (scheduling or calendar), records your business income and expenses (bookkeeping), and organizes and files correspondence and ideas (word processor).

Stay Organized

When you follow the advice in these pages, you will get busy. That is as it should be, but doesn't come without its own set of problems. You need to keep on top of matters. You need a good system for managing your business. It makes life so much easier. Spending time each week to manage your business affairs will save time in the long run. Keep good records, copious notes, and learn to file well. I prefer storing *everything* on my computer. This reduces paperwork immensely, and I can search and find pertinent information quickly.

Keep meticulous records of all your conversations with prospects and clients in files on your computer. Preface these pieces with keywords to make searching for notes easier, such as *XYZ on-hold ideas, Al's Software CD notes*, etc. You might consider your note-taking as a sort of journal. Use this as a record of your business (and personal) life. Your journal can help you keep track of stuff (conversations, ideas, etc.), vent your anger or frustration, cheer you up, help you make decisions, open your eyes and feed your creativity, and appreciate and celebrate what you possess and have accomplished.

Watch out for procrastination. It's far too easy to put off important tasks. Manage your time wisely, too. Use delivery services and messengers to save time. Ignore the phone and modem so you can concentrate better, and avoid time-wasting long lunches. Tell your family and friends not to interrupt you. To be fair, provide a specific, future time that they can visit or talk with you. Create "to do" lists, and prioritize your urgent needs. Use and reuse when you can: develop generic phrases and letters, and use them when contacting clients and prospects. Set up templates for your MIDI and audio gear, too.

Make your paper handling quick and efficient. A shredder is a terrific piece of office equipment. Get one! Mail time is break time for me. Usually, after I've been at it for several hours, I take a break and deal with the mail and telephone calls. I go through the mail fast. All the junk mail, especially credit card applications, go right in the shredder, envelope and all. I deal with important matters right away. I file bills (after recording them in my accounts payable) for payment. I get checks ready for deposit. If there is mail to go, I get that together, then make one errand trip to bank, post office, and wherever.

Check e-mail at least three times each day. I usually answer them all immediately. That's why I use a lot of generic copy, as mentioned above, to answer the usual onslaught of music business questions filling my inbox. My phone is twelve inches from my left hand, so I often surprise people by getting them before the first ring finishes. If you're busy, let the voice mail get it. Always return calls promptly on the same day. If you can't return the call, send an e-mail or fax to say you received the call and will try to connect the next day.

Manage Your Stress

This creative work can consume you. Keeping your life as uncomplicated as possible goes a long way toward reducing this stress. You need frequent breaks sprinkled throughout your work days, and you also need longer stretches, such as a long weekend, mini-vacation, and full-fledged vacation(s). With the ups and downs of business, you can be afraid to turn down any work for any reason or take time off in fear you'll miss a gig. Some people suggest always taking the same time off every year, such as the last two weeks of the year or the last two weeks of July, and let all your best clients know that this is written in stone. Don't go back on your word. Let that time be sacred. You need and deserve it.

Music and reading are terrific refreshers for me, as is simply not doing anything for part of a day. Also, you can pursue a separate hobby as a way to recharge your mind, body, and spirit. Get out and exercise, soak in a hot tub, and/or snuggle with your significant other. According to author Laurence Boldt, you need "time to be (idle, play, experience), time to learn, think, and plan, time for creative expression, and time to relate (with other people)."

Work Well

Do your best work all the time, and maintain consistent quality. Always give more than expected. Also, give little extras to your best clients. Provide added value to every client, such a free hour of setup time when somebody books a full day at your studio. Be readily available to your best clients. Strive to be polite and personable. Remember clients are people first—treat them well. Follow up and follow through. Be neat, organized, and efficient. Try to always beat the deadlines. Correct problems fast, and make no excuses. Keep your feet on the ground, and make sure your head stays actual size. Have fun!

(12)
Pricing for Profit

I f *you want to run a profitable project studio,* you must possess a keen understanding of how the project studio business works today. Don't sell time at your project studio. Let me repeat that: *don't sell time at your project studio.* No matter what music and sound production products and services you sell, what you ultimately sell is your talent. You sell yourself and your ability to solve problems and meet the needs of other people. By carefully packaging your services, you have greater earning potential. In this new paradigm, your project studio functions as nothing more than the tool you need to get the job done right. You will charge your clients for your creative services only. The room and its gear are essentially free. You may feel that's crazy; nevertheless, that is how you must approach your project studio to really make it successful. When you begin to see yourself as a music and sound consultant rather than a room full of gear, you will realize the full impact of what I'm advising. You will command much higher rates than you could possibly charge for the room itself.

Your project studio doesn't need to be filled 24-7-365 to make money. A part-time venture, where you work and bill out only a few hours or days each month, still puts extra cash in your pocket. The key to pricing effectively is to know your real overhead—what it costs to be in business. Knowing this shows you what you have to generate each month, week, and day to meet your overhead and leave you with some profit.

When you know your general overhead, along with the costs of any products you sell, you are in a better position financially. With exact costs in hand, you can quote bids and offer deals that help you secure more work. Wouldn't you rather make 70 percent of something than 100 percent of nothing? For example, I invariably get calls about one of my books. After listening and answering questions, I'll often explain how my other books can help this person, too. Near the end of the conversation, I usually make an offer that gives the caller a significant discount if they order multiple products. Because I know what the products cost me, I can easily make an offer that's hard to resist. This way, the customer orders more (spends more money) with me than they would have otherwise.

When you know your expenses, you can turn your attention to profit. How do you define your profit? Is it the gross dollars you bring in before expenses or the net after paying your bills? Part-timers may prefer to measure the hours they worked and compare that to the dollars brought in. With the money you earn, you can either pay yourself a regular salary or keep whatever is left over after you pay all your business expenses.

Charge for Your Time

Don't sell studio time. Why? People try to buy the cheapest studio time they can find, but are willing to pay more for professional experience. Your music and sound production skills, coupled to your mastery of equipment, is a far more potent combination than your gear list alone. Too many people sell studio time and throw in their services for free. I'm suggesting you *take the opposite approach* and sell your professional expertise as a service and throw in the studio time for free. For example, you decide to do demo work and charge bands $25 an hour to record at your studio. This fee has to pay for your time and all the equipment. I'd suggest charging at least double that amount by acting as producer and engineer for their recordings, and give them the studio time free (a $25/hour value). In essence, you make more money than just selling studio time on its own.

You are a music and sound professional with his or her own tools. Therefore, transform your image and promotional approach to become a music and sound *consultant* people hire to solve their problems. One survey respondent said it best when asked about this issue: "It depends on how many of my skills are needed for a project. If I have to arrange, perform some or all of the parts, sing, and be the engineer, I will charge more than if I'm only engineering. I have no basic rates, but I will base my quote on the fact that I need to get $500 to $700 per nine-hour day. I bill usually per project, but if I feel I have a picky or indecisive client, I'll charge hourly."

Some project studio owners charge by the hour, while others charge by the project. You will be better off if you don't sell by the hour. Instead, bid by the project. J. Dennis Onopa charges "according to the project as a package, not by the hour. I do not rent time in my facility. It is for my company's use only."

"One of the things that sells people is that instead of selling time by the hour, I bid on the project, and then we take as much time as needed to get done," said David Conley. "This helps the clients, because they know I am committed to the quality of the project, and they aren't worrying about looking at the clock every ten minutes or so. I *do* have a price list, but frequently deviate from it. It's all in my computer, so when I bid, they can see what they would have paid, and then they see what I will charge them. They feel like they are special and getting a deal."

As a member of both SAG and AFTRA, Harlan Hogan's voice talent rates are determined by the union, based on the type of work. To that end, he doesn't charge for basic work in his project studio. His studio is essentially free. He does charge for materials and for editing time if the project goes beyond just basic, raw narration. And if the project needs the help of a commercial facility, he passes those costs on, too.

Determine Your Fees

Ask yourself first what you want to earn from your project studio work. One way is to compare yourself to a full-time position doing similar work. For example, you want to make $50,000 a year. You need to add in your business overhead (the costs of running your project studio) and the costs of benefits, such as health care. Let's say that adds 30 percent to your salary needs (if you know your actual expenses, use that figure instead). Your income goal must now be $65,000. About two thousand hours are available in a typical work year. You must deduct time spent promoting and administering your business, time lost to vacation, holidays, and sickness, and time when you are ready to work, but have no work to do. Let's say you can only bill about a thousand hours a year. So, if you want to earn $65,000, you need to make about $65 an hour, or a daily rate of $520. Check out the salary survey results at the end of this chapter for an idea of what your peers are charging for their project studio work.

Now, if you only have a Roland VS-series recorder and a Shure SM57 on a card table in the corner of your bedroom, you will not be charging

$500 a day for your project studio—unless you are really good (Bob Clear-mountain, Ed Cherney, Geoff Emerick good!). You'll probably be charging somewhat less for band and songwriter demos, maybe closer to that fee for radio spots, on-hold, etc. However, don't consider your track record the main factor when pricing your services. You obviously have the skills, desire, and enthusiasm, and so deserve to be paid fairly for your project studio creative services. It doesn't always pay to be the cheapest in town. That can get you in the door, but it can backfire on you, too. Ask around, and see what others are charging, then position yourself slightly lower than the average rate. Plus, rates often don't matter. Clients have budgets—very specific budgets—and it's up to you to decide if you can do what they need for the money they are prepared to pay. Let me add this canny wisdom: Decide on a price using my basic formula, and try it out on a few clients. Next, keep pushing your fees higher and higher with each subsequent project, until somebody really complains. Now, you've arrived at the top dollar your market will bear. You should also increase fees as your experience or success accumulates. And always remember to sell the value of what you offer, and not its cost to your clients.

When quoting projects, provide a fee estimate with a range (e.g., $2,500 to $3,250). Don't exceed these estimates. Make sure you understand the project's specs before giving your quote. Build in a margin of error and a contingency, in case too many changes are requested or the scope of the project changes entirely. You should build in enough leeway should you underestimate your costs or time. If you've never done a project before, add in a 40 percent margin of error, 20 percent if you know the client or the project better. If your client changes the specs of a project, make sure you update the fee estimate before proceeding any further. As with all major projects, you should get a formal agreement up front in the form of a letter of agreement, contract, or even a client purchase order. Also, if you publish a formal rate card, deviate only slightly from it. Offer no more than a 15 to 20 percent discount. If you subtract too much from your rates, you'll appear to have a rate card that gouges instead of informs.

Mark Up Other Costs

You should charge back your clients for the costs you incur on their behalf when helping them with their projects, such as when you hire independent contractors, purchase supplies, and so forth. Make sure that you mark up these costs somewhat. Also, make money by marking up the products and other amenities that you sell. David Conley adds that "expenses are frequently the responsibility of the clients. I'm candid about that. If I have to hire a musician or rent some equipment, I tell people in the bid what I may need and that these expense will be tacked onto my fee."

For a product that you manufacture yourself, mark it up about seven to eight times its cost. Since most products are sold to wholesalers and retailers at discounts of 50 percent or more, you must make your profit based on the discounted price. For example, a CD costs $2.00 to duplicate and package. Its retail price is $15.95, $8.00 wholesale. That leaves just $6.00 to pay for all the promotional costs, general overhead, and still leave something for your profit.

For products you purchase yourself at wholesale costs, consider pricing them at 2 to 2.5 times their cost. For example, buy blank CDs at $1.00 each, sell them for $2.50 to your clients. For products you buy at retail prices, add a 10 to 15 percent markup. For services you buy whose cost you will pass on to your clients, mark up the fee you paid by 10 to 20 percent. In other words, if a voice artist or musician charges you $100 to work on a track, charge your client $120 (or more).

One of my clients needed my work in a particular software format. He asked me to buy the software and bill him back for it. Though this was a client demand for specific gear, they paid for my upgrade. I was out no money whatsoever. This can often happen in both purchase and rental situations.

Minimum Fee

You might want to consider having a minimum fee for the projects you do take on. This is especially true for those who charge hourly. It often isn't worth the effort to turn on the gear for a thirty-minute session. If you decide to bill clients at an hourly rate, beware of its trap. Quick-and-easy projects don't pay very well. For example, I once spent a whopping ten minutes altering an existing music track for a new client. I slowed the tempo, used a different sound palette, deleted a lead instrument, remixed the track with some different effects and balance settings, and presto: a "new" music track. How could I bill for only that ten minutes of work? More importantly, how can I make any real money should I bill that little? Well friends, it took my entire life to get to this point where

I *could* significantly alter a music track in just six hundred seconds. Since you can't bill clients for all that time spent honing your craft, you need to make up for it now. Whether you bill hourly rates or by the project, make sure you have a minimum fee. Shoot for at least a two-hour minimum or a half-day's work (four times your hourly rate). And don't make the mistake of telling your client it only took you a few minutes to deliver his content. Some secrets we must all protect. An exception to this rule would be for a good client who just has a simple demand, such as to burn a quick CD of a rough mix. Go ahead and do that, and don't charge for it. Make sure the client knows you did it gratis, too.

Recording Packages

If you decide to record music productions for others, consider offering and promoting recording packages. Offer studio time, mixing, mastering, and duplication for one fee, such as sixteen hours recording time, four hours mixing, one hour mastering session, one CD-R master, and 100 bulk copies. Your client pays one price for the complete package. Alternatively, you could provide some services at a low rate and make up the difference in other areas: low-price recording, but high-price duplication. The low rate initially attracts many people, but they must pay a premium to finish the recording.

Dealing with the Cut Rate Service

If you do some basic research, you will know what to charge. There will always be somebody who is willing to undercut your price, though. If you want to be a little cheaper than the going rate, 85 to 90 percent is the best tactic. Instead, consider adding value to your services. Provide a little more to your clients that can substantiate your higher fee. If you can play on their sessions, that can be something you can provide as part of the room, for example.

Also, the way you present your fee can have an impact. Offer a package deal, not the hourly rate. This way, the client doesn't have to worry about the bill running up. There is no worse impediment to creativity than watching the clock. Each tick of the second hand is money down the drain. It's like the taxi ride from hell, where you watch the dollars tick by and still you're stuck in traffic, miles from your destination. If you are professional, chances are, you can get the job done faster, which usually translates to cheaper for the client.

Get Paid

There are several approaches when invoicing your clients. You can either bill on delivery or you can invoice (monthly, by the project, etc.) with terms or a payment plan. Billing upon delivery is ideal when you perform a single service—studio time, for example. You want to be paid at the end of the session (or don't release the tapes/files/CDs). However, you can offer some credit terms to your best clients. This lets the client pay you in the time frame offered by you, usually net 30 (total due in thirty days). I prefer to bill net 10 or 15, because shaving a few days off really helps the cash flow. If you choose to bill by the project, set one fee for the work performed. If the project is substantially complex and will take a significant amount of time, you may want to create a series of progress payments. The simplest payment schedule in this example would be half up front and half on delivery. It is good business to get these advances from new clients. This gives you some leverage should the client decide not to continue. Plus, this payment usually helps weed out the serious people from those who might try to take advantage of you.

Another way to bill is to create a retainer contract. Basically, you agree to perform a certain amount of work during a given time period for an agreed-upon sum. You usually agree to give the client first priority when he needs you, and he agrees not to bank hours (use them or lose them). For example, you might sell a half day each month on retainer. The client pays your fee, and you agree to provide the four hours when needed and in any way they are required. Any hours beyond that time would be billed and paid as usual. Keep your options open, and look at each gig on its own merits before deciding which billing method is most advantageous to you.

Contracts and Talent Releases

What kind of contract should you use when selling your project studio services? Keep it simple by recording your agreement with your client as a formal letter. Print this on your letterhead, and include these essential parts: At the top of the page, place the date of the contract, your client's name and address, and the name of the project. Next, list the services you will provide for the project and any specifications required. Indicate the date the agreement begins and the due date, when you will deliver the services you listed above. Next, indicate the total fee for the project and any payment terms (e.g., half up front, remainder on delivery). Also, indicate how additional expenses are to be reimbursed. Make sure to include a grant-of-rights section that clearly defines who owns the copyright to the work you do (you retain all rights, license some rights, or work for hire). Leave room for both your signatures, make two copies of the agreement, and sign them both. Ask your client to sign both copies, keep one, and return the other copy to you with a check for the amount of the advance (if any). You can easily develop standard contracts for your most common services. If you prepare this contract carefully, following a simple question-and-answer format, it can also function as the promotional document at the same time. Show any contracts you plan to use to your lawyer first for approval. If the project is too small to warrant a contract such as this, ask for a purchase order from your client instead.

When contracting musicians or other talent, it is a good idea to get a signed talent release from them. Print this sample talent release on your company letterhead, fill in the blanks, have the person sign and date the release, and exchange the release with their paycheck. Here's an example:

AUTHORIZATION OF RELEASE

For value received in the sum of $ (indicate amount), I, (insert their name here), the undersigned, give and grant (your company name here), its affiliates, successors, and assigns the unqualified right, privilege, and permission to reproduce in every manner or form, publish and circulate video, audio, or films of recordings of my (indicate voice, musical contribution, etc.) arising from the production titled (insert title here), and I hereby grant, assign, and transfer all my rights and interest therein. I specifically authorize and empower (your company name here) to cause any such video, film, or audio recordings of my (indicate voice, musical contribution, etc.) to be copyrighted or in any other manner to be legally registered in the name of (copyright holder name here). My contribution to this work shall be considered a work made for hire, and as such, I, my heirs, executors, administrators, and assigns, hereby remise, release, and discharge (your company name here) for and from any and all claims of any kind whatsoever on account of the use of such recordings, including, but not limited to, any and all claims for damages for libel, slander, and invasion of the right of privacy. I am of lawful age and sound mind, and have read and understand this Authorization of Release. Signed this first day of June 2001.

———————————————

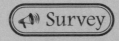

Where does your income come from and in what percentages (project studio, product sales, job, royalties, other)?

♪ Mostly production, then composition and orchestration.

♪ 100 percent from product sales.

♪ From my full-time job. I can't realistically count on the studio at this point.

♪ About 75 percent album/demo work, 25 percent radio production.

♪ 80 percent (full-time) job, 20 percent studio time.

♪ 60 percent studio, 25 percent sales (duplication), 25 percent miscellaneous and producer fees.

♪ 75 percent (full-time) day job, 20 percent custom music composition, 5 percent performance.

♪ Band performances 50 percent, studio 40 percent, royalties 10 percent.

Do you have a formal pricing structure? What are your basic rates for your project studio? (Be specific.) How do you bill (hourly, project, royalties, other)?

♪ Around $20 to $25 per hour, usually hourly, sometimes per day; sometimes per project.

♩ $45 an hour for production of any kind or recording, $50 for consultation, $3,999 a recorded minute for compositional buyout. Billed mostly by the project.

♩ The deals I sign with artists vary between 50/50 split to $1.50 per CD for the artist. Every deal is different.

♩ $399 per finished minute of instrumental music. The longer the production, the lower the rate. For theatrical productions, depending on the number of cues, usually around $600 to $1500 per production. By the project.

♪ $25 per hour or our $300 block rate. Hourly.

♪ $40 per hour, down to $25 if purchasing a forty-hour block within one week. Hourly.

♪ $35 per hour for bands, $75 for corporate, $500 per finished minute for video and multimedia. Billed mostly hourly.

♪ I'm experimenting and learning as I go. But right now, I'm getting $289 per minute for one-time rights agreements, and $578 per minute for buyout music. Billed by the project.

♪ Lessons $20 a half an hour. For studio work, it varies: $30 an hour.

♪ My studio hourly rate is currently $70 per hour.

♪ Around $50 per hour. Mainly hourly, but some projects have a flat fee.

♪ $30 per hour, plus media for archiving, Web site sound design will vary per site, probably a minimum of $395 per site.

♪ Basically $20 per hour, but I am flexible and willing to work within people's budgets.

♪ $15 to $30 per hour for college students.

♪ Engineers usually charge $30 to $75 per hour for low-budget demo recordings and $75 to $125 for larger budgets. They usually require a three-hour minimum, though a daily rate is probably more likely.

♪ Nonunion musicians typically charge $50 to $75 per hour for buyout, while nonunion voice artists charge $65 to $125 per hour for a buyout. These require a one-hour minimum, which means, if the session only takes ten minutes (something that often happens), you still pay for the whole hour. The union rates are somewhat higher, depending on the use and time involved.

♩ For music composers, local jingles run between $2,500 and $5,000, while national jingles can be between the $5,000 to $50,000 range, usually as a package deal. Game music and sound design falls in the $5,000 to $25,000 range, again as a package. TV scoring is usually between $7,500 and $25,000+, always as a package deal, while film scores can start at $25,000 and move upwards of $250,000. Independent films and videos fall between $5,000 and $50,000 as a package. Note that music played on TV earns performance royalties, which can be quite substantial for multiple reruns on a major network. Music playing in theaters does not earn performance royalties in the United States (until the film plays on TV). Library music single CDs range from $59 to $199, always as a buyout.

♪ On-hold message tape (six minutes) charge: $325.

♪ Music for two thirty-second cable spots = $1,000.

♩ Piano lessons: $40 an hour, or $25 a half-hour. "There are lots of parents willing to pay for their kids to study piano, and I keep them interested. I found that the number of my students *doubled* once I raised my rates from $30 to $40 an hour."

♪ Video game: 2 percent of net profits from the game.

♩ This last rate clearly illustrates why you need to get serious about earning real money from your project studio. A band in New York City received $1 per head at the front door of a club that specifically mentioned their name, $2 per head above twenty or twenty-five people. Last two shows were thirty-one people ($70) and sixteen people ($16). They split that between four members. Ouch! Of course, I once made $15 one night for three forty-five-minute sets. It was a solo gig, so I kept the whole $15. However, I did buy two soft drinks ($2) and a new set of strings for my acoustic guitar ($5), so my net was far lower!

13

Make the Most of Your Project Studio Profits

S*tudy this chapter carefully,* and commit right now to taking charge of your financial situation with the ultimate goal of becoming financially self-sufficient. You need to make the most money you can from your project studio endeavors. Work hard to keep more of that money by controlling your personal and business expenses and living within your means. Reduce your personal and business taxes using every legal means available. Manage your finances effectively. Get rid of debt, because it interferes with your creative endeavors. And finally, make the most of your money by investing your resources for growth and future income.

There are only two forms of income: passive and active. Active income is the money you make actively pursuing your project studio business: You sell a TV score and get paid. Passive income is the money you make through your investments (bank CD, bond, mutual fund, stock, etc.). Aside from their initial purchase, you do very little to maintain them. Interest gets credited to your account, a stock pays a dividend, your fund goes up 20 percent, and so forth. The important thing to recognize right now is that a certain portion of your active income *must* be used to build your passive income. It is this passive income that ultimately becomes the key to your financial independence.

Let's say your humble little project studio lets you earn $50 a month, $600 a year. You would need $10,000 in the bank earning 6 percent interest to make the same six hundred bucks in a year. Of course, it can be hard to save $10,000. If your project studio business nets you just $100 a month and you sweep that into an investment paying 6 percent a year, you will have your $10,000 in 6.8 years. You will have accumulated a capital base that pays a $600 dividend each year—$50 a month without further intervention on your part. Add that to the $100 your project studio earns actively, and in less than seven years, your small business and investments provide you an income of $150 each and every month—$100 you earn by actively pursuing your business and the other $50 you earn passively from your investments. I know what you are thinking: "Jeffrey, nobody is going to get rich on $150 a month!"

You are correct, but you are missing the crucial point. *It is this combination of earning, saving, and investing that creates a moneymaking machine for you.* Take the same strategy from above and multiply the figures by ten. Can you use your project studio to make and save an extra $1,000 a month? In the same 6.8 years, you will have $100,000 paying you a whopping $6,000 a year in interest. That's $500 a month without touching the original hundred grand. (Note: this is a simplified example that doesn't include the tax impact of your savings or interest or whether you can consistently earn a 6 percent return—you may do better or worse.)

If you could earn enough money passively to cover your basic living expenses, wouldn't a whole new world open up to you? You'd be financially independent, because you wouldn't have to work to pay for your lifestyle. Accumulating the substantial savings needed to generate such income can take a long time, often your entire adult life. What is important to recognize are the various stages of financial independence that you can reach along the way. Going back to that first example, let's say the $600 yearly income generated by your savings and investing is one-third of your total monthly expenses. You could honestly say that you are 1/36th of the way toward financial independence! These kinds of milestones can make the journey to real financial independence somewhat more palatable and rewarding.

Maximize Your Income

Your project studio can help you earn a substantial income—especially when you diligently follow the advice in this book. As you already know from reading this far, you must focus on several profitable ventures that let you earn the most income you can. Using your time wisely and choosing better-paying projects are proven methods for elevating your earnings. Promoting regularly both to past buyers and new prospects also ensures a steady flow of cash into your business.

The most obvious way to earn more is to get more clients. There are two issues you must consider: promoting hard-to-land new clients and offering additional products and services that let you attract new and different clients. Also, make sure you work to find the right clients. You can make some dough recording demos and such for $25 an hour, or you can promote the hard-to-land big corporate clients who will pay you over $500 for a half-day's work. You can compose and record local jingles for $2,000 or work hard to get the national gig that pays ten times that amount.

Get more business from existing clients. Again, promoting and expanding your products and services are key elements here. Recently, I needed an infusion of cash to cover some upcoming expenditures (namely, tax payments and retirement plan contributions). Rather than worry about it, I got on the phone and went to work finding sources for the money. First, I called some past clients and proposed new projects to them. Next, I asked for a short extension on a bill owed a vendor (this helped the cash flow temporarily). Then, I sent a simple promotion to some warm prospects, making deals I knew they couldn't refuse. Finally, I redoubled my efforts to complete my *Melomania* royalty-free, buyout music library, so that initial sales of this new product would provide extra capital. So, with a little hard work, a few creative strategies, and some perseverance, I was quickly able to get the funds I needed before the deadlines. Remember this advice: Always keep looking for new business, and make sure you build strong relationships with existing clients. If you get in a pinch, you can execute a program that instantly brings in the cash you need to keep going.

The fees you charge are directly related to your experience. As you become more successful and acquire skills that let you offer more to your clients, the fees you command should rise accordingly. When you figure fee increases, first look at your years of experience and the value you bring to many of your main, anchor clients. Even being more expensive, you may be cheaper to them in the long run, because you already know your client's business and what they expect. You will deliver what they need faster and of higher quality with fewer misses.

Minimize Expenses

How much do you spend to support your current lifestyle? If you don't know this number, there is no way to know what your current or future income requirements are or will be. Without a clear picture of today's situation, you can never hope to establish goals and work to fulfill them. If you manage to earn a substantial salary from your project studio, you'll never be truly successful if you squander every penny you make. If you earn a million dollars a year, but spend $999,999 of it, you are *not* a millionaire. You must control both your business and personal expenses to generate the savings or capital base you need to ensure your financial independence.

You need two expense statements: one that shows your typical business expenses and another that shows your personal expenses. The business is easy. If you follow the advice later in this chapter and keep accurate records (which you need for tax purposes anyway), you will always have a clear picture of your business expenses. Once in a while, there will be some aberrations (new, major equipment purchases come to mind), but the regular expenses should even out over time!

For the business, take a long, hard look at your purchases and typical fixed expenses. Can you see ways to trim the fat? Cutting business expenses is a double-edged sword. You want to reduce your tax burden through prudent business expenditures, but on the other side, you don't want to waste money either. Look for obvious places to trim and eliminate, such as rent, telephone charges, gear habits, and so forth. Don't cut your promotional expenses too much, unless they are costing you too much money and generating very little return.

Personal expenses, because so little of them really affect your taxes, are often much harder to discover. You should know your mortgage or rent, car payment, and utilities right off the top of your head. It's the fast food, trendy clothing, entertainment, and other money dribbles and drabbles that you need to diligently track down and record. First, see if some of your personal expenses can be converted to business expenses. For instance, your industry magazine subscription might be a legitimate business tax deduction for you. Second, turn your attention to your typical monthly expenses. These include: housing (mortgage or rent), transportation (car loan or lease), food, clothing, personal care, entertainment and recreation, medical, car maintenance and gasoline, electric, heating and cooking gas, oil, water and sewer, telephone, maintenance, health insurance, car insurance, and property insurance. Some expenses may not occur monthly (insurance premiums, for instance), so you need to do the division to arrive at a suitable monthly number. As you gather all these figures, look for ways to both eliminate frivolous spending and reduce regular bills.

Save More

As you continue to expand your income and correspondingly control your expenses, you will begin to accumulate extra cash—your savings. It is these savings that you will invest for growth and to support your lifestyle in the future.

Keep Good Financial Records

Basic bookkeeping is crucial because it provides useful insight into how your business is doing. How can you possibly make informed, educated, and proactive decisions about pricing and purchasing if you don't know your true financial position? These records help you easily spot your growth from quarter to quarter and year to year. You'll notice seasonal patterns and trends. Is it always slow December to February? It's either a great time for a vacation or you need to promote harder in November to keep your project studio busy during the winter. You'll know your overhead, those pesky fixed expenses that come due whether you work or not. Best of all, you see which products and services are making money and which ones are *not*.

You need to keep track of the money flowing both into and out of your project studio business for several reasons. First, to make sure you are collecting the money due to you. Second, to make sure you are paying your bills. Third, to make sure you are actually making a profit. And fourth, to keep track of your money situation for tax purposes. Business income is money for your pocket. Business expenses also put money in your pocket, because they reduce your business income, and therefore the money you pay in taxes. If you miss a legitimate business deduction, you throw money away. And though it can be boring to keep track of all this detail, it is for your own best interests.

There are two types of accounting: cash and accrual. In the cash system, each transaction, income or expense, is recorded the minute it is received or incurred. If you get paid for a session, you record it in Accounts Receivable. If you purchase a business item, you record that in your Accounts Payable. If you invoice a client with credit terms (where they pay you in the future), you wouldn't record the transaction until the money is actually received. This fact of the cash system can work in your favor at year end (discussed later in this chapter). The accrual system is more complicated and was designed with built-in checks and balances required by larger companies. Choose the cash system, as it is the easiest, most efficient method for handling your bookkeeping.

You need specific evidence to back up your business income and the expense claims you make to the IRS. That means you must keep accurate records. It also implies you must keep those pesky receipts. According to the IRS, you don't need the receipt on business expenses below $20, provided you document the expense in some other way. However, you may discover that the vast majority of your project studio expenses are under $20 anyway. If you have to write all those little purchases down, you may as well keep the receipt, too. Set aside some time each week for keeping your records up-to-date. Use either a multicolumn ledger or a computer program to do your bookkeeping.

Typical Accounts Receivable (A/R)

This is money you earn (income) from a variety of sources (sales, royalties, etc.).

- Studio time and/or production services
- Sound and music consulting services
- Gigs (solo, band, etc.)
- Composing and arranging scores and jingles
- Session playing
- Product sales
- Equipment sales and rentals
- Lessons and teaching
- Royalties
- Writing revenues
- Other income sources specific to your situation

Typical Accounts Payable (A/P)

This is money you spend (expenses) to operate your project studio. The following categories are from the Schedule C tax form, which applies to most project studio owners. These categories work for any business form (corporation, sole proprietor, partnership).

- Advertising (ads, promotional material, Web site hosting)
- Car and truck (business mileage, depreciation, interest, lease payment)
- Commissions, fees (independent contractors)
- Depreciation and section 179 deductions (capital purchases, see below)
- Insurance (business insurance, such as liability, specific riders, but *not* health insurance; corporations can deduct 100 percent of health insurance premiums, while the self-employed can only deduct a percentage [60 percent in 2001, 70 percent in 2002, and 100 percent in 2003] of their premiums on their form 1040, *not* the schedule C)
- Interest mortgage, other (interest on business property and equipment loans)
- Legal and professional (accountants, lawyers)
- Office expense (costs of running your project studio: postage, copies, Internet connection charges, and so forth)
- Rent/lease (business equipment, property, studio time elsewhere)
- Repairs and maintenance
- Supplies (items you buy for the project studio, such as musical supplies, paper, tapes, blank CDs)
- Taxes and licenses (business license)
- Travel
- Meals and entertainment (only 50 percent deductible)
- Utilities (electricity, telephone—see home office deduction below; you can't deduct your personal telephone for the business; get a line specifically for business, and you can deduct its full cost)
- Wages, salaries (paid to employees)
- Other (business education expenses, for example)

The IRS defines a business deduction as any expense you incur that helps you to earn additional income. These expenses must be reasonable and customary for your business. With careful documentation, you can be rather aggressive when it comes to legitimate business deductions. For example, you can't really deduct the clothes you wear to work. However, put your logo on a polo and wear it every day as a "uniform," and you would have a stronger case. Better still, sell the same polo as an add-in product to further demonstrate your willingness to use an expense to produce income. Play guitar? Your strings and ax maintenance would be deductible. Lessons to improve your playing skills, and therefore your marketability, would also be deductible. Buy software for your business computer, and its expense would be deductible, provided you use it for business. An accounting program would qualify, mahjong would not. Buying this book to further your professional education would be another example of a legitimate business deduction. Did you save your receipt?

The real advantage of running your own project studio as a small business is that you can essentially deduct a portion of your current lifestyle by converting personal expenses into legitimate business expenses. If you are not already in business, you may not know that the money you spend on gear, education, books, supplies, and so forth can be deducted against your business income. You can save a bundle on your taxes. Those already in business usually know the distinct advantages, and if you don't, you will when you finish this book. Everything you buy to operate your business and everything you do to make it successful can be expenses that you use to offset your business income.

Now, some people may look at this and say, "If I pretend to be in business, I can write off all my expenses and save a bundle on my taxes." Hold on, Buckaroo! The IRS has a hobby loss rule that says your business must turn a profit three out of every five years. If you don't meet this criterion, your "business" will be considered a hobby, and all your business deductions will be forfeit. If you are just starting out, it may be fine to take a loss. After all, you are building your business from scratch, and that can take time to come to fruition. But beyond that first year, you really need to start showing a reasonable profit. Also, you can't make $50,000 and spend $49,999 every three out of five years without causing suspicion, either.

Day-to-Day Bookkeeping Made Simple

Categorizing both your income and expenses by the A/P and A/R accounts listed above helps you better monitor and control your financials. Keep running totals of all these income and expense accounts to track the profitability of any given venture. If you see that you are spending too much time on activities that produce little financial reward, rethink your approach.

To keep track of your income, assign it to an A/R account that represents the work performed (e.g., production services). Issue an invoice for every session, even if it's COD. Keep one copy, and give the other copy to the client. Make copies of the checks you receive, and staple this check copy to the corresponding invoice copy. File these invoices in date order in a three-ring binder. Record the transaction in your ledger or computer software.

To keep track of expenses, retain the receipt for every item you purchase. Record the A/P account on the top of the receipt (e.g., Supplies). Record the transaction in your ledger or computer software. Make sure you include the account reference there, too. File the receipt in date order in an envelope that corresponds to its account.

Reduce Your Tax Burden

You will pay taxes on the money you make from your project studio. You will owe federal income tax, perhaps state and local taxes, and self-employment tax. This last tax is your share of Social Security and Medicare that all workers pay. As a self-employed business owner, you have to pay both the employee and employer share, which amounts to 15.3 percent of your business income. You do, however, get half the amount you pay as a deduction on your form 1040. Taxes can take a substantial bite out of your profits. Thankfully, there are many ways to reduce them.

The project studio survey clearly showed that although most owners felt they were taking advantage of all the business deductions they were due, very few knew exactly what those deductions really were. You must know what expenses are deductible, otherwise, you won't make prudent decisions for your project studio business. For instance, a purchase may not be deductible for a number of reasons. If you know this in advance, it will most assuredly affect your decision on whether to buy the item or not.

Business expenses work to offset your business income. Therefore, any business purchase you make reduces your taxable income by the same amount. If you are in the 28 percent federal tax bracket, pay 3 percent to your state, and pay the full 15.3 percent self-employment tax, that means a $100 business purchase only costs you $53.70 in after-tax dollars. You reduce the $100 by the 46.3 percent you would pay in taxes if it was all income. I know it's only a paper transaction, but the value is real nonetheless.

Ironically, what actually occurs is, you really *do* start making some decent money—and your expenses go down considerably. Right now, my expenses average just about 26 percent of my income. That means it only costs me 26 cents to earn a dollar. Try as I may to spend more, it gets increasingly difficult to offset my income. Therefore, I must pay more taxes. That, my friend, is the taxman's ultimate revenge. The IRS is happy to help you out along the way with all these expense deductions, because they know that, in the end, they'll get it all back in taxes as your income increases substantially.

Home Office Deduction

The much-touted home office deduction is another positive lure for many project studio owners. In essence, if you use your home for business, you can deduct some of your home-related expenses as a business deduction. It's usually easy to qualify for the home office deduction if you have a legitimate, permanent studio in your home. The IRS is rather strict on this issue, which means you must use an area of your home *exclusively and regularly* for business, and it must be your principal place of business. And though you may occasionally use other rooms of your home, the main part is what the IRS talks about here. If you meet the restrictions for the home office rules, you can deduct your housing costs at the percentage occupied by the home office. For example, if your house is two thousand square feet and your project studio occupies a spare 200 square-foot bedroom, your business use is 10 percent. That means you can deduct 10 percent of your housing costs (rent or mortgage interest, utilities, property taxes, repairs, insurance, and so forth) as a business deduction.

Sounds great, right? For renters, this can be a terrific deduction. However, for homeowners, well, there is a recapture clause that kicks in when you sell your residence. Any profits you make on the home sale will be profits for the business *at the same percentage* as the deductions. Using the example from above, should you make $20,000 on your house sale, you will have to record 10 percent, or $2,000, as business income (subject to self-employment and income taxes). That means you pay about $926 in taxes (28 percent federal rate, 3 percent state tax, 15.3 percent self-employment tax) on your house sale. The IRS figures that since you used the home office as a deduction, you should use your home sale profits as business income as well.

Figure out how much the home office deduction will save you each year. Weigh this against how much profit you expect from the sale of your house. Will you come out ahead? There is another opt-out, too. If you convert your home back to just a home (stop taking the home-office deduction) for at least two years before the sale of your home, you are not subjected to this recapture rule. Also note, you can *still* deduct gear and other business supplies you use exclusively for your project studio business even if you don't take the "space" deduction itself.

Hire the Family

Hire your kids, and pay them up to the standard deduction allowed each year. Your business gets the tax deduction for the wages you pay, and your kids earn some money for themselves. Plus, if they make the same amount or less than their standard deduction, they reduce their taxable income to zero and owe no income taxes. You essentially shift some of your income from your tax bracket into your child's. This must be earned income—wages, not dividends—and you must pay a reasonable wage for the work they perform. You can't employ a two-year old, but eight on up may work out fine. Children can actually earn an additional $2,000 tax-free if they put it in a traditional IRA. This probably won't apply, because young people should use the nondeductible Roth IRA, with its potential for expansive, long-term growth and tax-free withdrawals at retirement.

Car/Truck Expenses

Chances are, you won't use a vehicle just for your project studio business. You'll probably divide its use between business and personal driving. That means you need to keep track of your use in order to deduct the business portion as a business expense. The IRS lets you choose between two ways to deduct your business vehicle use: actual expenses or standard mileage. If you deduct actual expenses, follow the instructions above to record all your automobile expenses. You will also need to determine your business use percentage with a diary (see below), which you'll use when calculating your depreciation.

If you deduct the standard mileage, use a diary to record your business trips (date, mileage, destination, and purpose). The standard rate varies each year; it's currently around $0.32 per mile. On January 1, write down the odometer reading; do the same at year end. The difference between these numbers is the total mileage you drove for the year. Add up the business miles from your diary, and subtract that from the total miles. This shows you the percentage of business versus personal use of your vehicle. If you incur tolls or parking charges, record those separately as regular expenses. These are deductible whether you choose actual expenses or the standard mileage deduction on your taxes. One often-overlooked deduction for those who take the standard mileage deduction is the interest you pay on your car loan. You can deduct the amount you pay in interest at the same percentage as the business use you determine above. For example, if you pay $400 in interest on your car loan in a given year, and you use your car 50 percent for business use, you can deduct $200 more from your business taxes.

Depreciation and Section 179 Deductions

When you purchase something for your project studio, you can deduct its full cost for the tax year in which it was purchased. You "write off" the expense. However, larger capital purchases must be depreciated, where you essentially deduct a portion of the expense over several years. Capital expenses are assets that have a life beyond simple consumption. In other words, you buy paper for your printer and typically consume it right away. The paper is not an asset; it is a consumable item, fully deductible as an office expense. However, when you buy a new $2,000 computer, it has a useful life beyond one single consumption. It is a deductible capital asset that must be depreciated, typically over five or seven years—for example, $400 each year for the next five years. This is oversimplified, as actual depreciation is somewhat more complicated. Consult a tax adviser for details. Now, a case can be made for a stapler, which obviously has useful life beyond simple consumption. However, the stapler's minuscule cost lets you treat it as a consumable in this case.

That's why most companies differentiate between straight deductions and depreciable assets at a specific dollar amount, say $200. For example, the new computer gets depreciated, while the software you buy to run on it would be an office supply and expensed fully.

Thankfully, the IRS gives small business owners a break by letting them choose to expense the entire cost of larger, capital items *instead* of depreciating them. Section 179 of the tax code lets you fully deduct business expenses that would otherwise be depreciated. Currently, you can expense capital purchases up to $20,000, rising to $25,000 by 2003. Here's how investing in your project studio can save you money you would otherwise pay in taxes. Let's say you finish a gig that pays you $2,000. If you are in the 28 percent federal tax bracket, pay the 15.3 percent self-employment tax, and have a 3 percent state income tax, your net income, after taxes, is $1,074 ($2,000 x .537). You owe the government $926! If you spent the two grand on a piece of new gear, you reduce your income to zero on this gig, because you can deduct its purchase under Section 179 (minding the total dollar limit). While you've still spent the money, you saved 46.3 percent on the gear, as this is the money you would have paid to the tax man. More importantly, you've made your project studio better through a prudent equipment purchase. Obviously, you could make and spend $20,000 in a year and owe no taxes. That can let you put together your project studio quite quickly. Just don't forget the hobby loss rule mentioned earlier. When you're contemplating a major business purchase, always consider the tax advantages of the purchase. In this example, you save nearly half of the cost of everything you buy for your business!

Quarterly Taxes

Self-employed individuals must pay estimated income taxes quarterly (April 15, June 15, September 15, and January 15) and make up any shortfall (including penalties for having a shortfall) on April 15 of each year, when you file your taxes. Consult a tax adviser for details, or visit the IRS Web site (see below). Some people don't pay their quarterly taxes and instead invest the money during the year. They then pay the whole amount on April 15, including the penalties. Usually, you can earn more on your money than the penalties, so you come out ahead by a small margin. However, to beat the penalty percentage (about 5 percent), you must be in stocks. And while I believe stocks are the only way to invest for the long term, they can really beat you up in the short term. Your precious "income tax fund" might not be worth as much as you need, when you need it. Plus, selling the stock incurs a capital gain, and if it is less than a year, it is subject to a higher tax rate itself. This fact usually negates any small gain you would have anyway. So, although I despise sending in the quarterly payments (where the money no longer works for me), it is still the most fiscally prudent move. However, there is nothing wrong with parking excess cash in a good money market account (paying about 5 percent) during the intervening months between quarterly payments.

Tax Advisers

Beware, as there is a lot of bad tax advice out there. For example, if you purchased equipment and expensed it (wrote it off) for tax purposes and later you decide to donate it to charity, you can't write off the donation, because you already recovered the full price in the original expense. I see this "donate-gear-to-charity-thing" all the time as a last-minute tax strategy. It just doesn't apply for sole proprietorships. Another often-misunderstood tax trap is this: If you buy equipment and write it off, and later sell the gear, this sale generates income that must be reported on your Schedule C (ouch!). This doesn't apply to personal items, only business equipment that you expensed. If you're new to the vagaries of business taxes, seek the talents of a qualified tax consultant. It may be the most important advice you'll ever get.

- Go to the IRS Web site (*www.irs.gov*) for some useful, free information booklets: Tax Guide for Small Business #344, Business Use of Your Home #587, Business Expenses #535, Self Employment Tax #533, and Tax Withholding and Declaration of Estimated Tax #505.

Invest for Growth and Future Income

If you continue to maximize your income, reduce your expenses, and save the difference, you will begin to accumulate a capital base of money. You must begin to invest the first dollar you save, and every subsequent savings dollar, for maximum growth. First, let's determine how much money you need invested and producing income to support today's current lifestyle. Following the advice earlier in this chapter, let's say you determine that your monthly expenses total $2,000. How much savings do you need to generate that amount? You would need $240,000 earning 10 percent to meet your monthly bills today ($240,000 x 10 percent = 24,000 / 12 months = $2,000).

I can hear you all screaming, "There's no way I can save $240,000!" Well, how much money do you make each year? You may discover that if you save 10 to 15 percent of your income for the next twenty years, you will be able to accumulate the nest egg you need. Unless you do the math, you won't know for sure. Investing means looking beyond today. Where do you want to be in twenty, thirty, and forty years? My financial calculator shows this: If you start with $0 and deposit $3,971 annually over twenty years (at a 10 percent compounded rate of return), you will save $240,000. In just two decades, you'll accumulate enough capital that, in turn, can generate enough income to pay for your current basic living expenses. If you are thirty, you'll get there by age fifty. Ironically, the $3,971 is just $29 shy of the maximum annual contribution allowed for a married couple in a traditional or Roth IRA ($4,000 in 2001). Go ahead, kick in the extra $29 bucks! I hope this clearly shows that you can grow your own nest egg easily.

With investments, you can either own something, such as stocks, stock mutual funds, real estate, and tangible assets (gold and silver, collectibles), or you can loan money and earn interest, such as a savings account, certificate of deposit, savings bonds, treasury bonds, municipal bonds, and corporate bonds. Owning typically gives greater returns, but with increased risk. Loaning generally has lower returns with less risk. You need a balance of both types of investments that reflect both your risk tolerance and timeline. The younger you are, the more you can weather the ups and downs of the stock market. The older you are, the more you might prefer the nonvolatility of more predictable investments.

Where you specifically choose to put your money is beyond the scope of this book. Let me provide this essential advice: start today, invest as much as you can afford, and keep going. Consider setting up an automatic investment program, so you don't have to do anything to keep your investments running smoothly and regularly. In *Eight Steps to Seven Figures*, author Charles B. Carlson profiled the investment strategies of the wealthy: "1) Start investing NOW!, 2) establish a goal, 3) buy only stocks and stock mutual funds, 4) swing for singles (don't try to hit homers), 5) invest every month, 6) buy and hold and hold and hold, 7) take what Uncle Sam gives you, and 8) limit shocks to your finances." This is good, sensible, and proven advice that you should consider following with your investments.

Investment Plan

Before you start investing for your financial independence, make sure you take care of the following matters first. If you are already in debt, channel your initial savings toward paying it down before you start saving for retirement and financial independence. Pay off your pesky credit cards first. The high interest rates are sapping your money resources. While it is okay to have a mortgage, try to avoid other debt. Additionally, try to pay down your mortgage sooner by adding a little extra money to your monthly payment to reduce your principal. Even just $50 more each month can save you thousands of dollars over the term of the loan and enable you to pay off your mortgage years earlier.

Accumulate an emergency fund. Make sure you have enough money to cover three months of your basic living expenses in a safe, interest-bearing account. A high-interest money market account is a good choice here. If you have an emergency or some lean months, you will rest better knowing you have savings to rely on. Also, have another source of quick cash for an immediate, dire emergency (medical or other catastrophes), such as a home equity credit line, credit card, or some other method of getting cash.

Invest for your retirement first. There are specific tax advantages when you invest in certain tax-deferred investments, such as personal IRAs and other retirement plans. You can start and contribute to a traditional IRA that gives singles a $2,000 and couples a $4,000 tax deduction each year. The interest on your nest egg grows tax-deferred until you make withdrawals after age fifty-nine-and-a-half. Conversely, the Roth IRA gives you no immediate tax break, but the growth is tax-free upon retirement. Your actual allowable contributions can vary, depending on your actual tax situation.

Another option for sole proprietors and partnerships is a Simplified Employee Pension Plan (SEP). A SEP is easy to start, as it lets you contribute to it just like a personal IRA. The real advantage is, you can sock away up to 15 percent of your income, to a total of $22,500 (for 2001). That sure beats the meager $2,000 offered by an IRA. The expense for you (and your employees) is deductible, and the money earns tax-deferred interest until withdrawal, just like a traditional IRA. What's nice about a SEP is, if you have a profitable year, you can contribute more cash; in tough times, you can scale back. After maxing out your retirement plan, turn your attention toward investing for your financial independence, though your retirement plan will probably fund most, if not all, of your future needs.

Manage Your Cash Flow

When you are in business, your erratic income will rarely align perfectly with your rather-regular expenses. Here are a few strategies to smooth the ride. Let me remind you that these strategies are *only* for managing your cash flow. I'm a firm believer of paying cash for items and financing very little. Think twice before spending, unless you either have the money or know the money is forthcoming (like an invoice due in the future, quarterly royalties, and so on).

Should you keep extra cash in your business checking account or bleed it dry? Many accountants suggest that you pay yourself a regular salary. The problem with this business is that some months are rather lean and others are virtual bonanzas. Also, some months, your bills may be high, other times, average. It never seems to even out, and there always seems to be way too much cash in the business account. In case you didn't already know, business accounts don't pay interest, so the money just sits there like a shoebox in the closet. What I decided to do was leave just enough cash in my business account to pay upcoming bills plus a small contingency (10 percent over projected expenses), and transfer the rest as my salary to my personal account. If an unexpected bill comes up, I use my business credit card, and then pay it off when the credit card statement arrives. My salary still often fluctuates wildly (though I've become a little more adept at smoothing out the bumps), but it's better than having thousands in the bank doing nothing for either the company or my personal life.

After this tip appeared in my weekly e-mail newsletter, several people mentioned that they had way too much money in their business accounts and proceeded to move the money into more sensible places. Jimmy Graham wrote, "I had a float of $3 to 4K on hand, and your tip got me to get off my butt to invest it in short-term investments to at least make 3 to 4 percent on the cash, while still having complete access to it. I am also investing my income tax money I put away each week into a one-year investment, to make 5 percent on money that will eventually go to the tax man. Better that I profit from it than them!"

Creative credit can also help your cash flow, since you are not paying for expenses until after your clients pay you. One technique you might consider is the '"same-as-cash"' deals offered by many companies. This is essentially an interest-free payment plan. You order the product for something akin to three payments of $29.95. The company takes your credit card number and charges you equal installments spread over time, usually once a month for three to six months. They bill you the same day each month, too, until the amount is paid in full. Combining this technique with the grace period on your credit card can let you get gear or supplies today and pay for them over time (without incurring finance charges or interest). That gives you more time to earn (or collect!) the cash you need.

Get and use a single credit card for your project studio purchases. Having one can simplify your bookkeeping and also help you manage your cash flow. Use your credit card's grace period to your advantage by waiting for the statement rollover to make large purchases. That can give you a thirty-day billing cycle plus a twenty-day grace period before you have to pay the bill. Watch your use of credit carefully, though. Don't carry balances on your credit cards, because the interest rates are far too high.

Review Your Financials Regularly

While you should monitor your income and expenses regularly, there is a particular strategy you can use once each year. On the Friday after the Thanksgiving holiday, gather up your income and expense reports, and also grab a copy of your business goals, specifically your plans for the next year. Look for ways to reduce your tax burden before the end of the year. You have only two legitimate methods: delay your income and accelerate your expenses. You should both reduce the money you have coming in *and* uncover any purchases you can make before New Year's Day. Bill your clients later, and offer liberal credit terms. This lets you put off the income you would receive in December to January of the next year. If you use the cash accounting system, hold on to any checks you get the last week of December and wait to deposit them in January, too. Contemplating new gear? Need to print and mail a promotional campaign? Spend the money before December 31, and get the tax break from a legitimate business expense. Don't just look for major purchases either. Stock up on office supplies, stamps, blank CDs, and anything else you buy regularly. You are not just blowing away money to save a few nickels next April. Only buy those items you planned on buying early in the next year anyway. It's funny. Every small business knows about this advice. Everybody takes advantage of it, but nobody talks about it—as if it's some dirty little secret. This is not some tax dodge! It is a legitimate, albeit creative, way to reduce your tax burden late in the year. When April 15 rolls around, you'll be happy you took my advice the previous December.

Getting Help

If you don't feel comfortable handling your finances effectively, hire someone else, such as a professional bookkeeper, to do your work. Because investing your capital is so important, you may need help to find your way through the fog of money. Hire a financial planner who can help you map out your savings and investing plan. Choose a fee-only financial planner, because they do not earn commissions from the investments they recommend. These commissions often bias the recommendations some planners make to their customers.

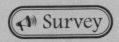

Do you have an expense budget for your project studio?

Not surprisingly, most project studio owners do not work from a formal budget. Many know their basic expenses and work to cover them.

- ♪ I [have a] budget for equipment purchases and replacement, ongoing expenses, wages, etc.

- ♪ I know what my bills are and make sure there's money in the business account to cover them.

- ♪ It costs about $2,500 per month to keep the doors open and the equipment from being repossessed.

- ♪ Basically, I just purchase supplies and equipment as needed.

- ♪ I purchase wisely and don't buy anything unless I really need it.

Do you handle the finances, or does another watch the books? About how much time do you spend each month managing your business finances? Do you use a computer to manage your business finances? If so, what software? Do you prepare your own taxes or hire a professional?

This multipart question revealed that, on the whole, project studio owners prefer to handle their own finances and average an hour a week on the task. Some had bookkeepers and accountants, but these were the rare exception. All but two used a computer, and the software of choice included the big three: Money, Peachtree, and Quicken. The clear majority hired a professional for income tax preparation.

Do you take advantage of the tax breaks given to businesses? If yes, which ones?

A disturbing point arose from the survey, where some project studio owners said they took the tax breaks, but didn't really know what they were. I'm not sure you can successfully run a project studio business without some idea of the tax advantages. Thankfully, a few respondents were quite clear on this issue.

♪ I deduct all my business expenses and depreciate all major purchases.

♪ I write off as much as I can.

(14)
Ready. Set. Go!

Your *project studio can help you* live the successful life you want, need, and deserve. When you follow the advice presented in these pages, you can achieve your dreams on your own terms. The more you can do working from your project studio, the more products and services you provide, and the more talent and experience you bring to your clients, the more money you can make. And never lose sight of the most important part of your life: *enjoy the journey!*

Although I hope this book provides just enough impetus to get you moving in the right direction, I'm not so bold as to believe it will be the substitute for your own real-world education. As Ralph Waldo Emerson said, "All of life is an experiment. The more experiments you make, the better." So, get started right now looking for opportunities. Learn all that you can. Even the grunt work of today can pay off for you down the road. Don't sit on your hands waiting for the big break. Make your own breaks, and find your own path to success. Do something today—anything!—that in some way moves you closer to your goal. You will learn a lot during the process, gain some invaluable experiences, and you just might be successful.

I hope you continue to use this book and that it inspires you to make your project studio endeavors successful. I'd welcome hearing from you about both your milestones and your setbacks. I'm also happy to answer questions you may have about this material. And you can get additional advice through my free e-mail newsletter and at my Web site. Send e-mail to *jpf@jeffreypfisher.com* or stop by *www.jeffreypfisher.com*. I look forward to hearing from you very soon.

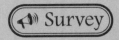 Survey

The best way to close this book is to review the words of the people who work the magic from their project studios.

What do you consider to be your business philosophy?

♪ If it doesn't make money, then it doesn't make sense.

♪ Make things sound good quickly and for a reasonable rate.

♩ Our philosophy is try to make every project (from the lamest karaoke session to the most fun major-label album projects) kick ass in every way, which includes top-notch sound quality, cutting-edge ideas, ON-TIME delivery, the most comfortable facility, the most knowledgeable (and easy-to-work-with) engineers, and most importantly, after-support, so once the album is in their hands, they're not left standing there with them wondering what the hell to do next.

♪ To provide a quality product at a fair price.

♩ Always focus on the customer's needs, be his one-stop audio soundtrack shop, always give something gratis beyond what is negotiated.

♪ With knowledge and persistence, you can pay the bills.

♩ To deliver quality work at fair prices. To use new (and old) technology in a creative, innovative, organic way. To be professional at all times, on every level. To be creative and innovative within the restrictions of any project.

What was the biggest mistake you ever made or worst thing that every happened with your project studio?

♩ Spent $900 on a CD-burner, not knowing that it wouldn't work with my setup. Had to sell it for $450 and buy another CD-burner for $420. So, I look at it as breaking even.

♪ I lost all the projects on my VS 880 hard drive once (and hopefully only once).

♪ Hiring the electrician that I did when I built the building. Didn't know zip about studios, I found out later.

♪ Turned down jobs, because I didn't feel I could handle them.

♪ Waiting so long to get it up and running. I wasted too many years pursuing pipe dreams.

♪ I didn't take it seriously enough in the beginning.

♪ Taking on a partner.

♪ I took it for granted and neglected my career goals.

What was your greatest accomplishment or the best thing that ever happened with your project studio?

♪ Learning the Akai MPC2000XL. There is so much to it. I still haven't used its full potential yet.

♪ Hearing stuff I produced on TV or radio, but has happened so many times now, not really a thrill.

♪ Some really, really great recordings.

♪ My greatest accomplishment is that every day, I collect money to do what I love.

♪ All our compilation CDs have charted.

♪ I've recently finished composing and recording a piece that I'm quite proud of.

If you could start over today, what would you do differently about/with your project studio?

♪ Would've started sooner.

♪ Do it sooner.

♪ I would get a bigger board with more inputs.

♪ Do it myself.

♪ Push harder to get clients.

♪ Buy the top of the line instead of buying pieces "just for now."

What do you consider to be your greatest challenge about your project studio?

♪ Getting time to get in and use my equipment.

♪ Setting it up/putting it away, so my fiancée isn't upset with it taking over the living room.

♪ Finding time to do *my* compositions.

♪ Getting the work.

♪ Getting big sound out of small boxes.

♪ Getting potential clients to use my studio.

♪ Getting paid.

♪ Keeping up on the marketing and getting new clients.

♩ Financing the dream. I'm developing the facility from scratch, and it's been difficult to complete different segments of the construction without the funding being available at one time.

♪ Learning all the different gear capabilities and software.

♪ Budgeting my time and money.

♪ Working with so little equipment.

What advice would you give to someone just starting a project studio?

♪ Don't give up. Just make do with what you've got, and try and use it to its full potential.

♩ Buy used stuff off the Internet for less than the cost of new gear; hire a pro to consult before putting it together, so you don't buy useless or bad gear; hire a pro engineer for a project or two, so you can watch and see another (possibly better) way of using your gear to its maximum potential.

♩ Try as best as possible to anticipate your needs by a close examination of what you wish to do; ask questions of people who have done what you want to do; and research, research, research your gear before you buy.

♩ Don't expect too much when you first start promoting your business. In my city, the giants seem to rule the earth. People have this idea that us little guys can't possibly put out good products, so they continue going to the big production houses to get the same old garbage as everyone else.

♪ Be very cautious with your credit cards!

♪ Don't purchase hardware or software unless you absolutely need it for a current project.

♪ Study—study—study. A successful business is more about people than being a "cool studio cat."

Is there anything else you would like to add?

♩ What a great industry! They keep giving us all these really fine toys to play with, and we get to listen to great music. Because we don't hire out, I get to listen only to music that I already know that I love.

♩ Be willing to write any kind of music. Keep banging on doors, because I think sooner or later, someone will need your services.

♪ Remember there are NO Rules! Anything can work if you MAKE IT WORK!

♩ Learn to develop your ideas on the computer. One keyboard, a computer, some software, and a lot of time. Get to understand music theory and sampling, and just sit down and decide what you want to be.

♪ Learn as much as you can. Network as much as you can. Be prepared to work your butt off.

Index

Books from Allworth Press

The Art of Writing Great Lyrics
by Pamela Phillips Oland (paperback, 6 x 9, 272 pages, $18.95)

How to Pitch and Promote Your Songs, Third Edition
by Fred Koller (paperback, 6 x 9, 208 pages, $18.95)

Creative Careers in Music
by Josquin des Pres and Mark Landsman (paperback, 6 x 9, 224 pages, $18.95)

Moving Up in the Music Business
by Jodi Summers (paperback, 6 x 9, 224 pages, $18.95)

The Songwriter's and Musician's Guide to Nashville, Revised Edition
by Sherry Bond (paperback, 6 x 9, 256 pages, $18.95)

Making It in the Music Business: The Business and Legal Guide for Songwriters and Performers, Revised Edition
by Lee Wilson (paperback, 6 x 9, 288 pages, $18.95)

Making and Marketing Music: The Musician's Guide to Financing, Distributing, and Promoting Albums
by Jodi Summers (paperback, 6 x 9, 240 pages, $18.95)

Booking and Tour Management for the Performing Arts, Revised Edition
by Rena Shagan (paperback, 6 x 9, 272 pages, $19.95)

The Copyright Guide: A Friendly Guide to Protecting and Profiting from Copyrights, Revised Edition
by Lee Wilson (paperback, 6 x 9, 208 pages, $19.95)

The Trademark Guide: A Friendly Guide to Protecting and Profiting from Trademarks
by Lee Wilson (paperback, 6 x 9, 208 pages, $18.95)

Artists Communities: A Directory of Residencies in the United States That Offer Time and Space for Creativity, Second Edition
by the Alliance of Artists' Communities (paperback, 6 x 10, 256 pages, $18.95)

Please write to request our free catalog. To order by credit card, call 1-800-491-2808 or send a check or money order to Allworth Press, 10 East 23rd Street, Suite 510, New York, NY 10010. Include $5 for shipping and handling for the first book ordered and $1 for each additional book. Ten dollars plus $1 for each additional book if ordering from Canada. New York State residents must add sales tax.

To see our complete catalog on the World Wide Web, or to order online, you can find us at *www.allworth.com*.